JOURNAL FOR THE STUDY OF THE OLD TESTAMENT
SUPPLEMENT SERIES

409

Editors
Claudia V. Camp, Texas Christian University
and
Andrew Mein, Westcott House, Cambridge

Founding Editors
David J. A. Clines, Philip R. Davies and David M. Gunn

Editorial Board
Richard J. Coggins, Alan Cooper, John Goldingay,
Robert P. Gordon, Norman K. Gottwald, John Jarick,
Andrew D. H. Mayes, Carol Meyers, Patrick D. Miller

The Levitical Authorship of Ezra–Nehemiah

Kyung-jin Min

T & T CLARK INTERNATIONAL
A Continuum imprint
LONDON • NEW YORK

Copyright © 2004 T&T Clark International
A Continuum imprint

Published by T&T Clark International
The Tower Building, 11 York Road, London SE1 7NX
15 East 26th Street, Suite 1703, New York, NY 10010

www.tandtclark.com

British Library Cataloguing-in-Publication Data
A catalogue record for this book is available from the British Library

Library of Congress Cataloging-in-Publication Data
A catalogue record for this book is available from the Library of Congress

Typeset by ISB Typesetting, Sheffield
Printed on acid-free paper in Great Britain by CPI Bath

ISBN 0-567-08226-1

ACKNOWLEDGEMENTS

The present work is a minor revision of my doctoral dissertation submitted for the PhD degree at the University of Durham, England, in 2002.

I was privileged to receive the superb supervision of Dr. Stuart Weeks, whose comments were always invaluable and of great help in each stage of the work's growth. The dissertation was even more elaborated on after having been examined by Professors Robert Hayward at Durham and William Johnstone at Aberdeen. They gave me immensely worthwhile tips for further scholarly studies. In addition to those scholars, I would also like to express my warm appreciation to my previous teachers, of whom three should be especially mentioned here: Professor Joon-surh Park at Yonsei University, Seoul, Korea; Professor Dong-hyun Park at Presbyterian College and Theological Seminary, Seoul, Korea; and Professor Hugh Williamson at Oxford. The publication of this insignificant work is an outcome totally made of their brilliant teaching and loving concerns.

I wish to share this joy with my children, Ye-sul and Jae-won, as well as my colleagues at Busan Presbyterian University who will walk along the path of scholarly life with me.

Above all, this book is sincerely dedicated to my wife, Kyung-sun, as a small token of my gratitude for her unflagging support and inestimable sacrifices that cannot be repaid.

Gimhae, South Korea
June 20, 2004

CONTENTS

Part II
LITERARY CONTEXT

Part III
HISTORICAL CONTEXT

ABBREVIATIONS

AB	Anchor Bible
ABD	David Noel Freedman (ed.), *The Anchor Bible Dictionary* (New York: Doubleday, 1992)
ABR	*Australian Biblical Review* (Melbourne)
AJSL	*American Journal of Semitic Languages and Literatures* (Chicago)
ALGHJ	Arbeiten zur Literatur und Geschichte des hellenistischen Judentums (Leiden)
ALUOS	Annual of Leeds University Oriental Society
AnBib	Analecta biblica
AnBoll	Analecta Bollandiana
ANEP	James B. Pritchard (ed.), *Ancient Near East in Pictures Relating to the Old Testament* (Princeton: Princeton University Press, 1954)
ANET	James B. Pritchard (ed.), *Ancient Near Eastern Texts Relating to the Old Testament* (Princeton: Princeton University Press, 3rd edn, 1969)
Ant.	Josephus, *Jewish Antiquities*
ASTI	*Annual of the Swedish Theological Institute* (Leiden)
ATD	Das Alte Testament Deutsch (Göttingen)
BA	*Biblical Archaeologist* (New Haven)
BBB	Bonner biblische Beiträge (Bodenheim)
BDB	Francis Brown, S.R. Driver and Charles A. Briggs, *A Hebrew and English Lexicon of the Old Testament* (Oxford: Clarendon Press, 1907)
BEvT	Beiträge zur evangelischen Theologie (Munich)
BHS	*Biblia hebraica stuttgartensia*
BHT	Beiträge zur historischen Theologie (Tübingen)
BJS	Brown Judaic Studies (Atlanta)
BWANT	Beiträge zur Wissenschaft vom Alten und Neuen Testament (Stuttgart)
BZ	*Biblische Zeitschrift* (Paderborn)
BZAW	Beihefte zur *ZAW* (Berlin)
CBQ	*Catholic Biblical Quarterly* (Washington, DC)
CRBS	*Currents in Research: Biblical Studies* (Sheffield)
DSB	The Daily Study Bible (Edinburgh)

DSD	*Dead Sea Discoveries* (Leiden)
EvTh	*Evangelische Theologie* (Munich)
ExpTim	*Expository Times* (Edinburgh)
FOTL	The Forms of the Old Testament Literature (Grand Rapids)
FRLANT	Forschungen zur Religion und Literatur des Alten und Neuen Testaments (Göttingen)
GKC	*Gesenius' Hebrew Grammar* (ed. E. Kautzsch, revised and trans. A.E. Cowley; Oxford: Clarendon Press, 1910)
Grammaire	Paul Joüon, *Grammaire de l'hebreu biblique* (Rome)
HAR	*Hebrew Annual Review* (Columbus, OH)
HAT	Handbuch zum Alten Testament (Tübingen)
HdA	Handbuch der Archaologie (Munich)
HeyJ	*Heythrop Journal* (London)
HSM	Harvard Semitic Monographs (Missoula)
HUCA	*Hebrew Union College Annual* (Cincinnati)
ICC	International Critical Commentary (Edinburgh)
IDB	George Arthur Buttrick (ed.), *The Interpreter's Dictionary of the Bible* (4 vols.; Nashville: Abingdon Press, 1962)
IDBSup	*IDB*, Supplementary Volume (Nashville)
ITC	International Theological Commentary (Edinburgh)
JANES	*Journal of the Ancient Near Eastern Society of Columbia University* (New York)
JAOS	*Journal of the American Oriental Society* (New Haven)
JBL	*Journal of Biblical Literature* (Philadelphia)
JESHO	*Journal of the Economic and Social History of the Orient* (Leiden)
JETS	*Journal of the Evangelical Theological Society* (Leiden)
JJS	*Journal of Jewish Studies* (Oxford)
JSJSup	Supplements to the *Journal for the Study of Judaism* (Leiden)
JSOT	*Journal for the Study of the Old Testament* (Sheffield)
JSOTSup	*Journal for the Study of the Old Testament*, Supplement Series (Sheffield)
JTS	*Journal of Theological Studies* (Oxford)
KAT	Kommentar zum Alten Testament (Gütersloh)
KHAT	Kurzer Hand-Kommentar zum Alten Testament (Tübingen and Leipzig)
NCB	New Century Bible (London)
NEB	*New English Bible* (Würzburg)
NICOT	New International Commentary on the Old Testament (Grand Rapids)
NIDOTTE	Willem A. VanGemeren (ed.), *New International Dictionary of Old Testament Theology and Exegesis* (5 vols.; Grand Rapids: Zondervan, 1997)
OBO	Orbis biblicus et orientalis (Freiburg and Göttingen)
OLZ	*Orientalistische Literaturzeitung* (Berlin)

OTG	Old Testament Guides (Sheffield)
OTL	Old Testament Library (London)
OTM	Oxford Theological Monographs (Oxford)
OTS	*Oudtestamentische Studiën* (Leiden)
RB	*Revue biblique* (Paris)
SAT	*Die Schriften des Alten Testaments in Auswahl* (Göttingen)
SBL	Society of Biblical Literature
SBLDS	SBL Dissertation Series (Atlanta, Georgia)
SJOT	*Scandinavian Journal of the Old Testament* (Copenhagen)
SUNVAO	Skrifter utgitt av Det Norske Videnskaps-Akademi I Oslo (Oslo)
TGUOS	*Transactions of the Glasgow University Oriental Society* (Glasgow)
ThWAT	G.J. Botterweck and H. Ringgren (eds.), *Theologisches Wörterbuch zum Alten Testament* (Stuttgart: W. Kohlhammer, 1970–)
TOTC	Tyndale Old Testament Commentaries (Leicester)
TynBul	*Tyndale Bulletin* (Cambridge)
VT	*Vetus Testamentum* (Leiden)
VTSup	*Vetus Testamentum*, Supplements (Leiden)
WBC	Word Biblical Commentary (Waco)
WMANT	Wissenschaftliche Monographien zum Alten und Neuen Testament (Neukirchen–Vlein)
WTJ	*Westminster Theological Journal* (Philadelphia)
WUNT	Wissenschaftliche Untersuchungen zum Neuen Testament (Tübingen)
ZAW	*Zeitschrift für die alttestamentliche Wissenschaft* (Giessen and Berlin)

INTRODUCTION

Until a few decades before the end of the twentieth century, Ezra–Nehemiah had not generally attracted the attention of Old Testament scholarship; indeed, it has had little impact historically on either Jewish or Christian interpretation.[1] In recent years, however, there has been an upsurge in interest in the book, and great strides have been made in E–N studies. This has been reflected in both a number of key publications and several ongoing projects.[2] One of the most important reasons for this change in attitude has been the separation of E–N from the book of Chronicles.[3] The relative lack of past scholarly interest in E–N may be attributed to a sense that the principal value of any historical literature lies in its *historicity*. E–N has conventionally been treated as part of the Chronicler's work, most of which was believed to be of little use for historical reconstruction.[4] With a growing

1.   Cf. Hugh G.M. Williamson, 'Ezra and Nehemiah, Books of', in J.H. Hayes (ed.), *Dictionary of Biblical Interpretation* (Nashville, TX: Abingdon Press, 1999), pp. 375–82, esp. pp. 375–77. See also Rodney K. Duke, *The Persuasive Appeal of the Chronicler: A Rhetorical Analysis* (JSOTSup, 88; Sheffield: Almond Press, 1990), pp. 12–18.

2.   For a useful summary of scholarly achievements in this area, see Ralph W. Klein, 'Ezra and Nehemiah in Recent Studies', in F.M. Cross *et al.* (eds.), *Magnalia Dei: The Mighty Acts of God: Essays on the Bible and Archaeology in Memory of G. Ernest Wright* (Garden City, NY: Doubleday, 1976), pp. 361–76; Geo Widengren, 'The Persian Period', in J.H. Hayes, and J. Maxwell Miller (eds.), *Israelite and Judaean History* (London: SCM Press, 1977); Tamara C. Eskenazi, 'Current Perspectives on Ezra–Nehemiah and the Persian Period', *CRBS* 1 (1993), pp. 59–86; Eric M. Meyers, 'Second Temple Studies in the Light of Recent Archaeology: Part I: The Persian and Hellenistic Periods', *CRBS* 2 (1994), pp. 25–42; H.G.M. Williamson, 'Exile and After: Historical Study', in D.W. Baker, and Bill T. Arnold (eds.), *The Face of Old Testament Studies: A Survey of Contemporary Approaches* (Grand Rapids: Baker Books, 1999), pp. 236–65. For current projects, see Eskenazi, 'Current Perspectives on Ezra–Nehemiah', p. 81, where she speaks of: 'the 'Chronicles, Ezra, Nehemiah Section', the 'Sociology of the Second Temple Period Group', and the 'Literature and History of the Persian Period Group' in the Society of Biblical Literature; the Achaemenid History Workshops; and the *Association pour la recherche sur la Syrie-Palestine à l'Epoque Perse* (ASPEP) in Paris'.

3.   Cf. Sara Japhet, 'The Supposed Common Authorship of Chronicles and Ezra–Nehemiah Investigated Anew', *VT* 18 (1968), pp. 330–71. For a more detailed discussion, see the first section of Chapter 1 below. Another important reason for this change may be the recent boom in studies of the Achaemenid period. Cf. Williamson, 'Exile and After', pp. 236–37, which examines this recent concern for the Persian period; Charles E. Carter, 'The Changing Face of the Persian Period', in *The Emergence of Yehud in the Persian Period: A Social and Demographic Study* (JSOTSup, 294; Sheffield: JSOT Press, 1999), pp. 31–74. With new archaeological evidence, and a new, more socio-political approach to history, there has been a greater opportunity for biblical scholars to reconstruct the Jewish history of this period.

4.   See, for example, Wilhelm M.L. de Wette, *Beiträge zur Einleitung in das Alte Testament*

consensus that it has an independent origin, however, E–N is now increasingly read as a discrete composition, subject to its own ideology rather than to that of the Chronicler. This has not only opened up the possibility that E–N is more 'historical' than Chronicles,[5] but has also forced scholars to launch a thorough re-evaluation of critical issues taken for granted in the past.

Some progress has already been made on the historical background of E–N and its relationship to Chronicles. Nevertheless, there are still many issues to be resolved in the light of this new paradigm, and this present study sets out to examine one of the most important: the authorship of E–N.[6]

The issue of authorship is, of course, bound up with broader questions of setting, purpose and perspective, and is of more than simple antiquarian interest for any study of the highly partisan post-exilic period. In the current state of E–N studies,

---

(2 vols.; Halle: Schimmelpfennig, 1806–1807); Charles C. Torrey, *The Composition and Historical Value of Ezra–Nehemiah* (BZAW, 2; Giessen: Ricker, 1896). Cf. William Johnstone, 'Which is the Best Commentary?: 11. The Chronicler's Work', *ExpTim* 102 (1990), pp. 6–11, esp. p. 7; John W. Kleinig, 'Recent Research in Chronicles', *CRBS* 2 (1994), pp. 43–76, esp. p. 68. As well as the dearth of historicity, E–N may have been disregarded, probably because of Protestant scholarly antipathy toward cultic matters such as temple service, sacrifices, and priesthood, with which the Chronicler's work is filled.

5.   E–N, of course, claims to include some portions of the *ipsissima verba* of historical figures, Ezra and Nehemiah. These are often called 'Memoirs' and are presented as eye-witness testimonies. If so, the work contains some of the most important sources for the historical reconstruction of the Achaemenid period in Palestine, whatever its editorial ideology. Certain scholars, however, do question the historical reliability of the Ezra and Nehemiah Memoirs. Thus, Ulrich Kellermann, *Nehemia: Quellen Überlieferung und Geschichte* (BZAW, 102; Berlin: Töpelmann, 1967), doubts the existence of any Ezra material containing his *ipsissima vox* (cf. pp. 56–69), though not denying the historicity of Ezra himself. Torrey, *Composition*, pp. 57–63, goes farther and denies Ezra's existence. Likewise, there are a few scholars who doubt the authenticity of the Nehemiah Memoir. See, especially, David J.A. Clines, 'The Nehemiah Memoir: The Perils of Autobiography', in *What does Eve do to Help?: And Other Readerly Questions to the Old Testament* (JSOTSup, 94; Sheffield: JSOT Press, 1990), pp. 124–64. Many other scholars, however, believe them to be historically reliable. Cf. Wilhelm Rudolph, *Esra und Nehemia* (HAT, 20; Tübingen: Mohr, 1949), pp. xxiii–xxiv; H.G.M. Williamson, *Ezra, Nehemiah* (WBC, 16; Waco, TX: Word Books, 1985), pp. xxiv–xxxii.

6.   Judson R. Shaver, 'Ezra and Nehemiah: On the Theological Significance of Making Them Contemporaries', in E. Ulrich *et al.* (eds.), *Priests, Prophets and Scribes: Essays on the Formation and Heritage of Second Temple Judaism in Honor of Joseph Blenkinsopp* (JSOTSup, 149; Sheffield: JSOT Press, 1992), pp. 76–86, identifies the critical issues unresolved in E–N scholarship as 'the genre and historical reliability of the book's sources, its date and editorial history, the nature and extent of literary dislocations in the text, and the relationship of Ezra–Nehemiah to Chronicles' (p. 76). To these, some scholars have added the authorship issue, since it is agreed that the author of E–N is unknown. Cf. David A. Smith, 'Ezra, Book of', in W.E. Mills (ed.), *The Lutterworth Dictionary of the Bible* (Cambridge: The Lutterworth Press, 1990), pp. 285–86; S. Japhet, 'Composition and Chronology', in T.C. Eskenazi, and Kent H. Richards (eds.), *Second Temple Studies*: II. *Temple and Community in the Persian Period* (JSOTSup, 175; Sheffield, JSOT Press, 1994), pp. 189–90; M. Patrick Graham, 'The "Chronicler's History": Ezra–Nehemiah, 1–2 Chronicles', in S.L. McKenzie, and M.P. Graham (eds.), *The Hebrew Bible Today: An Introduction to Critical Issues* (Louisville, KY: Westminster John Knox Press, 1998), pp. 201–15, esp. pp. 212–13; Mark A. Throntveit, 'Nehemiah, Book of', in D.N. Freedman *et al.* (eds.), *Eerdmans Dictionary of the Bible* (Grand Rapids: Eerdmans, 2000), pp. 955–57.

however, many commentators have gone no further than to discuss issues of unity, or the relationship with Chronicles, under the heading of authorship.[7] The only specific nomination has appeared in Hugh Williamson's work, where priestly authorship is more implied than demonstrated.[8]

It will be our contention in this book that E–N was, in fact, composed by the rival clerical class of Levites, or at least by somebody who was so strongly pro-Levitical that we might as well describe them as a Levite.[9] In terms of earlier scholarly assumptions, this is not a novel position. E–N shares its favourable attitude toward Levites with the work of the Chronicles, where scholars have often detected a conspicuous emphasis on Levitical concerns.[10] Many have, therefore, argued that Chronicles–Ezra–Nehemiah was composed as a unified work in Levitical circles.[11] It is, perhaps, because of this earlier association with theories of a unified Chronicles–Ezra–Nehemiah, that more recent scholars have been reluctant to take E–N's interest in the Levites as evidence of authorship.[12] Correspondingly, we should, perhaps, be more specific: the contention of this book will be that E–N

---

7.   E.g., Derek Kidner, *Ezra & Nehemiah: An Introduction & Commentary* (TOTC; Leicester: IVP, 1979), pp. 136–39; F. Charles Fensham, *The Books of Ezra and Nehemiah* (NICOT; Grand Rapids: Wm. B. Eerdmans Publishing Company, 1982), pp. 1–4; J. Gordon McConville, *Ezra, Nehemiah and Esther* (DSB; Edinburgh: The Saint Andrew Press, 1985), pp. 3–4; Antonius H.J. Gunneweg, *Esra* (KAT 19.1; Gütersloh: Gerd Mohn, 1985), pp. 21–28; Fredrick C. Holmgren, *Ezra & Nehemiah: Israel Alive Again* (ITC; Edinburgh: The Handsel Press, 1987); Joseph Blenkinsopp, *Ezra–Nehemiah: A Commentary* (OTL; London: SCM Press, 1988), pp. 47–54; M.A. Throntveit, *Ezra–Nehemiah* (IBC; Louisville: John Knox Press, 1989), pp. 8–10.

8.   H.G.M. Williamson, 'The Composition of Ezra i–vi', *JTS* 34 (1983), pp. 1–30, esp. pp. 26–29.

9.   In spite of long discussions about the historical relationship between the priests and the Levites, no consensus has been reached. This is mainly because biblical texts which speak of the clerical group are too inconsistent and incoherent for us fully to delineate the relationship. Cf. Julia M. O'Brien, 'Priest and Levite in Malachi' (unpublished PhD dissertation, Duke University, 1988), pp. 5–55. It is widely agreed, however, that a feuding relationship between the groups, which may have begun with Josiah's radical reformation, lasted until the post-Achaemenid period. For a recent substantial study which argues for this position, see Joachim Schaper, *Priester und Leviten im achämenidischen Juda: Studien zur Kult- und Sozialgeschichte Israels in persischer Zeit* (Tübingen: Mohr–Siebeck, 2000), pp. 79–129, 162–302.

10.   See, for example, Edward L. Curtis and Albert A. Madsen, *A Critical and Exegetical Commentary on the Books of Chronicles* (ICC; Edinburgh: T&T Clark, 1910), p. 5.

11.   E.g., W.M.L. de Wette, *A Critical and Historical Introduction to the Canonical Scripture of the Old Testament* (trans. T. Parker; Boston: Little and Brown, 1843), pp. 277–82; Samuel R. Driver, *An Introduction to the Literature of the Old Testament* (New York: Charles Scribner's Sons, 1906), p. 519; Gerhard von Rad, 'The Levitical Sermons in I and II Chronicles', in *The Problem of the Hexateuch and Other Essays* (Edinburgh and London: Oliver & Boyd, 1966), pp. 267–80.

12.   For example, Williamson notes the promoted position of the Levites in E–N, but simply asserts, somewhat on insufficient grounds, that their position in Chronicles is even more promoted than in E–N. Having taken this position, he does not discuss the authorship issue on the basis of the marked feature of the Levites described in E–N. Cf. H.G.M. Williamson, *Israel in the Books of Chronicles* (Cambridge: Cambridge University Press, 1977), p. 69; *idem*, 'The Composition of Ezra i–vi', pp. 26–29. For a more detailed discussion, see section 2.3 below.

was composed as an *independent* work in Levitical circles, regardless of the origin of Chronicles.

The importance of such a conclusion goes beyond interpretative issues. In many respects, the Achaemenid period in Palestine remains mysterious, but, as we shall see, an understanding of the Levites and their role can shed a significant amount of light on some of the key events. The historical significance extends to later periods: manuscript discoveries have improved our understanding of Jewish clerical groups and traditions in the post-Achaemenid, Hellenistic era,[13] but discussion has been handicapped by a lack of consensus about the starting-point in Persian times, and the roles of the Levites immediately after the Return.[14]

There are a number of issues which need to be resolved before we can discuss Levitical authorship in detail, or look at the historical questions. The first chapter of the book, therefore, is intended to prepare the ground by reviewing the key compositional assumptions: after rehearsing and examining the arguments for treating E–N as a work independent of Chronicles, it will present those which support internal unity between the books of Ezra and Nehemiah. Chapter 2 will assess current theories of authorship, focusing in particular on the possibility of a priestly origin. These two chapters have been grouped together as Part I of the book, dealing as they do with preliminary considerations.

Part II turns to the literary evidence for Levitical authorship. Chapter 3 examines a range of biblical material to determine the ways in which priestly and Levitical texts each portray the Levites, and shows that a reasonably consistent picture emerges, characterizing each perspective. Chapter 4 then compares the presentation in E–N, to show that the book is more likely to have been written from a Levitical than a priestly viewpoint; it also introduces some more tangential indications of Levitical origins.

Finally, Part III tackles the issue from a very different direction, by endeavouring to demonstrate that the Levites are the group most likely to have shared the political ideology represented in E–N. Chapter 5 begins by delineating that ideology, in terms of the Persian Empire and what we know of its strategies. Chapter 6, correspondingly, attempts to trace the relationship between the Persians, on the one hand, and the priestly and Levitical groups on the other.

---

13.   For a useful survey, see Michael A. Knibb, 'Perspectives on the Apocrypha and Pseudepigrapha: The Levi Traditions', in F.G. Martínez *et al.* (eds.), *Perspectives in the Study of the Old Testament and Early Judaism: A Symposium in Honour of Adam S. van der Woude on the Occasion of his 70th birthday* (VTSup, 73; Leiden: Brill, 1998), pp. 197–213, esp. pp. 197–201.

14.   Cf. James Kugel, 'Levi's Elevation to the Priesthood in Second Temple Writings', *HTR* 86 (1993), pp. 1–64; Robert A. Kugler, *From Patriarch to Priest: The Levi-Priestly Tradition from Aramaic Levi to Testament of Levi* (SBL Early Judaism and Its Literature 9; Atlanta: Scholars Press, 1996); Cana Werman, 'Levi and Levites in the Second Temple Period', *DSD* 4 (1997), pp. 211–25. This matter will be dealt with in more detail in the conclusion of this book.

Part I

Priestly or Levitical Authorship?

Discussions about the authorship of E–N have focused principally on issues of composition: in this first part, therefore, we shall begin by looking at the work's independence and unity, before turning to look at the suggested and likely candidates for its origin.

Chapter 1

EZRA–NEHEMIAH AS AN INDEPENDENT SINGLE WORK

This chapter deals with the issue of the boundaries of Ezra–Nehemiah, an issue surrounded by controversy. The controversy has centred on two sub-issues: (1) should E–N be viewed as a work independent of Chronicles?; and (2) should E–N be treated as a single book?

1.1 *Ezra–Nehemiah Independent of Chronicles*

1.1.1 *Introduction*
Ancient tradition attributes the composition of E–N largely to Ezra the Scribe and, furthermore, suggests that Ezra was the writer of Chronicles.[1] This traditional view has been accepted by a few modern scholars.[2] However, it was radically challenged

---

1.   Mainly on the basis of *Babylonian Talmud, Baba Bathra,* 15a, which says 'עזרא כתב ספרו ויחס בדברי הימים עד לו '. This text is suggested as the correct reading by David Talshir, 'The References to Ezra and the Books of Chronicles in *B. Baba Bathra* 15a', *VT* 38 (1988), pp. 358–60. According to him, the printed text, which has, instead of ויחס בדברי הימים above, ויחס של דברי הימים (literally, 'and genealogy belonging to the events [or the words] of the days'), is a corruption; for של indicates that יחס here is a *singular* noun, while the latter is never used in the singular form in Mishnaic Hebrew, thus making the sentence, syntactically speaking, abnormal. Therefore, he prefers to read ויחס as a verb, a reading which is attested in some manuscripts. ויחס, then, means 'and inscribed the genealogy' literally, but it can mean 'and wrote a history', since there is abundant evidence both that יחס is used with the meaning 'to write' (e.g., Numbers Rabba ii 20), and that 'genealogy' often means 'history', as in the case of תלדות. Talshir finally argues that *Baba Bathra* 14–15 is the section mentioning all the books of the Bible and their authors, and thus that דברי הימים refers necessarily to the books of Chronicles. The suggested text, therefore, may be construed as 'Ezra wrote his book [i.e., the book of Ezra and Nehemiah] and registered the genealogy (and history) [of Israel] in Chronicles up to him' (p. 359), thus ascribing both E–N and Chronicles to Ezra. On the other hand, another Jewish tradition ascribes E–N to *Nehemiah*. For example, *Babylonian Talmud, Sanhedrin* 93b says that 'the whole subject matter of Ezra was narrated by Nehemiah the son of Hachalia'. The subsequent section furthermore provides the rationale for why, then, *Ezra*'s name, instead of Nehemiah's, is attached to the book of E–N. According to this section, it is because Nehemiah claimed too much merit for himself (e.g., 'Remember me, O Lord'; Neh 13.31), making an excessive request of God that superseded David, and spoke ill of his predecessors in Neh. 5.15.

2.   E.g., Johann G. Eichhorn, *Einleitung in das Alte Testament*, vol. 2 (Leipzig: Weidmann, 3rd edn, 1830), pp. 579–601; William Foxwell Albright, 'The Date and Personality of the Chronicler', *JBL* 40 (1921), pp. 104–24; *idem, The Biblical Period from Abraham to Ezra: An Historical Survey* (New York: Harper & Row, 1963), p. 95; Gleason L. Archer, *A Survey of Old Testament Introduction* (Chicago: Moody Press, 1964), pp. 419–20.

by Leopold Zunz in 1832, who found that, at most, an eighth of the book of Ezra was written by Ezra himself and the remainder was written by earlier or later hands. Favouring the thesis of common authorship, Zunz concluded that it was *the Chronicler*, rather than Ezra, who composed E–N and Chronicles.[3]

This new theory long enjoyed a position of consensus within scholarship,[4] and faced few challenges before Sara Japhet's seminal article in 1968.[5] In this article, she attempted to shake the argument, based on linguistic similarities between Chronicles and E–N, which had been the principal foundation for the theory of common authorship.[6] Her pioneering thesis has since been supported in the influential work of Hugh Williamson,[7] and a growing number of scholars have been convinced by their arguments. Some, indeed, have elaborated different versions of their basic conclusions.[8]

---

3.   Leopold Zunz, 'Dibre-Hajamim oder die Bücher der Chronik', in *Die gottesdienstlichen Vorträge der Juden, historisch entwickelt: Ein Beitrag zur Alterthumskunde und biblischen Kritik, zur Literatur und Religionsgeschichte* (Berlin: Asher, 1832), pp. 13–36. For a concise summary of this article, see S. Japhet, 'The Supposed Common Authorship', pp. 331–32; *idem*, 'The Relationship between Chronicles and Ezra–Nehemiah', in John A. Emerton (ed.), *Congress Volume, Leuven 1989: International Organisation for the Study of the Old Testament Congress* (VTSup, 43; Leiden: Brill, 1991), pp. 298–313, esp. p. 299.

4.   It was Martin Noth, *Überlieferungsgeschichtliche Studien: Die sammelnden und bearbeitenden Geschichtswerke im Alten Testament* (Halle: Max Niemeyer, 1943), pp. 110–216 and W. Rudolph, *Chronikbücher* (HAT, 21; Tübingen: Mohr, 1955) who made Zunz's theory influential in present biblical scholarship. Cf. S. Japhet, *I & II Chronicles* (OTL; Louisville: Westminster/ John Knox Press, 1993), p. 6.

5.   Japhet, 'The Supposed Common Authorship', pp. 330–71.

6.   For a detailed discussion, see section 1.1.2.3 below. Before 1968, there had been some challenges to this theory, though not as strong as Japhet's: e.g., David .N. Freedman, 'The Chronicler's Purpose', *CBQ* 23 (1961), pp. 436–42, who noted that Chronicles is keenly interested in the house of David, a feature which is totally absent in E–N.

7.   Williamson, *Israel*, pp. 1–70. See also *idem*, *1 and 2 Chronicles* (NCB; London: Marshall, Morgan & Scott, 1982), pp. 5–11; *idem*, 'Did the Author of Chronicles Also Write the Books of Ezra and Nehemiah?', *Bible Review* 3 (1987), pp. 56–59.

8.   E.g., James D. Newsome (Jr.), 'Toward a New Understanding of the Chronicler and His Purpose', *JBL* 94 (1975), pp. 201–17; Roddy L. Braun, 'A Reconsideration of the Chronicler's Attitude toward the North', *JBL* 96 (1977), pp. 59–62; *idem*, 'Chronicles, Ezra and Nehemiah: Theology and Literary History', in J.A. Emerton (ed.). *Studies in the Historical Books of the Old Testament* (VTSup, 30; Leiden: Brill, 1979), pp. 52–64; Dennis J. McCarthy, 'Covenant and Law in Chronicles–Nehemiah', *CBQ* 44 (1982), pp. 25–44; William J. Dumbrell, 'Purpose of the Books of Chronicles', *JETS* 27 (1985), pp. 257–66; W. Johnstone, 'Guilt and Atonement: The Theme of 1 and 2 Chronicles', in J.D. Martin *et al.* (eds.), *A Word in Season: Essays in Honour of William McKane* (JSOTSup, 42; Sheffield: JSOT Press, 1986), pp. 113–38; T.C. Eskenazi, *In an Age of Prose: A Literary Approach to Ezra–Nehemiah* (Atlanta: Scholar Press, 1988), pp. 14–36; Simon J. De Vries, *1 and 2 Chronicles* (FOTL, 11; Grand Rapids: Eerdmans, 1989), pp. 8–10; Kim Strünbind, *Tradition als Interpretation in der Chronik: König Josaphat als Paradigma chronistischer Hermeneutik und Theologie* (BZAW; Berlin: de Gruyter, 1991); William Riley, *King and Cultus in Chronicles: Worship and the Reinterpretation of History* (JSOTSup, 160; Sheffield: JSOT Press, 1993); Martin J. Selman, *First Chronicles: An Introduction and Commentary* (Tyndale Old Testament Commentaries; Downers Grove: InterVarsity Press, 1994); Kent H. Richards, 'Reshaping Chronicles and Ezra–Nehemiah Interpretation', in J.L. Mays *et al.* (eds.), *Old Testament Inter-*

Nevertheless, the thesis of common authorship continues to be held, albeit in modified forms, by some scholars. While only a few maintain Zunz's original contention that Chronicles and E–N are a single work by the Chronicler as an individual author,[9] a number of modern scholars propose alternative theories, which, while differing in detail, share one common assertion: that E–N was not composed independently of the Chronicler. One group of these scholars argues that Chronicles and E–N were originally composed *by the same compiler but as two separate works*.[10] Another group maintains that Chronicles and E–N are one work but composed *by more than one author*. Some, who belong to this latter group, claim, on the basis of 1 Esdras and the witness of Josephus, that the extent of the original Chronicler's work did not include the so-called Nehemiah Memoir.[11] Others propose *two editors or the Chronicler as a circle,* or *the Chronicler as a school*.[12] Bob Becking has rightly noted that 'the common authorship of Chronicles–Ezra–Nehemiah is still defended', despite the growing influence of Japhet's work.[13]

---

pretation: Past, Present, and Future, Essays in Honor of Gene M. Tucker (Nashville: Abingdon Press, 1995), pp. 211–24; Georg Steins, *Die Chronik als kanonisches Abschlußphänomen: Studien zur Entstehung und Theologie von 1/2 Chronik* (BBB, 93; Weinheim: Beltz, 1995), pp. 49–82; Brian E. Kelly, *Retribution and Eschatology in Chronicles* (JSOTSup, 211; Sheffield: JSOT Press, 1996), pp. 13–26.

9.   E.g., F.C. Movers, *Kritische Untersuchungen über die biblische Chronik* (Bonn: T. Habicht, 1834); Noth, *Überlieferungsgeschichtliche Studien(=ÜS)*; Rudolph, *Chronikbücher*.

10.   E.g., Thomas Willi, *Die Chronik als Auslegung* (FRLANT, 106; Göttingen: Vandenhoeck und Ruprecht, 1972), p. 180; Peter Welten, *Geschichte und Geschichtsdarstellung in den Chronikbüchern* (WMANT, 42; Neukirchen–Vlein: Neukirchener Verlag, 1973), p. 4.

11.   E.g., Sigmund Mowinckel, *Studien zu dem Buche Ezra-Nehemia I: Die nachchronistische Redaktion des Buches. Die Listen* (SUNVAO. II. Hist. Filos. Klasse. Ny Serie. No. 3; Oslo: Universitetsforlaget, 1964), p. 19; Kellermann, *Nehemia*, pp. 89ff; Karl-Friedrich Pohlmann, *Studien zum dritten Esra: Ein Beitrag zur Frage nach dem ursprünglichen Schluß des chronistischen Geschichtswerkes* (FRLANT, 104; Göttingen: Vandenhoeck & Ruprecht, 1970), pp. 32ff; Wilhelm Th. In der Smitten, 'Zur Pagenerzahlung im 3. Esra [3 Esr. III 1 – V6]', *VT* 22 (1972), pp. 492–95.

12.   For the two-editor hypothesis, see Kurt Galling, *Die Bücher der Chronik, Esra, Nehemia* (ATD, 12; Göttingen: Vandenhoeck und Ruprecht, 1954), pp. 8-12. For the thesis of the Chronicler as a circle, see Arvid S. Kapelrud, *The Question of Authorship in the Ezra-Narrative: A Lexical Investigation* (Oslo: I Kommisjon Hos Jacob Dybwad, 1944), p. 97, while for that as a school, see Peter R. Ackroyd, 'Studies in the Book of Haggai', *JJS* 2 (1951), pp. 163–76, esp. p. 173; F.M. Cross, 'A Reconstruction of the Judean Restoration', *JBL* 94 (*1975*), pp. 4–18. For differences between 'circle' and 'school' in meaning here, see Japhet, 'The Relationship between Chronicles and Ezra–Nehemiah', p. 311, where she says: 'a "school" has a more literary and theological orientation than the sociological definition of "circle"'.

13.   B. Becking, 'Ezra on the Move ... Trends and Perspectives on the Character and His Book', in Martínez *et al.* (eds.), *Perspectives in the Study of the Old Testament and Early Judaism*, pp. 154–79, esp. p. 157. For more recent defenders of the unity of authorship, see A.J.H. Gunneweg, 'Zur Interpretation der Bücher Esra-Nehemia', in J.A. Emerton (ed.), *Congress Volume, Vienna 1980: International Organization for the Study of the Old Testament* (VTSup, 32; Leiden: Brill, 1981), pp. 146–61; *idem, Esra*, pp. 24–26; D.J.A. Clines, *Ezra, Nehemiah, Esther* (NCB; London: Marshall, Morgan & Scott, 1984), pp. 9–12; Steven L. McKenzie, *The Chronicler's Use of the Deuteronomistic History* (HSM, 33; Atlanta: Scholars Press, 1985), pp. 17–25; P.R. Ackroyd, 'Chronicles–Ezra–Nehemiah: The Concept of Unity', in O. Kaiser (ed.), *Lebendige Forschung im Alten Testament* (BZAW, 100: Berlin: de Gruyter, 1988), pp. 189–201; Blenkinsopp, *Ezra–*

Since no final scholarly consensus on the issue has yet been reached, this chapter seeks to re-evaluate the various arguments about the demarcation of E–N since the publication of Japhet's article in 1968. In what follows, the so-called *four principal arguments* for common authorship will be reinvestigated,[14] as they have been at the core of the discussion of the authorship issue.[15] These are:

(1)   the doublet in 2 Chronicles 36.22-23 and Ezra 1.1-3a;
(2)   the evidence of 1 Esdras;
(3)   linguistic similarities between the books;
(4)   similarity of ideology.

1.1.2 *Appraisal of the Four Arguments*
1.1.2.1 *The Doublet in 2 Chronicles 36.22-23 and Ezra 1.1-3a*
The end of Chronicles (2 Chron. 36.22-23) overlaps with the beginning of E–N (Ezra 1.1-3a) *verbatim*, apart from only a few small differences, as below.[16]

> In the first year of Cyrus king of Persia, that the word of the Lord by the mouth (Chron. – בְּפִי; Ezra – מִפִּי) of Jeremiah (C – יִרְמְיָהוּ; E – יִרְמְיָה) might be accomplished, the Lord stirred up the spirit of Cyrus (C – כּוֹרֶשׁ; E – כֹּרֶשׁ) king of Persia so that he made a proclamation throughout all his kingdom and also put it in writing: 'Thus says Cyrus (C – כּוֹרֶשׁ ; E – כֹּרֶשׁ) king of Persia, "the Lord, the God of heaven, has given me all the kingdoms of the earth, and he has charged me to

---

Nehemiah, pp. 47–54; Joachim Becker, *Esra, Nehemia* (NEB, 25; Würzburg: Echter Verlag, 1990), pp. 5f; Manfred Oeming, *Das wahre Israel: Die genealogische 'Vorhalle' 1 Chronik 1–9* (Stuttgart: Kohlhammer, 1990), pp. 41–47; Rex Mason, 'Some Chronistic Themes in the "Speeches" in Ezra and Nehemiah', *ExpTim* 101 (1989), pp. 72–76; *idem*, *Preaching the Tradition: Homily and Hermeneutics after the Exile* (Cambridge: Cambridge University Press, 1990), pp. 7–11; K.-F. Pohlmann, 'Zur Frage von Korrespondenzen und Divergenzen zwischen den Chronikbüchern und dem Esra/Nehemia Buch', in Emerton (ed.), *Congress Volume, Leuven 1989*, pp. 314–30; Klaus Koch, 'Weltordnung und Reichsidee im alten Iran und ihre Auswirkungen auf die Provinz Jehud', in P. Frei and K. Koch, *Reichsidee und Reichsorganisation im Perserreich; Zweite bearbeitete und stark erweiterte Auflage* (OBO, 55; Freiburg and Göttingen: Vandenhoeck & Ruprecht, 2nd edn, 1996), pp. 220–39; Antony Gelston, 'The End of Chronicles', *SJOT* 10 (1996), pp. 53–60, and more.

14.   Cf. Zunz, 'Dibre-Hayamim', pp. 13–36; Driver, *Introduction*, pp. 535–40; Curtis and Madsen, *Chronicles*, pp. 27–36; and Rudolph, *Esra und Nehemia*, p. xxii.

15.   Cf. Williamson, *Israel*, pp. 1–70; Eskenazi, *Age of Prose*, pp. 11–36; J.R. Shaver, *Torah and the Chronicler's History Work* (BJS, 196; Atlanta: Scholar Press, 1989), pp. 44–70; Steins, *Die Chronik als kanonisches Abschlußphänomen*, pp. 49–82.

16.   The differences are largely of spelling, but there is one substantial difference between the two texts: the Chronicles text has יהוה ('Yahweh'), but the Ezra text יהי ('may he be'). This difference may demonstrate that the former text depended on the latter rather than the reverse, since it is almost impossible to think that the copyists would have replaced the sacred name unnecessarily. Cf. Herbert E. Ryle, *The Books of Ezra and Nehemiah* (The Cambridge Bible for Schools and Colleges; Cambridge: Cambridge University Press, 1893), p. 6. According to Williamson, *Ezra, Nehemiah*, p. 4, this switch from יהי in Ezra 1.3a to יהוה in 2 Chron. 36.23 was intended to obviate the possibility that the following word אלהיו might come to mean a pagan god. At any rate, because the differences are not significant, they do not affect the widely held notion that the two passages are a doublet.

build him a house at Jerusalem, which is in Judah. Whoever is among you of all his people, may the Lord his God (C – יהוה; E – יהי) be with him. Let him go up." '

These overlapping passages have frequently served as evidence in favour of unity of authorship,[17] and are said to show that the Chronicler's single original work was split into two books in the course of canonization. At first, according to this theory, E–N alone was accepted into the canon as a proper continuation of the historical books (1 Samuel to 2 Kings), which had already been canonized but lacked any account of the post-exilic history of Israel. After a certain period of time, however, Chronicles, which had not previously been accepted because of its overlap with the Deuteronomistic History, became part of the canon. The doublet was then added to the end of Chronicles to indicate that the two works were originally one.[18]

This suggestion leaves many questions, however. Above all, such a history is entirely speculative, and has never been corroborated.[19] It is also improbable: there is neither any known evidence that redundancy was a concern in discussing canonicity, nor are there convincing examples of other books sliced up to avoid redundancy.

More recently, this argument has been revived in another form by Menahem Haran, who offers a different explanation for the separation of E–N from Chronicles.[20] From an observation of the prevailing practices in biblical times, he suggests that a single scroll was usually allotted to each complete book.[21] The Chronicler's work, however, exceeded the maximum length that a scroll could contain in those days and so was divided into two books. Because the work had to be separated in this way, the compilers indicated the original relationship between the two parts by employing the device of catch-lines, as was common in antiquity. Haran thus interprets the existence of parallel passages at the end of Chronicles and in the beginning of E–N as conclusive evidence for single authorship: they are catch-lines indicating continuity.[22]

This suggestion is problematic, however. Haran uses the split to establish the length of a scroll; but we know scroll lengths to have been extremely variable.[23] In

17.   Cf. Movers, *Kritische Untersuchungen über die biblische Chronik*, pp. 11–14; Curtis and Madsen, *Chronicles*, p. 3; Otto Eissfeldt, *Einleitung in das Alte Testament* (Tübingen: Mohr, 3rd edn, 1964), (ET *The Old Testament: An Introduction, including the Apocrypha and Pseudepigrapha and also the works of Similar Type from Qumran* (trans. P.R. Ackroyd; New York: Harper & Row, 1965), pp. 530–31.

18.   Curtis and Madsen, *Chronicles*, p. 3.

19.   Willi, *Die Chronik als Auslegung*, pp. 176–84. See especially p. 179.

20.   M. Haran, 'Catch-Lines in Ancient Palaeography and in the Biblical Canon', *Eretz-Israel* 18 (1985), pp. 124–29 (Hebrew); *idem*, 'Book-Size and the Device of Catch-Lines in the Biblical Canon', *JJS* 36 (1985), pp. 1–11; *idem*, 'Explaining the Identical Lines at the End of Chronicles and the Beginning of Ezra', *Bible Review* 2 (1986), pp. 18–20.

21.   Haran, 'Book-Size and the Device of Catch-Lines', pp. 1–11; *idem*, 'Explaining the Identical Lines', pp. 18–20.

22.   Haran, 'Explaining the Identical Lines', p. 18.

23.   Williamson, 'Did the Author of Chronicles Also Write?', p. 59, also points out that Haran

addition, catch-lines are not found where other books have been split (e.g., the Pentateuch or the Deuteronomistic History). In response, Haran argues that they had their own proper criteria of separation in terms of themes and history, which allowed for their division into separate scrolls. Williamson notes, however, that the break between 2 Samuel and 1 Kings is not satisfactorily explained with Haran's criteria, and if Haran's understanding of the function of catch-lines were correct, there should be catch-lines at the end of 2 Samuel to show its continuation in 1 Kings. Indeed, it is somewhat awkward that we find catch-lines in Chronicles when the divergent history and themes already show a clear-cut division from E–N.[24]

As a last resort, or counsel of desperation, proponents of common authorship sometimes point out that no other adequate explanation has been offered for the repetition.[25] This is not true, though, as several persuasive suggestions have in fact been made, of which the best is arguably Japhet's.[26] She claims that E–N was actually an earlier work than Chronicles and that the doublet in 2 Chron. 36.22-23 was cited from Ezra 1.1-3a in order to demonstrate a *reversal* of the temple destruction and the exile described in 2 Chron. 36.17-21. This implies that the doublet in Chronicles was not intended to mark any original compositional connection between the two books. The relative dating of the two books is still a controversial issue and in that respect, therefore, the force of her argument may be weakened. However, we can support her argument by adding the possibility that the authors of Chronicles and E–N were both aware of Cyrus's edict and both had access to it, so that the doublet in 2 Chron. 36.22-23 and Ezra 1.1-3a occurred coincidentally. Either of these two possibilities may explain the doublet. To sum up, proponents of the theory of common authorship of Chronicles and E–N have used the doublet as one of their arguments together with three propositions: (1) the original single comprehensive work by the Chronicler was divided into two books either in the process of canonization or because of physical constraints; (2) the so-called catch-lines in 2 Chron. 36.22-23 indicate that the continuation of Chronicles is found in E–N; and (3) opponents of this position have failed to satisfactorily account for the overlap.

We must conclude that the first two propositions have insufficient supporting evidence, for they are largely based on presuppositions which have not been verified. The third is simply false if there are satisfactory explanations and, as examined,

---

builds his argument on two unproven assumptions: one, that both Chronicles and E–N were authored by the Chronicler, and the other, that there was no scroll long enough to contain both Chronicles and E–N.

24. Williamson, 'Did the Author of Chronicles Also Write?', p. 59.

25. E.g., Steven J.L. Croft, 'Review of Williamson's *Israel in the Books of Chronicles*', *JSOT* 14 (1979), p. 69; Shaver, *Torah and the Chronicler's History Work*, p. 57.

26. Japhet, *I & II Chronicles*, pp. 1076–77. Another plausible explanation is offered by Williamson, who first argues that Chronicles originally ended with 2 Chron. 36.21, and that 2 Chron. 36.22-23 was a secondary ending borrowed from Ezra 1.1-3a. Slight changes were made in the borrowed text in order to match the style of the preceding texts. He believes the text was borrowed for a liturgical reason, and reflects a habit in those days for the beginning of Ezra to be read together with Chronicles, to inform the reader that the continuing story of the post-exilic period may be found in E–N. Cf. Williamson, *Israel*, pp. 8–10; *idem*, *1 and 2 Chronicles*, p. 419. However, this explanation seems to lack evidence because this habit does not occur elsewhere.

it is possible for us to understand the existence of the doublet without the aid of the traditional explanation given by those in support of common authorship. Therefore, although the above discussion does not in itself prove conclusively that Chronicles and E–N were written by different authors, it should be concluded, at least, that the doublet cannot be used as supporting evidence for common authorship.[27]

1.1.2.2 *The Evidence of 1 Esdras*

1 Esdras has also been used to corroborate the thesis of single authorship.[28] Proponents of this argument note the scope of that work, which encompasses 2 Chron. 35–36, Ezra, and Neh. 8.1-13, and present this as evidence that Chronicles was directly followed by E–N and was not a separate book. In addition, they observe that the opening and ending of the work seem abrupt; the first words, καί ἤγαγεν ('and he kept'; 1 Esd. 1.1), are unusual for an opening in Greek literature, while the last words, καί ἐπισυνήχθησαν ('and they assembled…'; 1 Esd. 9.55), are apparently incomplete, and thus unlikely to be the deliberate ending of a work. Believing, on the basis of this, that the extant work must be only *part* of a larger book, scholars in favour of the unity of authorship have concluded that 1 Esdras must be a fragment of a Greek translation of the Chronicler's original work, which included both Chronicles and E–N.[29]

Of these two arguments, the first one, based on the scope of 1 Esdras, is hardly conclusive: it is as easy to claim that the present scope resulted from a *compilation*[30] of Chronicles with E–N, and many scholars have asserted as much.[31] The

27. This position has been shared even by McKenzie, who is one of the advocates of the thesis of common authorship. See McKenzie, *The Chronicler's Use of the Deuteronomistic History*, p. 17, saying: that 'The presence of this doublet at the end of Chronicles and the beginning of Ezra does not establish either common or separate authorship; it can be interpreted either way'.

28. Ever since Zunz, 'Dibre-Hajamim', pp 28–29, this position has been developed, although with differences in details, by the following scholars: H.H. Howorth, 'The Real Character and the Importance of the Book of I Esdras', *The Academy* 43 (1893), p. 60; C.C. Torrey, *Ezra Studies* (Chicago: University of Chicago, 1910), pp. 11–36; Loring W. Batten, *A Critical and Exegetical Commentary on the Books of Ezra and Nehemiah* (ICC; Edinburgh: T&T Clark, 1913), p. 2; Rudolf Kittel, *Geschichte des Volkes Israel*, 3 (Stuttgart: Kohlhammer, 1929); Mowinckel, *Studien I*, pp. 7–28; Pohlmann, *Studien zum dritten Esra*; Cross, 'A Reconstruction of the Judean Restoration', pp. 7–8; McKenzie, *The Chronicler's Use of the Deuteronomistic History*, pp. 17–25, etc.

29. Cf. especially Mowinckel, *Studien I*, pp. 7–28; Pohlmann, *Studien zum dritten Esra*, pp. 14–26.

30. The terms, *fragment hypothesis* (*Fragmenthypothese*) and *compilation hypothesis* (*Kompilationshypothese*), which Pohlmann used to categorize the views on the nature of 1 Esdras, have been adopted in most of the current writings and so here. See, for example, Eskenazi, *Age of Prose*, pp. 34–35; Steins, *Die Chronik als kanonisches Abschlußphänomen*, pp. 76–79; H.G.M. Williamson, 'The Problem with First Esdras', in J. Barton *et al.* (eds.), *After the Exile: Essays in Honour of Rex Mason* (Macon, GA: Mercer University Press, 1996), pp. 201–16; Kelly, *Retribution and Eschatology in Chronicles*, pp. 17–20. In addition to these two hypotheses, there is another view to which less attention has been paid, arguing that the work was based on an earlier Greek rendition. Cf. Jacob M. Myers, *I and II Esdras* (AB, 42; Garden City: Doubleday, 1974), p. 5.

31. This compilation hypothesis is currently represented by Williamson. Cf. Williamson, *Israel*, pp. 12-36; *idem*, 'The Problem with First Esdras', pp. 201–16. For a list of scholars before Williamson who were in support of this hypothesis, see note 6 in Pohlmann, *Studien zum dritten*

second argument, established on the abruptness in the opening and ending of the work, is also far from compelling.

Is the opening of the work abrupt? Such a beginning is not a rare feature in the Old Testament itself, and is attested in several LXX texts (e.g., Lev 1.1; Num 1.1; 1 Chron 10.1-2): it can be understood 'im Lichte des Übersetzungstiles von I Esr'.[32] Furthermore, 1 Esdras 1.31, which, after Josiah's death, summarizes his life,[33] may offer evidence in favour of the originality of the beginning of the work.[34] This verse speaks of Josiah's deeds, both 'what he *did* earlier' and 'what *is* told of him here'. 1 Esdras 1.1-31 comprises three units of accounts: (1) Josiah's passover (vv. 1-20); (2) Josiah's piety (vv. 21-22); and (3) Josiah's death (vv. 23-31).[35] In the light of these divided units, 'what is told of him here' in verse 31 refers to the celebration of Passover in the first unit (vv. 1-20), with which 1 Esdras begins, while 'what he did earlier' most likely indicates the accounts in the second unit (vv. 21-22), testifying to Josiah's past works. Thus, this chapter in itself forms a complete structure, requiring no prior supplementary accounts. By the same token, as van der Kooij properly points out, the passage (vv. 21-22) has a parallel in 2 Chron. 34.19-28 in the Hebrew Bible, since both pose a contrast between the righteous king (Josiah) and the sinful people, and contain the mention of 'die Worte des Herrn'.[36] Hence, if we suppose, as proponents of common authorship argue, that 1 Esdras originally included 2 Chron. 34 as well as its preceding chapters, then 1 Esdras 1.21-22 is obviously redundant. This suggests that 1 Esdras 1.1 is the original opening.

What about the *ending* of the work? Van der Kooij also argues against those who think that the ending is abrupt and, therefore, not the original ending. To those who claim that the last two words, καί ἐπισυνήχθησαν, in 9.55 indicate an abrupt

---

Esra, p. 15. The recent important articles which defend or develop the argument of Williamson are: Robert Hanhart, 'Zu Text und Textgeschichte des ersten Esrabuches', in I.A. Shinan (ed.), *Proceedings of the Sixth World Congress of Jewish Studies* (Jerusalem: World Union of Jewish Studies, 1977), pp. 201–12; Zipora Talshir, 'The Milieu of I Esdras in the Light of its Vocabulary', in A. Pietersma *et al.* (eds.), *De Septuaginta: Studies in Honour of John William Wevers on his Sixty-fifth Birthday* (Mississauga: Benben Publications, 1984), pp. 129–47; Anne E. Gardner, 'The Purpose and Date of I Esdras', *JJS* 37 (1986), pp. 18–27; T.C. Eskenazi, 'The Chronicler and the Composition of I Esdras', *CBQ* 48 (1986), pp. 39–61; *idem*, *Age of Prose*, pp. 34–35, 171–85; Arie van der Kooij, 'Zur Frage des Anfangs des 1. Esrabuches', *ZAW* 103 (1991), pp. 239–52; *idem*, 'On the Ending of the Book of I Esdras', in C.E. Cox (ed.), *Seventh Congress of the International Organisation for Septuagint and Cognate Studies, Leuven, 1989* (Atlanta: Scholars Press, 1991), pp. 37–49, etc.

32.   Van der Kooij, 'Zur Frage des Anfangs des 1. Esrabuches', p. 251.

33.   'These things are recorded in the book of the histories of the kings of Judah; every deed that Josiah did which won him fame and showed his understanding of the law of the Lord, both what he did earlier and what is told of him here, is related in the book of the kings of Israel and Judah'(NEB).

34.   Cf. van der Kooij, 'Zur Frage des Anfangs des 1. Esrabuches', pp. 249–51. Williamson had thought that the present beginning of 1 Esdras had been lost and admitted that it is *not* original (cf. Williamson, *Israel*, pp. 14–21). Now, in the wake of van der Kooij, he argues that it *is* original (cf. Williamson, 'The Problem with First Esdras', pp. 201–16).

35.   For this division, see, for example, Myers, *I and II Esdras*, pp. 23–26.

36.   Van der Kooij, 'Zur Frage des Anfangs des 1. Esrabuches', p. 247.

termination, ending in the middle of a sentence, van der Kooij responses that they are best taken as part of the ὅτι clause of the verse, thus functioning as an appropriate ending, similar to 7.10-15, where the last verse (v. 15) also preserves the reason for a festival giving joy.[37] A similar position has also been held by Tamara Eskenazi, though she approaches the matter from a slightly different angle, noting that the ending of 1 Esdras is identical with that of Chronicles, which also has an unexpected ending but is normally regarded as a complete sentence.[38]

From these observations, we may say that the arguments based on the scope of the work and its abrupt beginning and closing are of no use as evidence in support of common authorship.

In relation to 1 Esdras, the testimony of Josephus (*Ant.* XI.1–158) has also been presented as evidence against separate authorship.[39] In view of the fact that his work follows 1 Esdras and does not include most of the Nehemiah narrative, it has often been argued that E–N in its *present* form never existed as a separate book in antiquity; if it had existed, Josephus would surely have used it or mentioned it in his work; the Nehemiah narrative must have been added to the existing Chronicler's work, then comprising Chronicles and the book of Ezra, which was the *Vorlage* to 1 Esdras.

This argument is also unpersuasive. First, the simple fact that Josephus follows 1 Esdras does not necessarily give any precise information on the original content of the work;[40] the possibility does exist that E–N in its present form was not available to Josephus. Second, the fact that 1 Esdras 5.7ff closely follows Ezra 2 challenges the argument based on Josephus' testimony. Since it is widely accepted that Ezra 2 is dependent upon Nehemiah 7, where the Ezra and Nehemiah materials have already been interwoven,[41] it is reasonable to think that the author of 1 Esdras also had knowledge of the combined form of the materials (i.e., Ezra 7–Neh. 13). This is in sharp contrast to the theory that the author of 1 Esdras was not aware of the Nehemiah material and that 1 Esdras is the original ending of the Chronicler's work.[42]

Judging from the examinations so far, the arguments based on the content of 1 Esdras and the testimony of Josephus are unconvincing. It is worth noting, in fact, that 1 Esdras has a tendency to omit the obscure matters in Ezra narratives and simplify what seems unclear.[43] this tendency can be adequately explained only by the *compilation* theory, which permits the compiler to enact a redactional strategy

---

37.   Thus, the text (1 Esd. 9.55) reads, '… not only because the teaching given them had been instilled to their mind, but also because they had been gathered together'; Van der Kooij, 'On the Ending of the Book of 1 Esdras', p. 45. He finds a parallel to this element in 2 Maccabees 2.18 (pp. 45–46).

38.   Eskenazi, 'The Chronicler and the Composition of 1 Esdras', pp. 39–61.

39.   Cf. Pohlmann, *Studien zum dritten Esra*, pp. 74–126. For more scholars in support of this position, see n. 28 above.

40.   Van der Kooij, 'On the Ending of the Book of 1 Esdras', p. 40.

41.   For a detailed discussion, see Williamson, 'The Composition of Ezra i–vi', pp. 2–8; *idem*, 'The Problem with First Esdras', pp. 206–208.

42.   Williamson, 'The Problem with First Esdras', pp. 205–208.

43.   Williamson, 'The Problem with First Esdras', pp. 210–11.

of clarification and simplification. We may conclude with Williamson that 'I Esdras is not just a fragment of the original ending of the Chronicler's work but a composition in its own right'.[44] Consequently, it is no longer possible to employ 1 Esdras as evidence in favour of the common authorship of Chronicles and E–N, although the book does not prove diversity of authorship, either.

1.1.2.3 *Linguistic Similarities between the Books*

Similarities of style and vocabulary between Chronicles and E–N have frequently been used more than any other argument for common authorship.[45] However, since Japhet's challenge,[46] an increasing number of scholars have doubted their appropriateness as evidence.[47]

According to Japhet, it is undeniable that there exist conspicuous linguistic similarities between the two books, but it is also undeniable that there are numerous important lexical *differences* between them (she lists 36), as well as differences in technical terminology and peculiarities of style.[48] On this basis, she concludes that, while the linguistic traits shared in both works simply show that they both emerge from a similar phase in the development of Hebrew, the differences show that Chronicles and E–N could not have been written by the same person.

Her pioneering work has been further elaborated by Williamson, who has analysed the lists made by Samuel Driver and by Curtis and Madsen,[49] which have often been cited in favour of single authorship.[50] Williamson shows that these scholars originally collected the lists merely to illustrate some *peculiarities and mannerisms* of the Chronicler's style, not to demonstrate common authorship.[51] All the same, he tests all the entries in the lists by applying to them criteria which he proposes for determining unity of authorship. He first sets up those criteria:[52] (1) a substantial number of words or stylistic peculiarities should be produced; (2) these peculiarities must be drawn from both Chronicles and E–N; (3) the evidence adduced should be confined exclusively, or at least overwhelmingly, to the books under discussion; (4) the words or expressions in question should preferably be expressed in other literature of the same period in a different way; and (5) words

44. Williamson, 'The Problem with First Esdras', pp. 212–13.

45. See especially Zunz, 'Dibre-Hayamim', pp. 19–30; Driver, *Introduction*, pp. 535–40; Curtis and Madsen, *Chronicles*, pp. 27–36.

46. Japhet, 'The Supposed Common Authorship', pp. 330–71.

47. E.g., E. John Revell, 'First Person Imperfect Forms with *WAW* Consecutive', *VT* 38 (1988), pp. 419–26; Eskenazi, *Age of Prose*, p. 20; Gwilym H. Jones, *1&2 Chronicles* (OTG; Sheffield: JSOT Press, 1993), pp. 88–92; Kelly, *Retribution and Eschatology in Chronicles*, pp. 20–22.

48. For example, (1) linguistic oppositions in the formation of the imperfect consecutive and in the lengthened imperfect consecutive ואקטלה, and in theophoric names ending with יהו; (2) specific technical terms such as התקדש־הטהר and כהן־הראש גדול; and (3) stylistic peculiarities between Chronicles and E–N. For a more detailed discussion, see Japhet, 'The Supposed Common Authorship', pp. 334–71.

49. Driver, *Introduction*, pp. 535–40; Curtis and Madsen, *Chronicles*, pp. 27–36.

50. For rough lists of works which reflect this position, see n. 1 in Williamson, *Israel*, p. 37.

51. Williamson, *Israel*, p. 38.

52. Williamson, *Israel*, pp. 39f.

that are found to satisfy the above criteria should further be checked to determine that they are used with the same meaning in both Chronicles and E–N. He concludes that only *six* out of Driver's forty-six and Curtis's one hundred and thirty-six items meet these criteria, and may therefore be used to assert single authorship.[53] Four of these six items, moreover, are of doubtful value. For example, the lists take the usage of ה for the relative to be a phenomenon peculiar to both Chronicles and E–N, but this usage is found in many passages outside these two books.[54] As long as we accept Williamson's criteria,[55] the paucity of the items that might advocate unity forces us to conclude, therefore, that the lists cannot be cited as decisive evidence in favour of common authorship.

Despite such compelling arguments put forward by Japhet and Williamson, several objections have been voiced to them. Taking his cue from Arno Kropat,[56] Robert Polzin explores the grammatical and syntactical features of the books in question rather than the lexicographical evidence examined by Japhet and Williamson. On the basis of a considerable number of grammatical and syntactical features shared by Chronicles and E–N, he does not hesitate to affirm that not only did these books originate in the same period of the development of Late Biblical Hebrew, but that we also have here an 'extremely strong case for similarity in the authorship of Chronicles and E–N'.[57] Henry Cazelles also attempts to defend common authorship by emphasizing that, despite Williamson's challenge, there *are* still the six items which have been classified as favouring unity.[58] Antonius Gunneweg discounts Japhet's contribution on the ground that she did not pay sufficient attention to the various levels of Chronicles, and that, since the language of Chronicles is not uniform, it would be misleading to use it as the basis for literary-critical judgments.[59]

Nevertheless, it should be said that the objections raised have not succeeded in reversing the current trend toward underlining linguistic *dissimilarities* between Chronicles and E–N, which favour diversity of authorship, and effective replies have been made to all of those objections.

These replies have focused mainly on Polzin's argument, since it has been considered the most influential. Williamson, for example, points out that it is, at best, *similarity* of authorship, not *identity* of authorship that Polzin proposes. According to him, Polzin's theory has a defect in that the features shared in Chronicles, Ezra, and the non-Nehemiah Memoir portions of Nehemiah also appear in the Hebrew

53.   Williamson, *Israel*, pp. 39–59. For the six items, see pp. 58–59.

54.   Williamson, *Israel*, pp. 59–60.

55.   As far as I am aware, few scholars have questioned the effectiveness of these criteria. For example, after a careful examination of Williamson's argument on this matter, Shaver, one of the proponents of *common* authorship, asserts that 'Williamson's presentation of the evidence is thorough and very accurate' (*Torah and the Chronicler's History Work*, p. 64).

56.   Arno Kropat, *Die Syntax des Autors der Chronik* (BZAW, 16; Berlin: Töpelmann, 1909).

57.   Robert Polzin, *Late Biblical Hebrew: Toward as Historical Typology of Biblical Hebrew Prose* (HSM, 12; Missoula, MT: Scholars Press, 1976), p. 71.

58.   Henry Cazelles, 'Review of H.G.M. Williamson's *Israel in the Book of Chronicles*', *VT* 29 (1979), pp. 375–80.

59.   Gunneweg, 'Zur Interpretation der Bucher Esra-Nehemia', pp. 147–48.

portions of Daniel, which is obviously not the work of the author of the former group.[60] After analysing, in the light of Williamson's five criteria, the fifteen linguistic features advanced by Polzin to affirm similarity of authorship, Mark Throntveit insists that 'only two can possibly be taken to do so, and they are both doubtful'.[61] Similarly, on the basis of more extensive literature than Polzin, Mark Rooker concludes that Chronicles and E–N have *differences* as well as similarities.[62]

The other objections to the arguments of Japhet and Williamson, by Cazelles and Gunneweg, can hardly be regarded as conclusive, either. Clines points out that Cazelles's argument cannot stand because 'while dissimilarities of style are *prima facie* evidence for difference of authorship, similarity of style can prove nothing, and is merely negative evidence'.[63] Eskenazi argues against Gunneweg, maintaining that his argument loses balance because he keeps 'silence over the paucity of genuine examples of unity in Curtis and Madsen's list'.[64]

From the discussions so far, therefore, we may again conclude that the argument based on linguistic analysis does not offer solid proof for common authorship.[65]

1.1.2.4 *Similarity of Ideology*

Another important argument for common authorship has been based on a perception that Chronicles and E–N have significant ideological similarities. Some scholars, however, believe that the items presented as similarities are more cogently interpreted as evidence for diversity of authorship, instead of unity. For example, Martin Noth presents, as evidence of unity, six features common to Chronicles and E–N:[66] (1) emphasis on David and the Davidic dynasty; (2) emphasis on the cult; (3) the idea of retribution as structuring human and divine acts; (4) the role of genealogies; (5) the view that the tribes of Judah and Benjamin form the true Israel; and (6) polemic against the Samaritans. As Becking points out, however, all but one[67] have been construed subsequently as showing *differences* of ideology between the two.[68]

---

60.   Williamson, *1 and 2 Chronicles*, pp. 7f. Cf. for another argument against Polzin, see Gary Rendsburg, 'Late Biblical Hebrew and the Date of "P"', *JANES* 12 (1980), pp. 65–80.

61.   M.A. Throntveit, 'Linguistic Analysis and the Question of Authorship in Chronicles, Ezra and Nehemiah', *VT* 32 (1982), pp. 201–16, esp. p. 215.

62.   Mark F. Rooker, *Biblical Hebrew in Transition: The Language of the Book of Ezekiel* (JSOTSup, 90; Sheffield: JSOT Press, 1990), pp. 182–83.

63.   Clines, *Ezra, Nehemiah, Esther*, p. 7.

64.   Eskenazi, *Age of Prose*, p. 20.

65.   This conclusion has also been shared by proponents of common authorship. See, for example, Blenkinsopp, *Ezra–Nehemiah*, pp. 49–51.

66.   Noth, *ÜS*, pp. 171–80. These six features are summarized by Becking, 'Ezra on the Move', pp. 156–57.

67.   Namely, the emphasis on the cult.

68.   Becking, 'Ezra on the Move', pp. 156–57, here says that his judgment is based on examinations made by scholars in support of separate authorship. But, as far as I know, their position has been that the emphasis on the cult is also insufficient evidence for either of the two opposing views of authorship. For example, Williamson, *Israel*, p. 60, says that, while it is true both books lay stress on the cult, the significance of this fact is at best to reveal the religious situation of that time, *not* to prove the same authorship. This position may be endorsed for two

This curious situation, where the same material is used to support two opposing arguments, calls for further examination. In what follows, therefore, we shall look briefly at the key themes identified as arguments against unity: (a) David and Solomon; (b) retribution; (c) concept of Israel; and (d) the future.

(a) *David and Solomon*: Ever since von Rad's substantial work,[69] it has generally been recognized that David and Solomon are significantly highlighted in the Chronicler's work.[70] This is not true, however, in E–N.

In Chronicles, David is depicted as the ideal, infallible king *par excellence* (e.g., 2 Chron. 29.1-2) as well as the initiator of Israel's new cult (1 Chron. 21–29). However, in E–N, his role appears quite limited and peripheral (Ezra 3.10; Neh. 12.24). For example, in Nehemiah 9, where Israel's history is retold, David and his contribution to the kingdom are never even mentioned. It is also noteworthy that the Davidic covenant, which dominates in Chronicles (1 Chron. 17.12; 2 Chron. 7.18; 13.5; 21.7; 23.3), is totally absent in E–N, where, by contrast, there is an emphasis on the Sinai covenant (Ezra 9; Neh. 1; 9).[71]

There is no consistency between the two books in the evaluation of Solomon, either. In Neh. 13.26, Solomon is described as an example of the sinner, rather than as an ideal and wise king, while in Chronicles his flaws are hardly visible in the light of his accomplishments. It is true that Neh. 13.26 belongs to the Nehemiah Memoir and may not, therefore, represent the views of E–N as a whole,[72] but it is also true that E–N nowhere contains any trace of an attempt to present Solomon as an ideal figure.

In the light of the fact that Chronicles and E–N show such different attitudes toward David and Solomon, it is most likely that these different descriptions are attributable to different authors rather than a single author.

---

reasons: (1) other contemporary biblical literature also shows an interest in the cult (e.g., the book of Malachi), but no one presumes common authorship from that fact (cf. Williamson, 'Did the Author of Chronicles Also Write?', p. 58); and (2) both books often differ in certain important descriptions of cultic personnel. For instance, the Nethinim and sons of Solomon's servants exclusively appear in E–N. Cf. concerning the reference to the Nethinim in 1 Chron. 9.2, see Japhet, 'The Supposed Common Authorship', pp. 351–54, where the argument is made that it borrowed from Neh. 11.3. Eskenazi, *Age of Prose*, p. 25, also reaches a similar conclusion by saying that 'the cultic similarities between Chronicles and Ezra–Nehemiah, though real, do not in themselves support common authorship'. Recently, Mark H. McEntire, *The Function of Sacrifice in Chronicles, Ezra, and Nehemiah* (Lampeter, Wales: Edwin Mellen, 1993), also noted the difference in the function of sacrifice between Chronicles and E–N. According to him, in the former, sacrifice serves as a vehicle to unify the community of Israel in crisis whereas, in the latter, it serves as a mechanism for developing community.

69.   G. von Rad, *Das Geschichtsbild des chronistischen Werkes* (BWANT, IV/3; Stuttgart: Kohlhammer, 1930).

70.   Cf. Noth, *ÜS*, pp. 171–80; Adrien M. Brunet, 'La théologie du Chroniste: Théocratie et messianisme', *Sacra Pagina* 1 (1959), pp. 384–97.

71.   Williamson, *1 and 2 Chronicles*, pp. 9–10.

72.   Shaver, *Torah and the Chronicler's History Work*, p. 65.

(b) *Retribution*: It is clear and widely recognized that Chronicles is informed by a doctrine of retribution,[73] which has been concisely formulated by von Rad as 'no disaster without guilt, no sin without punishment'[74] – a doctrine which appears to be quite absent in E–N. The nature of retribution in Chronicles is two-sided. On the one hand, it is *individual* and *immediate* (e.g., 1 Chron. 28.9; 2 Chron. 35.22-24). On the other hand, it also appears to be *collective* (2 Chron. 7.12-22),[75] or deferrable (on condition of repentance; 2 Chron. 12).[76] Although there are different aspects to, or interpretations of, retribution in Chronicles, there is no doubt that Chronicles is concerned with it as a theme.

In contrast, however, E–N retains neither of the two features of retribution detected in Chronicles. Ezra 9.6-15 and Neh. 9.6-37, though adumbrating the concept of retribution, cannot be treated as comparable to the retributive texts of Chronicles: the emphasis in Ezra 9 and Neh. 9 is on God's mercy, not on his punishment.[77]

In consequence, this remarkable contrast in the ideology of retribution between the two books again leads us to affirm separate authorship.

(c) *Concept of Israel*: For a long time, scholars contended that Chronicles and E–N share an exclusive view of the concept of Israel. That is, both books allegedly limit 'true' Israel only to the tribes of Judah and Benjamin, and have a corresponding anti-Samaritan polemic as one of their common features.[78]

It is apparent that the whole and true Israel in E–N is almost always represented by 'Judah and Benjamin' (e.g., Ezra 1.5; 4.1; 10.9; Neh. 11.4), not by the twelve tribes. The phrase, Judah and Benjamin, does occur in Chronicles, too, several times (1 Chron. 12.16; 2 Chron. 11.1, 3, 10, 12, 23; 15.2, 8, 9; 25.5; 31.1; 34.9), but there merely contains a geographical concept:[79] in Chronicles, the true Israel is spoken of as *all of Israel*, encompassing the twelve tribes (e.g., 2 Chron. 13.12, 16,

73. Cf. Noth, *ÜS*, pp. 172–73; W. Rudolph, 'The Problems of the Books of Chronicles', *VT* 4 (1954), pp. 401–409, esp. pp. 405–406; Robert North, 'Theology of the Chronicler', *JBL* 82 (1963), pp. 369–81, esp. pp. 372–74.

74. G. von Rad, *Theologie des Alten Testaments, Band I: Die Theologie der geschichtlichen Überlieferungen Israels* (München: Chr Kaiser Verlag, 1958), ET *Old Testament Theology: I. The Theology of Israel's Historical Traditions* (trans. D.M.G. Stalker; Edinburgh: Oliver and Boyd, 1962), p. 348. He provides many examples which show immediate and individual retribution (pp. 348–49).

75. Cf. Kelly, *Retribution and Eschatology in Chronicles*, pp. 46-63.

76. Braun, 'Chronicles, Ezra and Nehemiah', p. 55; Williamson, *1 and 2 Chronicles*, pp. 31–33; Raymond B. Dillard, 'Reward and Punishment in Chronicles: The Theology of Immediate Retribution', *WTJ* 46 (1984), pp. 164–72; S. Japhet, *The Ideology of the Book of Chronicles and its Place in Biblical Thought* (trans. A. Barber; Frankfurt am Main: Peter Lang [originally published in Hebrew; Jerusalem: Bialik, 1977], 1989), pp. 150–98; Kelly, *Retribution and Eschatology in Chronicles*, pp. 29–134.

77. Braun, 'Chronicles, Ezra and Nehemiah', p. 55.

78. Von Rad, *Das Geschichtsbild des chronistischen Werkes*, p. 10; Rudolph, 'The Problems of the Books of Chronicles', p. 404; J.M. Myers, *Ezra–Nehemiah* (AB, 14; Garden City, NY: Doubleday, 1965), p. 8.

79. E.g., Williamson, *Israel*, p. 99.

17, 18). Williamson notes the efforts of the Chronicler to advocate an inclusive attitude toward the concept of Israel, and offers as evidence the fact that Israel is always called 'Jacob', the father of the twelve tribes (1 Chron. 1.34; 2.1; 5.1, 3; 6.23; 7.29; 16.13, 17; 29.10, 18; 2 Chron. 30.6). This phrase rarely occurs in E–N where, instead, the use of the phrase, 'the tribes of Judah and Benjamin', is repeated frequently.[80]

Likewise, it is also obvious that the author of E–N harboured strong animosity toward the northern Israelites, as seen in the cases of the polemic in Ezra 4, and his strict attitude toward mixed marriages (e.g., Ezra 9–10; Neh. 13.26).[81] In Chronicles, however, there is no hint of this harsh treatment of the people of the northern kingdom. As noted by Japhet and Williamson, Chronicles probably intentionally lacks the account of 2 Kings 17, which mentions the apostasy of the northerners and must have been available to the Chronicler.[82] As for the problem of mixed marriages, Chronicles is again in clear-cut opposition to E–N in that the former alone shows a liberal attitude toward them.[83]

In the light of all this, we may conclude that Chronicles and E–N should be regarded as different works which have different understandings of Israel and consequently distinct attitudes toward mixed marriages.

(d) *The Future*: It has been widely recognized that E–N maintains an utter silence on the subject of Zerubbabel, a figure, apparently of Davidic lineage, who bears the hopes of Israel's restoration in the books of Haggai and Zechariah.[84] On the contrary it is apparently the Persian emperors in E–N who are understood to be the vehicle for actualizing God's will in Israel's restoration, and the work demonstrates no desire for any different dispensation.[85] It has generally been agreed, therefore, that E–N completely accepts the political *status quo*, lacks any advocacy for change[86] and, in this respect, is *antieschatologisch*.[87]

In contrast, Chronicles clearly desires a new order for the future, although there has been scholarly debate as to the precise nature of the book's expectations.

---

80. Williamson, *Israel*, pp. 61–62. Japhet, *Ideology*, pp. 267–351 and Braun, 'Chronicles, Ezra and Nehemiah', pp. 56–59, both express a similar opinion to Williamson on the basis of some references to the Chronicler's interest in the northern kingdom.

81. For a more detailed discussion of the exclusive nature of E–N in ideology, see Jonathan E. Dyck, *The Theocratic Ideology of the Chronicler* (Leiden: Brill, 1998), pp. 77–125.

82. Japhet, *Ideology*, pp. 326ff; Williamson, *Israel*, p. 67.

83. Japhet, *Ideology*, pp. 295–99; Williamson, *Israel*, p. 61.

84. S. Japhet, 'Sheshbazzar and Zerubbabel: Against the Background of the Historical and Religious Tendencies of Ezra–Nehemiah', *ZAW* 94 (1982), pp. 66–98, esp. pp. 71–72. These two prophets deliver great eschatological hope in the period of the restoration of the exiles who returned to Judah (see p. 76).

85. Japhet, 'Sheshbazzar and Zerubbabel', pp. 73–75.

86. Rudolph, *Esra und Nehemia*, pp. xxvii–xxx; Elias J. Bickerman, *From Ezra to the Last of the Maccabees: Foundations of Post-Biblical Judaism* (New York: Schocken Books, 1966), p. 30; Japhet, 'Sheshbazzar and Zerubbabel', pp. 72–80.

87. Cf. Rudolph, *Chronikbücher*, p. xxiii; *idem*, 'Problem of the Books of Chronicles', p. 408; J.M. Myers, 'The Kerygma of the Chronicler: History and Theology in the Service of Religion', *Interpretation* 20 (1966), pp. 259–73, esp. p. 266.

Scholars have variously argued that the Chronicler's hope for the future was characterized by one of the following descriptions: (1) a messianic expectation;[88] (2) a political restoration of the Davidic dynasty, with no specific eschatological or messianic expectation;[89] (3) a messianic and theocratic expectation of a Davidic messiah;[90] and (4) no restoration of the Davidic dynasty, but theocratic expectation.[91] Although different in detail, all these understandings agree that the Chronicler was dissatisfied with the status quo, and developed an expectation of a different future order, which is in radical contrast to the perspective of E–N on this matter.

Besides the items discussed so far, Chronicles and E–N are ideologically distinct in the following matters. In Chronicles, the roles of prophets and prophecy are conspicuous. In E–N, by contrast, they are minimized.[92] Furthermore, E–N describes the account of the return and later reforms in a matter-of-fact way, while Chronicles reports the history by exaggerating, idealizing, and presenting miracles.[93]

Based on the noticeable differences in ideology between Chronicles and E–N, we can positively conclude that E–N was composed separately from Chronicles.

1.1.3 *Conclusion*
Formulated by Zunz in 1832, the thesis of the common authorship of Chronicles and E–N was little questioned for about 150 years. As we have seen, however, a thorough reassessment of the four principal arguments on which common authorship was built has now led a number of scholars to find them unconvincing. The first argument which is based on a doublet in the two books is fragile; there is no evidence for the proposed process of canonization, nor does the presence of catch-lines necessarily show any original compositional connection between the two books. The second argument, related to the content of 1 Esdras, is also hard to use

88. Von Rad, *Old Testament Theology*, I, p. 123.

89. H.G.M. Williamson, 'Eschatology in Chronicles', *TynBul* 28 (1977), pp. 115–54; Oeming, *Das wahre Israel*, p. 209; Kelly, *Retribution and Eschatology in Chronicles*, pp. 135–233.

90. Tae-Soo Im, *Das Davidbild in den Chronikbüchern: David als Idealbild des theokratischen Messianismus für den Chronisten* (Frankfurt: Peter Lang, 1985), pp. 164–79.

91. Ernst M. Dörrfuss, *Moses in den Chronikbüchern: Garant theokratischer Zukunfts-erwartung* (BZAW, 219; Berlin: Walter de Gruyter, 1994), p. 282. There are more opinions. E.g., 'Restaurativer Messianismus' argued by Ingeborg Gabriel, *Friede über Israel: Eine Untersuchung zur Friedenstheologie in Chronik I 10–II 36* (Klosterneuburg: Osterreichisches Katholisches Bibel-werk, 1990), p. 202, or 'the restoration of the Temple cultus rather than the Davidic dynasty' by Riley, *King and Cultus in Chronicles*, p. 201, or 'the restoration, not of the Davidic dynasty but of the people' by Donald F. Murray, 'Dynasty, People, and the Future: The Message of Chronicles', *JSOT* 58 (1993), pp. 71–92, or 'the restoration of Israel's fortunes' by Japhet, Ideology, pp. 501–504. Cf. Piet B. Dirksen, 'The Future in the Book of Chronicles', in P.J. Harland *et al.* (eds.), *New Heaven and New Earth Prophecy and the Millennium: Essays in Honour of Anthony Gelston* (Leiden: Brill, 1999), pp. 37–51, esp. pp. 42–44.

92. Newsome, 'Toward a New Understanding of the Chronicler and His Purpose', p. 213, says: 'Haggai and Zechariah are twice mentioned in connection with their interest in the erection of the Second Temple (Ezra 5.1; 6.14), but the notices are brief and hasty, not at all of the same intensity or depth as the Chronicler's prophetic notices surrounding the building of the First Temple.'

93. Williamson, *Israel*, p. 68; Otto Kaiser, *Einleitung in das Alte Testament* (Gerd Mohn: Gütersloher Verlagshaus, 1984), p. 193.

as evidence for common authorship. As we saw, the present version of 1 Esdras is best read as the original compiled form, which had no more text than now, rather than as a fragment of some original work including both Chronicles and Ezra (or E–N). The third argument, grounded in linguistic similarities, also fails to provide evidence for common authorship, since there are just as many linguistic dissimilarities.

    None of these three arguments stands up to scrutiny, although their weakness does not necessarily imply separate authorship. In this respect, the last argument, regarding ideology, is more significant: not only is it untrue that Chronicles and E–N share several ideological features in common, but between the two there seem to be overwhelming differences in ideology. These differences can never be explained by a theory of common authorship, and it may be concluded, therefore, that E–N should be treated as a work independent of Chronicles, rather than as part of the Chronicler's work.

1.2 *Ezra–Nehemiah as a Unified Work*

In the preceding section, we affirmed the view that E–N should be treated as a work independent of Chronicles, and thereby provided both a foundation and a justification for our study of its authorship. Before we can move on to that issue, however, it is necessary to address another problem, which arises from our rejection of the link between Chronicles and E–N, and to explain our reasons for regarding E–N as one *single unified* work: some scholars have proposed that it should be treated as two distinct compositions, as it is usually presented in the Bible. If E–N were to be read as two separate books, then our question would have to be altered to: who are the *authors* of each of the two books? We now turn, therefore, to the issue of the unity of E–N: first, by summarizing and evaluating the opinions of those who argue for the separation of Ezra from Nehemiah and, secondly, by considering other points related to this issue.

1.2.1 *Views Treating Ezra and Nehemiah as Separate Compositions*
Because there is both internal and external evidence supporting the view that E–N was originally composed as a *single* work, its unity has rarely been questioned. Indeed, this unity is assumed in almost all major works discussing E–N, especially those written during the time when the authorship of E–N was universally ascribed to the Chronicler. For instance, Loring Batten writes:

> The books of Ezr. and Ne. were originally one, and ought really to be so combined now. The evidence of this is overwhelming. Two points suffice for a demonstration: (1) The story of Ezr. is partly in one book, Ezr. 7–10, and partly in the other, Ne. 7.70–8.12. In 1 Esd. these two parts are united in a single book. (2) At the end of each book of the Old Testament there are certain Masoretic notes, giving the number of verses, the middle point in the volume or roll, etc. There are no such notes at the end of Ezr., and those at the end of Ne. cover both books, showing that the two constituted a single work when those notes were made.[94]

---

94. Batten, *Ezra and Nehemiah*, p. 1.

This view has also been shared by opponents of the thesis of the common author-ship of Chronicles and E–N. Thus, Williamson echoes the same position by addressing the most telling reasons for the unity of E–N as follows:

> (1) In order to make sense of Josephus' enumeration of the biblical books (*Contra Apionem* § 40), it must be assumed that he counted Ezra and Nehemiah as one. (2) Melito, Bishop of Sardis, quotes Jewish sources in Palestine which speak of the whole work as 'Ezra'. (3) The Talmud includes the activities of Nehemiah in the book of Ezra and even asks, 'Why, then, was the book not called by his name?' (*Bab. Sanh.* 93b). (4) The Masoretes clearly regard the books as one because they count Neh 3.22 as the middle verse and add their annotations for the whole only at the end of Nehemiah. (5) The medieval Jewish commentators move directly from Ezra to Nehemiah without interruption. (6) In the earliest Hebrew manuscripts the books are not divided. (7) In the earliest manuscripts of the LXX the two books are treated as one.[95]

This widely held consensus has been criticized, however, by some scholars who prefer to see Ezra and Nehemiah as separate compositions, most notably James VanderKam and David Kraemer.[96] According to them, most of the above arguments for unity are untenable. Against Batten, for example, VanderKam reasonably suggests that the mention of one character in two different works does not necessarily mean that they were written by the same author, and he points out the possibility that two authors have recorded Ezra's career from different perspectives, comparing the various perspectives on Jesus in the Gospels.[97] Furthermore, he argues that the evidence based on Masoretic notes is inadequate proof of original unity, and is more pertinent to the history of transmission of the canon.[98] Arguing on rather different grounds, Kraemer acknowledges that the two books were recognized as a single work by the ancient believing community, but urges us to note the view of Origen, who divided E–N into two.[99]

These opponents of the unity of E–N have assembled the following arguments.[100] (1) the introduction to the book of Nehemiah, beginning with 'the words

---

95. Williamson, *Ezra, Nehemiah*, p. xxi, borrows heavily from Ryle, *Ezra and Nehemiah*, pp. ix–xiii.

96. VanderKam, 'Ezra–Nehemiah or Ezra and Nehemiah?', in Ulrich *et al.* (eds.), *Priests, Prophets and Scribes*, pp. 55–75; Kraemer, 'On the Relationship', pp. 73–92. A position similar to theirs has been opted for by Carl F. Keil, *Biblischer Commentar über die nachexilischen Geschichts-bücher: Chronik, Esra, Nehemia und Esther* (Leipzig: Doerffling und Franke, 1870), ET *The Books of Ezra, Nehemiah, and Esther* (trans. S. Taylor; Edinburgh: T&T Clark, 1873), pp. 5–14; Moses H. Segal, 'The Books of Ezra and Nehemiah' (Hebrew), *Tarbiz* 14 (1943), pp. 81–103; Shemaryahu Talmon, 'Ezra and Nehemiah', *IDBSup*, p. 318; Roland K. Harrison, *Introduction to the Old Testament* (London: The Tyndale Press, 1970), pp. 1149–50; Becking, 'Continuity and Community: The Belief System of the Book or Ezra', in B. Becking *et al.* (eds.), *The Crisis of Israelite Religion Tradition in Exilic and Post-Exilic Times* (*OTS*, XLII; Leiden: Brill), pp. 256–75, esp. p. 259.

97. VanderKam, 'Ezra–Nehemiah or Ezra and Nehemiah?', p. 61.

98. VanderKam, 'Ezra–Nehemiah or Ezra and Nehemiah?', p. 61. See also Talmon, 'Ezra and Nehemiah', p. 318.

99. Kraemer, 'On the Relationship', p. 76.

100. VanderKam, 'Ezra–Nehemiah or Ezra and Nehemiah?', pp. 61–75; Kraemer, 'On the Relationship', pp. 75–77; Cf. Keil, *Ezra, Nehemiah, and Esther*, p. 7; Segal, 'The Books of Ezra

of Nehemiah, the son of Hachaliah' (דברי נחמיה בן־חכליה; Neh. 1.1), clearly indicates that what follows is an independent composition; (2) the identical lists in Ezra 2 and Nehemiah 7 can be explained only when we propose separate authors for the two works; and (3) the books differ from each other in key respects, most notably their language, the ways in which they employ sources, and their themes.

This last argument requires a more detailed explanation. First of all, on the basis of the lists made by Driver and Curtis-Madsen,[101] VanderKam notes linguistic disagreements between Ezra and Nehemiah and concludes that more than half the entries for each list, which are relevant to the present context, clearly show serious *differences* in language between the two books.[102] He admits that this analysis has been done without consideration of the differences between sources and *editorial*[103] layers of the books. However, even when the examination is limited to the editorial portions alone, according to VanderKam, the same conclusion is reached. That is to say, after comparison with the passages which may be identified as the editor's contribution,[104] he maintains that, in spite of some resemblances, there are a number of remarkable differences, which compel us to consider Ezra and Nehemiah as separate literary units. For instance, the temple is referred to by its common name, בית האלהים, in both books (Ezra 3.8, 9; Neh. 12.40), but another name for it, בית יהוה, is found only in Ezra (3.8, 11). Also, the divine title, אלהי ישראל, is noted in Ezra alone (1.3; 3.2; 4.1, 3, 6, 21; 5.1; 6.14, 22; 7.6, 15; 8.25; 9.4, 15).[105] These linguistic differences, he argues, can be reckoned as conclusive evidence against the common authorship of Ezra and Nehemiah.

Secondly, VanderKam insists that the two books are similar in that they both rely heavily upon numerous sources, but are fundamentally different in the way they use them.[106] Ezra contains official documents (1.2-4; 4.17-22; 6.3-12; 7.12-26) and utilizes them as a means of authorizing the Jewish community to complete the restoration project. This practice is totally absent in Nehemiah, however, which does not quote or refer to any official royal documents even in places where we

and Nehemiah', pp. 93–96, 103; Harrison, *Introduction*, p. 1136; Talmon, 'Ezra and Nehemiah', p. 318; Becking, 'Ezra on the Move', p. 159.

101. Driver, *Introduction*, pp. 535–40; Curtis and Madsen, *Chronicles*, pp. 27–36.

102. '(a) Driver gives 46 entries; of these, 11 show no examples from either Ezra or Nehemiah and are thus irrelevant to the present context. Of the remaining 35 entries, 18 (in whole, or in part where the entry has subcategories) reveal differences between Ezra and Nehemiah in the sense that one book has the item in question while the other does not. Consequently, about one half of Driver's entries show linguistic distinctions between Ezra and Nehemiah. (b) Curtis and Madsen compiled a list of 136 items. Of these, 58 include no examples from either Ezra or Nehemiah. Of the remaining 78, 40 show disagreement between the two books.' VanderKam, 'Ezra–Nehemiah or Ezra and Nehemiah?', pp. 62–63.

103. In this book, I use the term *author*, rather than editor, compiler, or redactor, for the person who wrote and compiled E–N in its present form. Where I speak of or outline original works of those who prefer to use terms other than author, however, I employ them unamended.

104. Based on Williamson's analysis, the editorial passages he compares are: Ezra 1.1, 5-8; 3; 4.1-5; 4.23–5.5; 6.1-2, 13-22; 7.11, 27-28; Neh. 9.1-5 (?); 10.1, 29-40; 12.44-47. Cf. VanderKam, 'Ezra–Nehemiah or Ezra and Nehemiah?', p. 63.

105. For other examples, see VanderKam, 'Ezra–Nehemiah or Ezra and Nehemiah?', pp. 64–65.

106. VanderKam, 'Ezra–Nehemiah or Ezra and Nehemiah?', pp. 66–69.

would expect it (e.g., in Neh. 6.1-9, where 'he [Nehemiah] encounters the same sort of local opposition as befell the builders and restorers in Ezra'[107]).

Lastly, the themes of Ezra, according to VanderKam, are markedly different from those of Nehemiah because the former emphasizes the restoration of temple and people, whereas the latter emphasizes the rewalling and repopulating of Jerusalem.[108] Kraemer supports VanderKam by arguing that 'Ezra is a work of the priesthood, one that limits the realm of the most sacred to the Temple and the priesthood. Nehemiah, in contrast, is a lay composition that sees the Torah as the focus of the sacred.'[109]

From these various arguments, the opponents of the unity of E–N unhesitatingly conclude that the two books were independently composed by different authors, who possessed distinct and opposing ideologies.

1.2.2 *Evaluation of the Views*

Let us consider whether these arguments against the unity of E–N are compelling.[110]

First, opponents of unity regard the introductory words, דברי נחמיה בן־חכליה, in Neh 1.1 as the marker for an independent book. However, this sort of phrase in Old Testament literature does not always serve to indicate the beginning of a new book. While they may often play that role, as in Jeremiah 1.1, Hosea 1.1 or Joel 1.1, it is also common, however, for such headings to be used as sub-headings in the *middle* of books, as in the Psalter.[111] In such cases, a heading can show that the chapter following, though it has been included *within* the same book, is different from the preceding chapters in its *original* authorship. If it is assumed that Nehemiah is a work independent of Ezra, therefore, then the heading in Nehemiah may be used to confirm that assumption. But, in a situation where the literary relationship between the two books has not yet been decided, it is rash to present the heading as evidence for the separation of Nehemiah from Ezra: sub-headings may correspond to later *perceptions* of separate authorship which are not grounded in historical fact.

There is, in fact, reason to believe that, when the author composed Nehemiah, it was originally attached, in its present form, as a sequel to the Ezra material. In the second half of Neh. 1.1, there is a defective date, שנת עשרים ('the twentieth year'), with no mention of the king, who, from the context, must be the king Artaxerxes mentioned in Neh. 2.1.[112] It is quite difficult to suppose that in the heading of a book a writer would date the story so vaguely, assuming that the reader will come to discover the precise date later on (here in 2.1). Therefore, this dating can be

---

107. VanderKam, 'Ezra–Nehemiah or Ezra and Nehemiah?', p. 66
108. VanderKam, 'Ezra–Nehemiah or Ezra and Nehemiah?', pp. 69–75.
109. Kraemer, 'On the Relationship', p. 92.
110. The following discussion is focused largely on internal evidence which has been challenged by the proponents of the disunity of E–N. For a useful discussion of the external evidence, see Eskenazi, *Age of Prose*, pp. 11–13.
111. Cf. James Limburg, 'Psalms, Book of', *IDB*, vol. 5, pp. 522–36.
112. Rudolph suggests that the original text had the reference to ארתחשסתא המלך ('Artaxerxes, the king'). Cf. Rudolph, *Esra und Nehemia*, p. 102 and the apparatus on p. 1431 of the *BHS*. It is hard to adopt his suggestion, however, since there is no textual evidence to argue that this was dropped. Cf. Williamson, *Ezra, Nehemiah*, p. 166.

properly understood only when we assume that the author thought that the king's date would be recognized by the reader who had encountered it already in Ezra 7 as the time of Artaxerxes.[113]

The addition of this verse was probably motivated by the desire to indicate that the first person in the following narratives is Nehemiah, not Ezra who was portrayed as the main character in the preceding chapters (Ezra 7–10). In contrast, the absence of the same introductory words in Ezra 7.1, where the Ezra narratives begin, may indicate that there was no possibility of confusion between Ezra 6 and 7 in terms of the protagonist.

In conclusion, while it is true that the introductory words in Neh. 1.1 probably indicate an editorial perception of a different original author for the subsequent source material, there is insufficient evidence to suppose that this reflects either genuinely different authorship or a quite separate composition.

Secondly, the argument based on the duplicate lists of returnees in Ezra 2 and Neh. 7 also has some flaws. The repetition of the list, according to the opponents of unity, cannot fully be comprehended without supposing separate authors of the two works. In particular, VanderKam criticizes Eskenazi's proposal that the repetition plays the role of an *inclusio*, which unifies the material and is therefore a clue, rather than an obstacle, to the understanding of the structure of E–N,[114] claiming that her argument simply presupposes the unity of E–N.[115] However, VanderKam is himself by no means exempt from much the same sort of criticism. Indeed, after pointing out the absurdity of Eskenazi's assumption that the same editor was responsible for the lists in Ezra 2 and Neh. 7, which seem incompatible with each other in a historical sense,[116] he swiftly proposes that we should believe that there were two editors: 'one editor for the book of Ezra and another for the book of Nehemiah'.[117] This proposal is also apparently based on a presupposition – that of separate authorship. The theory that the lists were inserted by different editors may be acceptable, but why, then, cannot we here suppose an editor *for each editorial part, not for each book*, since an editorial division between Ezra 1–6 and Ezra 7–Neh. 13 is widely favoured?[118] Surprisingly, however, he states his conclusion without any discussion of the problems which might occur with such a division.[119]

---

113. For a similar argument, see Williamson, *Ezra, Nehemiah*, p. 166.

114. For other functions of the repetition of the lists, see T.C. Eskenazi, 'The Structure of Ezra–Nehemiah and the Integrity of the Book', *JBL* 107 (1988), pp. 641–56, esp. pp. 646–50.

115. VanderKam, 'Ezra–Nehemiah or Ezra and Nehemiah?', pp. 67–69.

116. If the same editor was responsible for both, the 'seventh month' of the texts becomes inexplicable, because it refers to a year in Cyrus's reign in the case of Ezra 2 and simultaneously to a year in Artaxerxes' reign in the case of Neh. 7. See VanderKam, 'Ezra–Nehemiah or Ezra and Nehemiah?', p. 68.

117. VanderKam, 'Ezra–Nehemiah or Ezra and Nehemiah?', p. 68.

118. E.g. Williamson, 'The Composition of Ezra i–vi', pp. 1–30; Eskenazi, 'The Structure of Ezra–Nehemiah', p. 645; Throntveit, *Ezra–Nehemiah*, p. 11. Cf. Gelston, 'The End of Chronicles', pp. 53–60, where he regards Ezra 1–6 as the end of Chronicles and accepts the division between Ezra 1–6 and Ezra 7–Nehemiah 13.

119. If we adopt the currently favoured division, the force of the evidence VanderKam proposes

On the other hand, it should also be noted that explanations for the twofold citation of the lists have been provided in quite cogent ways by those who accept the aforementioned editorial division. Of several explanations for the repetition, the following two are the most plausible. One is that the repetition of the lists was devised to show the continuity between the community which first returned and built the temple (Ezra 2) and the purified community (Neh. 7).[120] The other is that of William Dumbrell, who affirms Kurt Galling's view that the list in Ezra 2 was a register supplied to Tattenai of returnees who were authorized to build the temple.[121] Dumbrell further maintains that, despite its presence in Neh. 7, the list had to be repeated in Ezra 2 to demonstrate that in circumstances where the work was opposed by the people of the land (4.4), 'we' (4.3) *alone*, with reference to the list in Ezra 2, were authorized to participate in the work.[122]

On this basis, therefore, we cannot accept the argument based on the repetition of the lists as evidence for viewing E–N as two separate works.

Lastly, VanderKam argues that differences in language and the ways of employing sources offer weighty evidence for separate authorship. However, his arguments present many problems. For example, he lays stress on the exclusive use of בית יהוה in Ezra, but this phrase is also found in Neh. 10.36, which is one of the editorial passages he compares. Both books also share certain technical terms, i.e., נתינים ('temple servants')[123] and יד אלהים על ('the hand of God upon …'),[124] which are not found in any other books of the Old Testament.[125]

VanderKam also tries to show differences in themes between Ezra and Nehemiah. In doing so, he has to argue against Eskenazi, who maintains that the theme of the house of God is interrelated in both books and takes this as evidence for the unity of E–N. According to VanderKam, Eskenazi may be right when she highlights the temple theme in Ezra, but is fatally wrong when claiming that this theme is expanded to Neh. 1–7.[126] However, his argument is weak. While the theme of the

---

may be lost. For instance, he argues that the title of the king of Persia (מלך פרס) frequently occurs in Ezra (1.1, 2, 8; 3.7; 4.3, 5, 7, 24; 6.14; 7.1; 9.9), but not in Nehemiah (only in Neh. 12.22). If we apply our division, however, the contrast in frequency of the title is notably abated: nine times in Ezra 1–6 and three times in Ezra 7–Neh. 13.

120. Gunneweg, 'Zur Interpretation der Bucher Esra-Nehemia', p. 156; Williamson, *Ezra, Nehemiah*, p. 269.

121. K. Galling, 'The "Gōlā List" According to Ezra 2/Nehemiah 7', *JBL* 70 (1951), pp. 149–58, esp. 153–54.

122. W.J. Dumbrell, 'The Theological Intention of Ezra–Nehemiah', *The Reformed Theological Review* 45 (1986), p. 66. This view was likewise expressed to Carl Schultz, 'The Political Tensions Reflected in Ezra–Nehemiah', in C.D. Evans *et al.* (eds.), *Scripture in Context* (Pittsburgh: Pickwick, 1980), pp. 221–43, esp. p. 227.

123. Ezra 2.43, 58, 70; 7.7, 24; 8.17, 20 and Neh. 3.26, 31; 7.46, 60, 72; 10.29; 11.3, 21. Regarding the reference to it in 1 Chronicles 9.2, see n. 68 above.

124. Ezra 7.9; 8.18, 31 and Neh. 2.8.

125. Michael W. Duggan, 'An Exegetical, Literary, Theological, and Intertextual Study of the Covenant Renewal in Ezra–Nehemiah (Neh 7.72b–10.40)' (unpublished PhD dissertation, Catholic University of America, 1996), p. 50.

126. 'Eskenazi's intriguing attempt to inflate the meaning of "the house of God" should therefore be rejected. The themes of the book of Ezra will not accommodate the contents of the

house of God may not be shared, the theme of the *restoration* of the post-exilic community is clearly shared in the two books.[127] VanderKam may argue that the restoration should be understood independently, i.e., within the confines of Ezra's 10 chapters and Nehemiah's 13 chapters,[128] but the restoration in Ezra is closely connected with that in Nehemiah. For example, the restoration of community which commenced with Ezra is accomplished when Ezra reads the Law. This is recorded in Neh. 8, not in Ezra.

Kraemer's view, similar to that of VanderKam, is also open to criticism: its fundamental fault lies in a misunderstanding of the concerns found in each book. Kraemer contends that Ezra, as a priestly book, is concerned with the priesthood and Levites, whereas Nehemiah, as a lay book, sometimes shows 'antagonism to priestly concerns'.[129] It is misleading, however, to characterize the book of Ezra as a more priestly-inclined book, when the book of Nehemiah shows as strong an interest in priests and Levites as does Ezra. For instance, the typical phrase, הכהנים והלוים, which may show the *close* relationship between the clerical orders, recurs throughout Ezra as well as Nehemiah.[130] Also, since the book of Nehemiah includes the Nehemiah Memoir, which has a strong pro-Levitical inclination (e.g., Neh. 13.4-23),[131] it is not unreasonable to think that Nehemiah is concerned with the promotion of Levites, which presumably would not have been a concern of lay people.[132]

In short, the opponents of the unity of E–N have made attempts to challenge the thesis of unity by advancing three main arguments focused on: (1) the introductory phrase in Neh. 1.1; (2) the identical lists in Ezra 2 and Neh. 7; and (3) differences between the two books in language and themes. All of them, however, are unconvincing.

1.2.3. *Other Considerations*
If the opponents of the unity of E–N have failed to undermine the literary connection of Ezra and Nehemiah, there are also several positive indications of shared

---

book of Nehemiah.' VanderKam, 'Ezra–Nehemiah or Ezra and Nehemiah?', p. 74. Cf. Eskenazi, *Age of Prose*, pp. 60–77.

127. E.g., P.R. Ackroyd, *Exile and Restoration* (London: SCM Press, 1968), pp. 138–39.

128. VanderKam, 'Ezra–Nehemiah or Ezra and Nehemiah?', p. 74.

129. Kraemer, 'On the Composition', p. 77.

130. Ezra 1.5; 2.70; 3.8, 12; 6.16, 20; 7.7, 13, 24; 8.29, 30; 9.1; 10.5, and Neh. 7.72b; 8.13; 10.1, 29, 35; 11.3, 20; 12.1, 30, 44; 13.30. For a detailed discussion on this matter, see sections 4.1.2.1 and 4.2.3 below.

131. For a more detailed discussion on this matter, see section 6.1.3.2 below.

132. Also, it should be noted that, in contrast to Kraemer's argument, 'On the Relationship', pp. 79-83, Ezra is designated as scribe and priest in Nehemiah, as well (Neh. 8.1, 2, 4, 5, 9, 13; 12.26, 36). The inadequacy of Kraemer's argument has been pointed out by Richards, 'Reshaping Chronicles and Ezra–Nehemiah Interpretation', p. 214, who says 'Nehemiah's concern with the Torah and Ezra's interest in the more priestly matters reflect major issues of Persian period Judah, but not necessarily, distinct literature', and by Lester L. Grabbe, *Ezra–Nehemiah* (London and New York: Routledge, 1998), pp. 105–106, who argues that the central themes in Ezra, such as the priesthood and the maintenance of the temple and cult, are continued in Nehemiah, too, and the perspectives between the traditions about Ezra in Ezra and those in Neh. 8 are not different.

authorship, which ultimately lead us to accept E–N as a unified work. We have already noted the external evidence cited by Batten and Williamson. To this we may add the internal evidence in support of the unity of E–N put forward by Michael Duggan, who believes that the book of Ezra requires Nehemiah for its narrative integrity, and vice versa. He adduces as evidence the following:

> The unadorned mention of 'Ezra, the scribe' as the addressee of the people's request (Neh 8.2) requires the narrator's prior introduction of this important figure (Ezr 7.6, 10, 11). The same holds true for the phrase 'the book of the Torah' (Neh 8.1), which is never mentioned in Nehemiah 1–7 and therefore requires the introduction provided by Ezra (7.6, 10, 11, 12, 21; 10.3; cf. 3.2; 6.18). The weeping of the people in reaction to Ezra's reading (Neh 8.9) makes no sense without a prior knowledge of his dealings with them over the matter of marriage reforms (Ezr 10.1). Likewise, the brief references to 'separation' from foreigners in Nehemiah 9.2; 10.29 presume a previous treatment of the issue (Ezr 9.1; 10.8, 11, 16: בדל: niphal). Similarly, since concern for the temple is notoriously absent in Nehemiah 1–9 (cf. 6.10; 8.16), the concentration on temple-related issues in the written oath of Nehemiah 10.33-40 presupposes the prior attention to the temple found in Ezra (see, e.g., Ezr 1.2-4, 5-11; 2.68–3.13; 6.2b-12, 13-22; 7.15-20; 8.24-36). Lastly, Nehemiah's linking of the eras of Zerubbabel and Jeshua with the days of Ezra and Nehemiah by using lists (Neh 7.5-72a; 12.1-26) and narrative comment (12.47) presumes familiarity with Ezra's story of Zerubbabel and Jeshua (Ezr 2.1–5.2).[133]

This argument receives additional support in the work of two other scholars. First, on an analysis of E–N's structure, Eskenazi observes that a few themes are internally combined throughout the whole book, thus confirming the unity of E–N.[134] For example, the centrality of the community as a whole runs from the beginning to the end of the work. Second, according to Throntveit, the literary devices, i.e., *concentricity*, *parallel panels*, and *repetitive resumptions*, are found from the beginning of E–N to its end: they are not found solely in Ezra or in Nehemiah, but in both.[135] Furthermore, the so-called *name theology*,[136] which is almost exclusively prevalent in Deuteronomy and the Deuteronomistic History, appears in both books (Ezra 6.12; Neh. 1.9).

These findings may corroborate the proposition that E–N should be treated as a unified work, not as two separate works.

1.2.4 Conclusion

A few scholars have presented arguments in favour of regarding Ezra and Nehemiah as two separate compositions. A close examination, however, shows that these arguments are far from compelling, and that there are numerous indications supporting common authorship: the books of Ezra and Nehemiah are internally

---

133. Duggan, 'An Exegetical', pp. 49–50.

134. Eskenazi, *Age of Prose*, pp. 37–126. For a detailed discussion about her view, see section 2.2.1 below.

135. Cf. Throntveit, *Ezra–Nehemiah*, pp. 4–8.

136. I.e., the notion that Yahweh's presence is not confined to the ark but everywhere on earth. Cf. G. von Rad, *Studies in Deuteronomy* (London: SCM Press, 1953), pp. 37ff.

dependent upon each other, and are structured coherently and consistently. This enables us confidently to claim that E–N is a *single unified* work.

1.3 *Summary*

So far, as a prelude for the main study, we have examined issues of the authorship and boundaries of E–N. In the first section of this chapter, the leading question was whether or not E–N should be treated as part of the Chronicler's work. From our analysis of the principal arguments favouring common authorship of Chronicles and E–N, we concluded that this theory is established on shaky ground, and that it is easier to conclude that E–N was composed as a work independent of Chronicles. We then focused on arguments for viewing E–N as two separate works, a possibility which was also discounted on several grounds. We shall, therefore, continue to treat E–N as a single unified composition for the purpose of this book.

With these conclusions in hand, we shall now proceed to a discussion of the authorship of E–N. There has been very little previous work done on this issue from the perspective of E–N as a single work, separate from Chronicles. Before a thorough examination of that issue, however, we shall seek to narrow down potential authors of E–N, since prior research reveals that there are limited possibilities which deserve attention. These will be presented in chapter 2.

Chapter 2

PRIESTLY OR LEVITICAL AUTHORSHIP?

Having concluded that E–N is a work independent of Chronicles as well as one unified by internal coherence and consistency, let us now focus our discussion on its authorship, which is the prime concern of this book.

Although, as we shall see, several different proposals have been put forward, most of these are unpersuasive. After a survey of previous research, therefore, we shall focus principally upon Williamson's hypothesis of priestly authorship, before turning to explore some possibilities hitherto neglected in recent studies. We shall begin the chapter, however, by investigating the *date* of E–N, as a preliminary to the ensuing discussions; a number of issues are closely linked to this matter, and problems may arise if it is not discussed.

2.1 *The Date of Ezra–Nehemiah*

E–N's composition has traditionally been dated to about 400 BCE; the last event described in the book is Nehemiah's second visit (cf. Neh. 13), dated around 433 BCE, and Jaddua, found in the list of Neh. 12.10-11, 22-23, may be dated to the time of Darius II Ochus (424–405).[1]

This proposed date has been challenged by scholars who assign a late date to the mission of Ezra (i.e., 398 BCE). They argue that the *terminus a quo* must be, at the earliest, in the early fourth century BCE, and that the compositional date should probably be placed around the mid fourth century BCE.[2] There are also scholars who rely upon Josephus' claim that Jaddua lived in the early Greek period (i.e., in the time of Darius III Codomannus [336–331] in Persia, and of Alexander the Great in Greece; cf. *Ant.* xi, vii, 2), and consequently reach a similar conclusion, that the work should be dated no earlier than the fourth century BCE.[3]

The argument from the date of Ezra's mission raises some well-known problems.

Of three major proposals, dating Ezra to 458 BCE, 428 BCE, or 398 BCE respectively,[4] the popularity of the second has waned in recent decades, since it relies on

---

1. E.g., Rudolph, *Esra und Nehemia*, pp. xxiv–xxv; Freedman, 'The Chronicler's Purpose', pp. 436–42; Cross, 'A Reconstruction of the Judean Restoration', pp. 11–12; Myers, *Ezra–Nehemiah*, p. lxx; Clines, *Ezra, Nehemiah, Esther*, pp. 12–14.

2. E.g., P.R. Ackroyd, *I & II Chronicles, Ezra, Nehemiah: Introduction and Commentary* (London: SCM Press, 1973), pp. 25–26; Shaver, *Torah and the Chronicler's History Work*, pp. 71–72.

3. E.g., Torrey, *Ezra Studies*, pp. 30–35; Batten, *Ezra and Nehemiah*, pp. 2–3; Noth, *ÜS*, pp. 150–55.

4. For a helpful summary of these proposals for Ezra's date, see John Bright, *A History of*

emending the 'seventh' year for Ezra's return in Ezra 7.7-8 to the 'thirty-seventh' year, an emendation which is based utterly on unsupported conjecture.[5] The dating to 398 BCE was once prevalent but has also been seriously challenged in more modern scholarship. The weightiest argument in its favour is that Eliashib was the high priest in Nehemiah's time (Neh. 3.1, 20-21; 13.28), while Jehohanan, the son of Eliashib, is described as a contemporary of Ezra in Ezra 10.6,[6] thus implying that Ezra belonged to a later period than Nehemiah, whose date is agreed to be 445 BCE.[7] As Williamson has pointed out, however, this argument glosses over certain difficulties. It is, indeed, uncertain whether or not Ezra 10.6 refers to the *high-priestly* family. There is a discrepancy in the lists between Ezra 10.6 and Neh. 12.11-12, 22, the latter of which is part of a genealogy of high priests; in the first, Jehohanan/Johanan is son while, in the second, *grandson*. Furthermore, in Neh. 13.4, Eliashib is described as one 'appointed over the chambers of the house of our God'. It is highly unlikely that a high priest functioned as a caretaker and this shows that there was another person, named Eliashib, in Nehemiah's time who was not a high priest, while mention of a 'chamber' in Neh. 13.4 links it to Ezra 10.6 which also contains the same word. Here, of course, if both verses refer to the same Eliashib, Ezra should be dated later than Nehemiah. But since the practice of papponymy was prevalent at that time, it is also possible to think that the Eliashib in Neh. 13.4 might be the grandson of that in Ezra 10.6 (thus, Eliashib [Ezra 10.6] → Jehohanan [a contemporary of Ezra] → Eliashib [Neh. 13.5; a contemporary of Nehemiah]), showing that the late date for Ezra is not the only and best possibility.[8]

By contrast, the traditional view dating Ezra to 458 BCE has survived persistent attacks. After a careful examination of the arguments against this traditional view, Williamson contends that all are unconvincing. For example, in Ezra 9.9, Ezra

---

Israel (Philadelphia: Westminster Press, 3rd edn, 1981), pp. 391–402. Among the most complete bibliographies of prior discussions about this matter is Leslie McFall, 'Was Nehemiah Contemporary with Ezra in 458 B.C.?', *WTJ* 53 (1991), pp. 263–93, esp. nn. 1–13 on pp. 263–65.

    5.   Cf. J.A. Emerton, 'Did Ezra go to Jerusalem in 428 BC?', *JTS* n.s. 17 (1966), pp. 1–19.

    6.   In addition to this, some scholars have favoured Ezra's late date based on a few more arguments: for example, they argue that when Nehemiah reviewed the census of the returnees (Neh. 7.5-73), he was completely ignorant of those who returned with Ezra (Ezra 8.1-14). Cf. Albin van Hoonacker, 'Néhémie et Esdras: Nouvelle hypothèse sur la chronolgie de l'époque de la restauration', *Muséon* 9 (1890), pp. 151–84, 317–51, 389–401; 'La succession chronologique Néhémie-Esdras', *RB* 32 (1923), pp. 481–94; H. Cazelles, 'La Mission d'Esdras', *VT* 4 (1954), pp. 113–40; Harold H. Rowley, 'The Chronological Order of Ezra and Nehemiah', in *The Servant of the Lord and Other Essays* (Oxford: Blackwell, 2nd edn, 1965), pp. 137–68; Widengren, 'The Persian Period', pp. 503–509. These arguments, however, have already been critically examined by many scholars. Cf. John S. Wright, *The Date of Ezra's Coming to Jerusalem* (London: Tyndale Press, 1958); U. Kellermann, 'Erwägungen zum Problem der Esradatierung', *ZAW* 80 (1968), pp. 55–87; W. Th. In der Smitten, *Esra: Quellen, Überlieferung und Geschichte* (Studia Semitica Neerlandica 15; Assen: Van Gorcum, 1973), pp. 91–105; Williamson, *Ezra and Nehemiah*, pp. 59–64.

    7.   This agreement is based on an Elephantine papyrus, which shows that Sanballat, who had been Nehemiah's foe, was an old man in 407 BCE and that the Jerusalem high priest in 410 BCE was Johanan, who was the son of Eliashib, the high priest at the time of Nehemiah. For the papyrus mentioned, see Pritchard, *ANET*, p. 492.

    8.   Cf. Williamson, *Ezra and Nehemiah* (OTG; Sheffield: JSOT Press, 1987), pp. 63–64.

gives thanks to God for having given them a 'wall' in Judah and Jerusalem. On the basis of this, it has been argued that the work of Nehemiah had already been performed before Ezra came, which would suggest a late date for Ezra. As Williamson points out, however, it is also possible to interpret the use of the word here as metaphorical, just as in Psalm 80.12. Moreover, the common Hebrew word for a city wall is חומה, not גדר which is used here.[9]

There is strong biblical evidence to suggest that the early date is most plausible. For example, it would be hard to explain the widespread support which Ezra gained when tackling mixed marriages, if this was performed after Nehemiah's rigorous separation (Neh. 13.4-8, 23-28), which would have displeased many people (particularly the priests).[10] Moreover, as noted earlier,[11] the unqualified date, 'the twentieth year', in Neh. 1.1b presupposes that a king was referred to before this verse (here, in Ezra 7.7). This means that the king in Ezra 7 is the same king in the narrative following Neh. 1.1b. Since the king linked to Nehemiah is apparently Artaxerxes I Longimanus (464–425) and Ezra came to Jerusalem in the seventh year of the same king, his date should be 458 BCE. In short, the date of Ezra's mission is obviously one of the most difficult issues in current Old Testament scholarship and no consensus prevails,[12] but based on our research so far, we find the traditional date for Ezra (458 BCE) most plausible.

The mention of Jaddua is also problematic. If that individual is taken to have been a contemporary of Darius III or Alexander, the list in Neh. 12 produces an unusually long tenure for priesthood.[13] So, taking their cue from Cross' suggestion that the practice of papponymy was prevalent in ancient times, on one hand[14] many scholars suspect that there were a few, though not many, more high priests with the

---

9.   For Williamson's other critical arguments, see Williamson, *Ezra and Nehemiah*, pp. 59–62. Very recently, Schaper, *Priester und Leviten* (2000), pp. 244–49, has expressed support for a late date, and attempted to counter Williamson's argument on one point. It has long been argued that Ezra came later than Nehemiah because the committees in Ezra 8.33 and Neh. 13.13 are the same, and when Ezra arrived in Jerusalem he came across that committee, which is supposed to have been established by Nehemiah. Against this argument, Williamson (pp. 60–61) had held that the committee is not the same; the constitution of the committee is different: two priests and two Levites in Ezra while a priest (Shelemiah), a scribe (Zadok), a Levite (Pedaiah) and a layman (Hanan) in Nehemiah. Schaper argues, however, that the committee in Neh. 13 also consisted of two priests and two Levites ('einem Priester, eniem priesterlichen Schreiber und zwei Leviten, Pedaja und Hanan', p. 245). It is unclear whether Zadok was a *priestly* scribe, and Hanan may be a Levite as elsewhere in E–N (Neh. 8.7; 10.11), though not always (Ezra 2.46 [Neh. 7.49]; Neh. 10.23, 27): for that reason, Schaper's argument seems unconvincing.

10.   For more examples, see Williamson, *Ezra and Nehemiah*, pp. 64–68.

11.   See section 1.2.2.

12.   Cf. J. Maxwell Miller, 'Israelite History', in D.A. Knight *et al.* (eds.), *The Hebrew Bible and Its Modern Interpreters* (Philadelphia: Fortress Press, 1985), pp. 1–30, esp. pp. 17–19; Graham, 'The 'Chronicler's History': Ezra–Nehemiah, 1–2 Chronicles', pp. 204–205.

13.   The texts mention six high priests (Jeshua → Joiakim → Eliashib → Joiada → Jonathan [Johanan] → Jaddua). Therefore, if Jaddua was contemporary of Darius III (336–331), it means that there were about 240 years for only six priests, since Jeshua was probably born in *circa* 570 BCE. Cf. Cross, 'A Reconstruction of the Judean Restoration', p. 17.

14.   Cross, 'A Reconstruction of the Judean Restoration', pp. 9–18.

same name, on the other. Jaddua in Neh. 12 may therefore be equated with Jaddua II, born *circa* 420 BCE, not with Jaddua III, born *circa* 370 BCE, who is assumed to have been a contemporary of Alexander.[15] In addition, as pointed out by Ackroyd, there is no indication in E–N that Persian rule has come to an end. This forces us to date Jaddua before Alexander's age.[16] From this discussion, therefore, it may be better to view E–N's composition as in the late *fifth* century BCE.

In addition to these major arguments, a few miscellaneous points have been made in favour of a late date: (1) Rowley argues that the *Aramaic* in Ezra is later than the Elephantine papyri of the late fifth century BCE;[17] (2) it is suggested that some passages in E–N (especially Ezra 4) are out of order because the book was composed a very long time after the real events;[18] and (3) the animosity toward the Samaritans expressed in Ezra 4 is taken to presuppose the existence of a Samaritan community, which was only established after 350 BCE.[19]

These arguments are not firmly grounded, however. The character of the Aramaic in Ezra is still much debated and the issue is complicated by the possibility that a later copyist might have corrected it orthographically. Thus the language in Ezra remains a poor basis for any argument about the date of composition.[20] Ezra 4 seems indeed to be out of order, but the problem has convincingly been explained in other ways, as we shall see later.[21] The argument based on the date of the Samaritans is also weak since 'hostility between Jews and Samaritans may be traced much further back than the fifth century'.[22] In addition, it may be misleading to think that this kind of animosity prompted composition of the book. If so, we might as well connect the issue of compositional date to other resentments against, for example, the Ammonites or the Arabs, since Tobiah the Ammonite and Geshem the Arab were among the Israelites' main opponents.

To sum up, because the last event reported in E–N is Nehemiah's second visit, dated *circa* 433 BCE, and because it is most likely that Ezra returned to Jerusalem in 458 BCE, we agree that the book was probably composed in the late fifth century BCE.

15.   Kidner, *Ezra & Nehemiah*, pp. 143–46; Richard J. Coggins, *Ezra and Nehemiah* (Cambridge: Cambridge University Press, 1976), pp. 130–31; Bright, *A History of Israel*, p. 397; Clines, *Ezra, Nehemiah, Esther*, p. 225.

16.   Ackroyd, *I & II Chronicles, Ezra, Nehemiah*, p. 25. There has been a recognition that though Jaddua was a contemporary of Alexander it does not directly support the late compositional date of E–N; it is always possible to say that this list could have been added later by an editorial hand. Cf. L.H. Brockington, *Ezra, Nehemiah and Esther*, p. 25.

17.   H.H. Rowley, 'Nehemiah's Mission and Its Background', in *Men of God: Studies in Old Testament History and Prophecy* (London: Nelson, 1963), pp. 211–45, esp. p. 217.

18.   Cf. Ackroyd, *I & II Chronicles, Ezra, Nehemiah*, p. 25; Bright, *A History of Israel*, pp. 396–97.

19.   Georg Fohrer, *Einleitung in das Alte Testament* (Quelle & Meyer: Heidelberg, 1965), ET *Introduction to the Old Testament* (trans. David Green; London: SPCK Press, 1970), p. 239.

20.   See Kenneth A. Kitchen, 'The Aramaic of Daniel', in Donald J. Wiseman *et al.*, *Notes on some Problems in the Book of Daniel* (London: Tyndale, 1965), pp. 31–79. Cf. Clines, *Ezra, Nehemiah, Esther*, p. 13.

21.   E.g., Talmon, 'Ezra and Nehemiah', p. 322; Williamson, 'The Composition of Ezra i–vi', pp. 16–20. For a detailed discussion, see section 6.1.2.2.

22.   Clines, *Ezra, Nehemiah, Esther*, p. 13.

Our examination of challenges to this date has shown that most of them are unconvincing. Therefore, the dating of E–N to the late fifth century BCE is, at present, the best available. The ensuing discussions will be based on this date.

2.2 *Prior Research*

Because so many earlier scholars adhered to the belief that E–N was composed alongside Chronicles, there have been relatively few attempts to pinpoint the origin of the work on the basis of arguments specific to its own content. We can focus, therefore, on the views on authorship of four scholars: W.F. Albright, T.C. Eskenazi, S. Japhet, and H.G.M. Williamson. The last three obviously do favour the separation of E–N from Chronicles in terms of authorship, and have correspondingly proposed theories of authorship and composition which take account of this. Albright seems, on the face of it, however, to be a curious addition to this list, because he is a supporter of the common authorship of Chronicles and E–N. However, since he raises the possibility that the author of E–N might be Ezra – a possibility which has not been totally dismissed even by scholars favouring separate authorship[23] – Albright's views may be said to place a similar emphasis on the content of E–N, over against Chronicles.

In what follows, it is convenient to outline the views of these scholars by dividing them into two groups: Eskenazi and Japhet focus their studies on *how* E–N was composed, while Albright and Williamson focus on *who* composed it. Williamson's view will be considered separately in the next section, since it requires more detailed discussion.

2.2.1 *Tamara C. Eskenazi, A Focus on* How
Eskenazi tackles the authorship issue of E–N through a *synchronic* approach, which obliges us to conceive of the book primarily as literature rather than a historical text.[24] She first observes the repetition of the lists of the returnees in Ezra 2 and Neh. 7, and identifies this as a compositional technique, delimiting a unit in Ezra 1.5–Neh. 7.72.[25] On this basis, she divides E–N into three progressive parts dealing with: (1) *potentiality* in Ezra 1.1-4, where the objective of the work is defined; (2) *the*

---

23. E.g., Williamson, *Ezra, Nehemiah*, p. xxxi. Likewise, Nehemiah's authorship of E–N has also been noted by Myers, *Ezra–Nehemiah*, p. lxiii, on the basis of 2 Maccabees 2.13 and the Talmudic tradition (*Baba Bathra*, 16a), but this has received little support, and we shall not deal with it here.

24. See Eskenazi, *Age of Prose*. This synchronic approach to E–N has also been taken by Harm W.M. van Grol, 'Ezra 7,1-10: Een Literair-stilistische Analyse', *Bijdragen* 51 (1990), pp. 21–37; *idem*, 'Schuld und Scham: Die Verwurzelung von Ezra 9,6-7 in der Tradition', *Estudios Bíblicos* 55 (1997), pp. 29–52; Gordon F. Davies, *Ezra and Nehemiah* (Berit Olam; Collegeville, Minnesota: The Liturgical Press, 1999). Cf. Becking, 'Ezra on the Move', p. 168.

25. According to Eskenazi, 'The Structure of Ezra–Nehemiah', p. 645, the repetition here is neither an error, nor evidence for the separate authorship of Ezra and Nehemiah, but was 'a voluntary and thus presumably deliberate act of the author/compiler'. She observes six important functions of the lists in E–N. One of them is the function of *inclusio* which unifies material (p. 646; see pp. 647–50 for the other functions).

process of actualization in Ezra 1.5–Neh. 7.72, where the objective is realized; and (3) *success* in Neh. 8.1–13.31, where the objective is achieved.[26]

She goes on to argue, not only that the book is structurally organized in this way, but also that three fundamental issues ('people', 'house of God', and 'written documents') recur in each unit, and thus constitute the main themes of the work.[27] The first theme, the centrality of the *people*, is expressed in various ways.[28] The second theme, the building of the *house of God*, is also found throughout, although less obviously, since the concept of the house of God in E–N is expanded from the temple to the whole city (Ezra 6.14).[29] The last theme, the centrality of the *written documents* as a source of authority, is represented by the collection of archival texts in each unit, which give rise to both conflict and resolution, but ultimately to fulfillment.[30] In short, in relation to the composition of E–N, Eskenazi observes that (1) the book is structurally well organized; and (2) common themes recur in each unit of the book.

Eskenazi's work has not escaped criticism, either for its minor methodological inconsistencies,[31] or for more substantial problems. Her presupposition that E–N is

---

26.   Eskenazi, *Age of Prose*, pp. 38–39.

27.   Eskenazi, *Age of Prose*, pp. 40, 44.

28.   In the first unit (Ezra 1.1-4), for example, the focus is directed on to the people by Cyrus's decree, which was issued for all God's people, not confined to some specially ranked group (Ezra 1.3-4). In the second unit (Ezra 1.5–Neh. 7.72), while leaders and heroic figures are shunned, the people are emphasized in the lists of returnees, which embrace the whole people with considerable specificity and length (Ezra 2.1-67; Neh. 7.6-69). More attention to the people is also paid in the Ezra material (Ezra 7–10), where, for example, the reform in Ezra 10 was prompted by the request of the people who repented of their sins (Ezra 10.1-5), and also in the first work of Nehemiah (Neh. 1–7), e.g., in the list of those who built the wall (Neh. 3.1-32), which includes all the people. The third unit (Neh. 8–13) continues to highlight the people as a whole in the following reforming narratives by describing all the people as actors or subjects in various reformational events: i.e., the reading and implementations of Torah (Neh. 8), repentance (Neh. 9), pledging to Torah (Neh. 10), repopulating Jerusalem (Neh. 11.1–12.26), and the dedication ceremony (Neh. 12.27-42). Cf. Eskenazi, *Age of Prose*, pp. 48–53, 62–70, 79–83, 97–104, 111–19, 185–88.

29.   Such an understanding of the phrase ('house of God'), according to Eskenazi, can be justified on these grounds: (1) 'house of God' (בית אלהים) is used differently from 'temple' (היכל) (e.g., Ezra 3.6-8); (2) in Artaxerxes correspondence (Ezra 4.1-3, 24), the phrase is used for both 'the city and the walls' (4.12-13, 16, 21); (3) in Ezra 6.14 ('they built and finished it, according to the commandment of the God of Israel, and according to the command of Cyrus, Darius, and Artaxerxes king of Persia'), the building work is not completed until the time of Artaxerxes, who is associated with both the city wall and the reformation of the community; (4) the participation of the high priest in the building of the Sheep Gate shows that the building work of the city was regarded as consecrated like the temple area; (5) such temple personnel as gatekeepers and Levites, whose duty was limited to the temple inside, are now appointed to the whole city (Neh. 11.1); and (6) in the dedication ceremony, the walls (Neh. 12.30) are purified together with the priests and the Levites. Cf. Eskenazi, *Age of Prose*, pp. 53–57, 71–73, 83–87, 119–21, 188–89.

30.   E.g., Ezra 1.1-4 for the first unit; Ezra 7.12-26 for the second; and Neh. 10.2-28 for the third. Cf. Eskenazi, *Age of Prose*, pp. 43–44, 58–60, 73–77, 87–88, 109–11, 122, 180–82, 189–92. See also T.C. Eskenazi, 'Ezra–Nehemiah: From Text to Actuality', J.C. Exum (ed.), *Signs and Wonders: Biblical Tests in Literary Focus* (Atlanta: Scholars Press, 1989), pp. 165–97.

31.   Cf. Becking, 'Ezra on the Move', pp. 167–68, points out that Eskenazi incorrectly quotes a

systematically structured, for example, leads her to overstate the compositional significance of the census lists in Ezra 2.1-67 and Neh. 7.6-72, and to ignore the fact that the first list is attached to preceding narrative material (Ezra 1.5-11), which casts doubt on its role as a heading.[32] Moreover, it is commonly accepted that the narrative of the repopulation of Jerusalem in Neh. 7.4-5a, 11.1-2 is interrupted by the insertion of Neh. 7.5b–10.40.[33] This raises questions about Eskenazi's suggested structure, which attributes Neh. 7.4-5a and Neh. 11.1-2 to different literary parts: the former to Ezra 1.5–Neh. 7.72 and the latter to Neh. 8.1–13.31.[34]

If her comments on structure have won few supporters, however, Eskenazi's analysis of themes, by contrast, has much more to commend it. As we shall see later, in addition to the three recurrent issues which she picks out, E–N has a consistent emphasis on such themes as unity and cooperation between social classes, or dissatisfaction with the current religious status quo.[35] This suggests that E–N was probably composed by a single author, who collected the sources and arranged them according to his/her own purpose.[36]

To sum up, Eskenazi's specific proposals for the structure of E–N raise many problems. Her work does succeed, though, in emphasizing the thematic unity of E–N, with its implications for authorship.

2.2.2 *Sara Japhet, A Focus on* How

Some scholars, who approach the composition of E–N diachronically, are inclined to think that it was composed over a long period of time by different compilers, and thus lacks an internal structural logic.[37] Japhet argues, however, that the book does maintain ideological and structural consistency and believes that E–N was produced 'all at once, by an author, according to a clear plan'.[38]

Compared with other works which deal with the post-exilic period, E–N shows certain remarkable features which Japhet uses to identify its ideology. First of all, the book completely accepts the contemporary political situation and lacks any

---

reference for a definition of narrative present in E–N and that she wrongly conflates 'text-immanent' readings with 'referential' remarks.

32.   Cf. Duggan, 'An Exegetical', pp. 74–78.

33.   E.g., Williamson, *Ezra, Nehemiah*, pp. 268, 344; Blenkinsopp, *Ezra–Nehemiah*, pp. 277, 322–23.

34.   We may also add the fact that Neh. 7.72 is closely connected to, rather than separated from, Neh. 8, thus weakening Eskenazi's argument regarding the structure of E–N. Cf. Williamson, 'The Composition of Ezra i–vi', pp. 2–3.

35.   See section 5.2 below.

36.   Eskenazi, *Age of Prose*, p. 185, maintains that the purpose of the book was 'to exemplify the postexilic era as a time when Israel built the house of God in accordance with the divine word embodied in texts'.

37.   As representatives of this approach to the text, Japhet, 'Composition and Chronology', pp. 197–201, mentions Rudolph, *Esra und Nehemia*, pp. xxii–xxiii, and Williamson, *Ezra, Nehemiah*, pp. xxxiii–xxxvi (Williamson's view will be examined in more detail in the following section). The major attraction of this approach is, according to Japhet, that contradictions and inconsistencies in the work can be abated by reference to separate authors and editors ('Composition and Chronology', pp. 197–98).

38.   Japhet, 'Composition and Chronology', pp. 201–202.

desire for change. This statement can easily be corroborated by the fact that there is no mention of the origin of Zerubbabel, who was explicitly of Davidic lineage and thus seems to have been considered within some sections of Judean society, at least, the bearer of the hopes of redemption, as shown in other texts (e.g., Hag. 2.6, 21-23). While this silence is maintained about Zerubbabel's origin, the spotlight is instead cast on the Persian kings, who are themselves portrayed as the actualizers of the divine will (e.g., Ezra 1.1; 4.24; 7.27-28; 9.9; Neh. 2.8).[39] Another feature characteristic of E–N is that the author lays more emphasis on *the public* as a whole than on its leaders.[40] So, for example, no leader of the people is mentioned in the list of the returnees from the exile (Ezra 2; Neh. 7). The role of the public is notably highlighted frequently within the work (e.g., Ezra 6.16-22; Neh. 8), except in the autobiographical portions, i.e., the Nehemiah Memoir and the accounts of Ezra.[41] In short, then, the author's tendency is to accept the political status quo and to view the Persian kings as vehicles of God's grace, while placing emphasis on the Jewish public rather than its leaders.[42]

Besides this ideological feature retained throughout E–N, the work is structurally well organized, leading us to believe that the composition as a whole was planned in advance. Japhet substantiates this by looking at the structure as clearly divided into two units: Ezra 1–6 and Ezra 7–Neh. 13. Each not only expressly relates to one generation,[43] but also asserts that the people were led by two leaders.[44] She concludes, therefore, that this division was based on the author's own historiographical ideology, and further argues that, since this ideology is preserved and shared in both units, we have every reason to claim that it was a single author who was responsible for the whole composition of E–N.

In summary, through their emphasis on thematic unity, then, both Eskenazi and Japhet have pointed to the probability that we are dealing with a single author for E–N. They have not, however, attempted to identify that author except in terms of the interests and ideology revealed in the work.

2.2.3 *William F. Albright, A Focus on* Who
In his thorough study of E–N, Charles Torrey observed that the Hebrew narratives of Ezra 7–10 and Neh. 8–10 share the Chronicler's stylistic and thematic peculiarities.[45]

---

39.   Japhet, 'Sheshbazzar and Zerubbabel', pp. 71–80. This position has been expressed by many scholars. Cf. Rudolph, *Esra und Nehemia*, pp. xxvii–xxx; Bickerman, *From Ezra to the Last of the Maccabees*, p. 30.

40.   This description sharply contrasts with the other sources of that period, such as Haggai and Zechariah, which lay great importance on the role of the leaders. Cf. Japhet, 'Sheshbazzar and Zerubbabel', pp. 86–87.

41.   For a more detailed discussion, see section 5.2.

42.   Japhet, 'Composition and Chronology', pp. 83–89.

43.   Namely, twenty-two years from the first year of Cyrus (538 BCE; Ezra 1.1) to the sixth year of Darius (517 BCE; Ezra 6.15) for the first unit; and twenty-six years from the seventh year of Artaxerxes (458 BCE; Ezra 7.7) to the thirty-third year of the same king (432 BCE; Neh. 13.6-7) for the second unit. Cf. Japhet, 'Composition and Chronology', pp. 208–209.

44.   Zerubbabel and Jeshua in the first unit, and Ezra and Nehemiah in the second. Japhet, 'Composition and Chronology', p. 209.

45.   See Torrey, *Ezra Studies*, pp. 238–48, who says 'there is no portion of the whole work

This observation led Torrey, who lived at a time when the notion that the Chronicler was responsible for both Chronicles and E–N was seldom questioned, to conclude that there existed no Ezra material; it was purely a fabrication of the Chronicler and Ezra was, therefore, a *fictional figure*.[46]

Albright was deeply impressed with Torrey's findings of stylistic similarities but, interestingly, reached a conclusion opposite to Torrey's about the authorship of the two books: if it is the case that the Ezra material shares the features of Chronicles, asserts Albright, then we can conclude that the Chronicler himself was Ezra.[47] In order to back up this assertion, he argues as follows.[48]

The Chronicler's general method of redacting existing sources (e.g., the books of Kings) was just to *supplement*, rather than to rewrite, and there is no compelling reason to see an exception in the case of the Ezra material. It is thus natural to think that each piece of material in the Chronicler's work was originally composed by its own author, implying that the Ezra narrative was penned by Ezra himself. If so, since its literary style and interest are, as rightly perceived by Torrey, very similar to Chronicles, the simplest way to explain this situation is to regard Ezra as the author of both the Ezra narrative and Chronicles.

Albright does recognize a serious chronological problem with this assertion. Ezra's return to Jerusalem has traditionally been dated to 458 BCE, but Albright himself believes that the book of Ezra was composed *circa* 400–350 BCE.[49] It is

---

Chron.-Ezra-Neh. in which the Chronicler's literary peculiarities are more strongly marked, more abundant, more evenly and continuously distributed, and more easily recognizable, than in the Hebrew narrative of Ezra 7–10 and Neh. 8–10' (p. 241), and 'he was a man precisely like the Chronicler himself: interested very noticeably in the Levites, and especially the class of singers; deeply concerned at all times with the details of the cult and with the ecclesiastical organization in Jerusalem; armed with lists of names giving the genealogy and official standing of those who constituted the true church; with his heart set on teaching and enforcing the neglected law of Moses throughout the land; and – most important of all – zealous for the exclusion of the 'people of the land', condemnation of mixed marriages, and the preservation of the pure blood of Israel! There is no garment in all Ezra's wardrobe that does not fit the Chronicler exactly' (p. 243). This view has been followed by numerous scholars: e.g., Noth, *ÜS*, pp. 146–47; Kapelrud, *The Question of Authorship*, pp. 95–97; Kellermann, *Nehemia*, pp. 68–69.

46. This contention was made, in addition to the stylistic and thematic similarities, on the basis of the absence of Ezra in Sirach 49.11-13, where heroes of the faith are listed. See Torrey, *Composition*, pp. 61–62. This critical idea of Torrey's had been advanced, a few years earlier, by E. Renan, *Histoire du peuple d'Israël*, vol. IV (Paris, 1891) and has subsequently been favoured by Gustav Hölscher, *Geschichte der israelitisch-jüdischen Religion* (Giessen: Alfred Töpelmann, 1922) and more recently by Giovanni Garbini, *History and Ideology in Ancient Israel* (trans. J. Bowden; London: SCM Press, 1988). Cf. J. Alberto Soggin, *An Introduction to the History of Israel and Judah* (Valley Forge: Trinity Press International, 1993), pp. 291–92. The evidence based on the book of Sirach has won little acceptance. Cf. Batten, *Ezra and Nehemiah*, p. 51, where he argues that Sirach omitted Ezra possibly 'because he was not in deep sympathy with the ruthless proceedings described in Ezr. 10', rather than because Ezra did not exist.

47. Albright, 'Date and Personality', pp. 104–24.

48. Albright, 'Date and Personality', pp. 119–24.

49. This date has been argued on these four grounds: '(1) the genealogy of Jeconiah, 1 Chron. 3.17-24; (2) the list of high-priests, Neh. 12.10-11, 22; (3) the supposed Greek loan-words; (4) the

most unlikely, therefore, that Ezra could possibly have lived long enough to compose the book. Albright seeks to solve this problem by accepting the thesis of Van Hoonacker, who placed Ezra after Nehemiah by viewing the Persian king in Ezra 7.7 as Artaxerxes II Memnon (405–359 BCE), not Artaxerxes I Longimanus (465–425 BCE), thus dating Ezra's return to 398 BCE.[50] A question may arise here of how we can understand certain verses which regard Nehemiah, whose date is generally agreed to be 445 BCE, and Ezra as *contemporaries* (e.g., Neh. 8.9; 10.2). Albright answers this simply by relying on the thesis of Torrey, who had previously argued that those verses are late glosses.[51]

There is, of course, a further chronological problem: if Ezra came back to Jerusalem later than Nehemiah, why does the former precede the latter in the accounts of Ezra and Nehemiah? It was inevitable, according to Albright, that Ezra, the author, should do so, because Nehemiah's Memoirs were available at a late stage of the composition of the book and all that Ezra could do, therefore, was to affix them to his own fragmentary compilation. In addition, he points out, Ezra's primary concern lay in ecclesiastical succession and theological orthodoxy, rather than in historical research according to chronological order.[52]

In brief, indebted to prior studies of scholars, particularly Torrey and Van Hoonacker, Albright reinvigorated the traditional view of the authorship of E–N, ascribing it to Ezra.

Albright's argument is untenable, however. It is heavily dependent upon Torrey's conclusion that Chronicles and the Ezra portion are related linguistically and thematically. As we have already seen,[53] however, it is highly questionable whether supposed linguistic and ideological similarities between the two books can possibly serve as evidence for common authorship. Essentially, Albright's thesis is virtually identical with the traditional view which assigns E–N to Ezra. It, thus, faces the same criticism by Zunz that only a few portions of the book were penned by Ezra and that most of it contains no evidence for the authorship of Ezra.[54]

Albright's thesis is undermined, of course, by his own late date for Ezra (398 BCE), which leads him into complicated and ultimately unconvincing arguments about chronology. In his later work, Albright himself corrected his view on Ezra's date by putting it not to 398 BCE but to 428 BCE.[55] In spite of such a switch, he continued to maintain the view that it was Ezra who wrote E–N, and that the work was composed between 400–350 BCE[56] This later position overcame some of the chronological problems, but if the book was indeed composed in 350 BCE, then Ezra would still have had to be an extremely old man when he wrote it.

---

language of the Aramaic letters'. For a more detailed discussion, see Albright, 'Date and Personality', pp. 107–18.

50. Van Hoonacker, 'Nehemie et Esdras', pp. 151–84.
51. Cf. Torrey, *Ezra Studies*, pp. 282–83.
52. Albright, 'Date and Personality', p. 123.
53. Cf. sections 1.1.2.3. and 1.1.2.4.
54. Cf. Zunz, 'Dibre-Hajamim', pp. 20–22.
55. Albright, *Biblical Period*, p. 93.
56. Albright, *Biblical Period*, pp. 94–95.

For all its elaborations, then, Albright's theory is essentially just a new presentation of a very old view. The same arguments can be mounted against it as against all attempts to attribute the work to Ezra, and his chronological assertions lead to some of the same problems of dating that we discussed earlier.

2.3 *Plausible Proposals*

2.3.1 *Priestly Authorship*
As we have seen, Eskenazi and Japhet both concluded that E–N was composed as a unity on the basis of the author's apparent motives. Their proposals, however, are mainly focused on *how* the book was composed rather than *who* composed it. Albright made a more specific claim by ascribing the composition of E–N to Ezra himself, but his view is little more than a restatement of the traditional view, which was long ago refuted by Zunz.

Hugh Williamson goes beyond other attempts simply to affirm unity of origin and offers a coherent argument for specific authorship of E–N. Laying more weight on the *historical* aspect of the text than its literary one, he begins his examination of the compositional question on the basis of one fundamental observation: Ezra 2 is dependent upon Neh. 7.[57] More specifically, since 'Nehemiah 7–8 is the point at which the originally independent accounts concerning Ezra and Nehemiah have been most clearly interwoven',[58] we have no choice, he asserts, but to conclude both that the editor responsible for Ezra 2 must have known the existing editorial body which encompasses Ezra 7 to Neh. 13 in its present form, and that there were two major editorial stages: one for Ezra 7–Neh. 13 and the other for Ezra 1–6.

Why and by whom, then, was each editorial part compiled? To begin with, Williamson insists that the incorporation of the Ezra and Nehemiah materials (Ezra 7–Neh. 13) was initiated in approximately 400 BCE. The efforts of the reformers (Ezra and Nehemiah) for the restoration of the community were fading away from memory, so the aspiration of the author was to reinvigorate the community by making their great work widely known. This motivation is reflected particularly in Neh. 8–10, which was composed to function as a climax of the work.[59]

As for the second editorial part (Ezra 1–6), Williamson argues that the editor may have had two major purposes for its composition. One of them was a concern

---

57. He presents the following four arguments: (1) in the continuation of the narratives, 'the seventh month'' of Neh. 7.72 is shown to be an integral part of its context by the reference to the same month in 8.2, whereas in Ezra 3.1 it is left completely in the air; (2) it is generally argued that Ezra 2.68-69 represents a summarizing of Neh. 7.69-71 rather than Nehemiah an expansion of Ezra; (3) the manner in which the date is given in Ezra 3.1 ('the seventh month') does not fit the practice adopted elsewhere in Ezra 1–6; and (4) within the usually shorter account of Ezra 2.68-69, v. 68 in fact constitutes a clear plus over Neh. 7.70. Williamson, 'The Composition of Ezra i–vi', pp. 2–8. For the argument against this view, see Blenkinsopp, *Ezra–Nehemiah*, pp. 43–44, and for Williamson's response to it, see Williamson, 'The Problem with First Esdras', pp. 206ff.

58. Williamson, 'The Composition of Ezra i–vi', p. 7.

59. Williamson, *Ezra, Nehemiah*, p. xxxiv.

with legitimacy, which he thought could be achieved only by showing contemporary readers the continuity which ran between the restored community and pre-exilic Israel, and between the second and first temples. The other purpose related to justification of the rejection of a request by the Samaritans to help with the building of the temple.[60]

Having analysed the motives for composition, Williamson then goes further, to seek the identity of the writers. He argues that Ezra 1–6 was composed around 300 BCE by an editor belonging to a *priestly* group who lightly redacted the books of Chronicles.[61] According to him, late in the Persian period, a substantial number of priests left Jerusalem for Shechem to establish what was later known as the Samaritan community and, as a result of this secession, the priests who remained in Jerusalem came to have a strong animosity toward the northern people. Since this animosity is clearly presented in the polemical rejection of northern participation in Ezra 4.1-3, he claims that priestly authorship can safely be endorsed.[62]

As regards the other editorial part (Ezra 7–Neh. 13), he does not mention its author directly, but the following points made in his works suggest that he also thinks that it originated in a priestly group, thus arguing for *priestly authorship* of the whole book of E–N:

(1)   Above all, he underlines that a pro-priestly inclination can be consistently detected throughout the book: for example, Neh. 3 highlights the *priestly* leadership under which the people are acting in concert to build the wall.[63]

(2)   According to Williamson, this priestly influence can also be detected at the beginning of Neh. 11. In the light of Neh. 7.4-5, which is part of Nehemiah's own account, we expect Nehemiah to organize the repopulation of Jerusalem on the basis of family (יחש) connections. However, in Neh. 11.1, which belongs to the editor's contribution, it is instead done by lot-casting, which, in ancient times, was a cultic and priestly affair, and is also mentioned in 1 Chron. 24.5, 7, 31; 25.8, 9; 26.13, 14, etc., all of which are attributed to a priestly reviser of the Chronicler's original work.[64]

60.   Williamson, *Ezra, Nehemiah*, pp. xxxiv–xxxv.

61.   Cf. H.G.M. Williamson, 'The Origins of the Twenty-four Priestly Courses', in Emerton (ed.), *Studies in the Historical Books of the Old Testament*, pp. 251–68, esp. pp. 267f; Williamson, *Ezra and Nehemiah*, p. 46; *idem*, 'The Composition of Ezra i–vi', pp. 26–29.

62.   Williamson, 'The Composition of Ezra i–vi', pp. 26–29. Cf. *idem*, 'The Origins of the Twenty-four Priestly Courses', pp. 267f.

63.   Cf. H.G.M. Williamson, 'Post-exilic Historiography', in R.E. Friedman *et al.* (eds.), *The Future of Biblical Studies: The Hebrew Scriptures* (Atlanta: Scholars Press, 1987), pp. 189–207, esp. p. 193; *idem*, *Ezra, Nehemiah*, pp. xxxiii and 201–203; *idem*, 'The Belief System of the Book of Nehemiah', in Becking *et al.* (eds.), *The Crisis of Israelite Religion Tradition*, pp. 276–87, where he distinguishes between the Nehemiah Memoir and the remainder of the material in the book of Nehemiah for which the author/editor was responsible, saying that the latter is characterized by an emphasis on priestly leadership (p. 277).

64.   Cf. Williamson, *Ezra, Nehemiah*, p. 346; *idem*, 'Post-Exilic Historiography', pp. 194–95, n. 11; *idem*, 'The Belief System of the Book of Nehemiah', in Becking *et al.* (eds.), *The Crisis of Israelite Religion*, pp. 276–87, esp. p. 283–84.

(3)   Lastly, Williamson argues that the location of the problematic letters in Ezra 4.7-23 shows that the editor responsible for Ezra 1–6, who belonged to a priestly group, joined this section to the existing work (Ezra 7–Neh. 13) as an introduction *without* making any editorial additions or changes. The passage is obviously out of context,[65] and its present location can be explained only when we suppose that the editor regarded the existing Ezra 7–Neh. 13 as inviolable, so that he could not place the passage into its chronologically proper location of Ezra 7–Neh. 13.[66] The implication of this observation is that, when finally combining and editing the existing material together with his own work, the editor found no incongruity in ideology, purpose or themes. Therefore, because he has argued that the editor responsible for Ezra 1–6 belonged to a priestly group, we may assume that Williamson would also accept priestly authorship of Ezra 7–Neh. 13.

To sum up, among those who treat E–N as a single work, Williamson is the first scholar to have dealt with the issue of origin in detail. He argues that the book underwent a *multi-staged* process in its composition: broadly speaking, first a compositional process for Ezra 7–Neh. 13 around 400 BCE and then another for Ezra 1–6 in about 300 BCE. He identifies the editor for the latter with a person who belonged to a *priestly* group. While he has not clearly specified the identification of the editor for the former part, a study of his work shows that he would probably be obliged to argue for a corresponding priestly authorship of Ezra 7–Neh. 13 as well.

His view has gained wide acceptance,[67] and may be supported both by the fact that the authorial portions[68] of the book clearly show clerical and religious interest, and by the probability that numerous sources found in E–N would have been preserved in temple archives, to which the clerical groups would have had easiest access.[69]

In this context, it is worth noting that the book exhibits a very high incidence of the word כהן, as shown in Table 2.1 below, where the first number in brackets indicates the occurrence of the word in each book and the second number indicates its occurrence per 10,000 words.[70]

65.   For a detailed discussion, see section 6.1.2.2.

66.   Williamson, *Ezra and Nehemiah*, pp. 44–45.

67.   E.g., Throntveit, *Ezra–Nehemiah*, pp. 8–10.

68.   For the extent of the authorial portions, see n. 86 below.

69.   Cf. Brockington, *Ezra, Nehemiah and Esther*, pp. 34–40, where he lists material from the temple (Ezra 1.9-11a; 2.1-70 [Neh. 7.6-73]; 8.1-14; 10.18-44; Neh. 3.1-32; 11.3-19; 11.25-36; 12.1-9; 12.10-11; 12.12-21; 12.24-26). See also Williamson, *Ezra and Nehemiah*, pp. 28–29; *idem*, 'Post-Exilic Historiography', pp. 193ff.; Richards, 'Reshaping Chronicles and Ezra–Nehemiah Interpretation', pp. 220–21.

70.   Cf. Francis I. Andersen, and A. Dean Forbes, *The Vocabulary of the Old Testament* (Roma: Editrice Pontificio Istituto Biblico, 1989), p. 341.

Genesis (7–3)	Exodus (11–7)	*Leviticus (194–162)*
Numbers (69–42)	Deuteronomy (14–10)	Joshua (37–37)
Judges (15–15)	1 Samuel (32–24)	2 Samuel (9–8)
1 Kings (29–22)	2 Kings (44–36)	Isaiah (6–4)
Jeremiah (41–19)	Ezekiel (24–13)	Hosea (4–17)
Joel (3–31)	Amos (1–5)	Micah (1–7)
Zephaniah (2–26)	*Haggai (8–133)*	Zechariah (6–19)
Malachi (3–34)	Psalms (5–3)	Job (1–1)
Ezra (34–91)	*Nehemiah (44–83)*	1 Chronicles (19–18)
2 Chronicles (89–67)		

Table 2.1

As can be seen in Table 2.1, E–N has the third highest frequency of the word after Leviticus and Haggai. Given that the principal focus of E–N is not on cultic regulation, as in Leviticus, it is odd for the word to occur so frequently unless the author belonged to a clerical group or was strongly interested in clerical matters. Conversely, this phenomenon is understandable and natural if the book originated in such a clerical group, or had a strong interest in the clergy.

E–N is not just strongly interested in the temple and the cult,[71] but also displays a technical knowledge of cultic matters.[72] This leads us positively to consider the possibility of clerical authorship, over against any suggestion that the author was simply a scribe who was familiar with, and interested in, cultic matters, since archiving and writing documents were scribal duties in ancient times.[73] In fact, it is quite doubtful that there ever existed an independent scribal group during the post-exilic period; during that period, scribes mostly appear to have overlapped with other groups such as priests or Levites.[74] For example, the scribal class, or part of it, is often identified with the Levites (e.g., 1 Chron. 24.6; 2 Chron. 24.11; 34.12-13; Neh. 35.3).[75] Ezra is also described as a *priest* and *scribe* (סֹפֵר, Ezra 7.6; Neh. 12.36).[76]

---

71. See, for example, Ezra 2.68-70; 3.1-13; 6.16-21; 8.30-35; Neh. 10.29-40; 12.33-36, 44-47, *et passim*.

72. Cf. Curtis and Madsen, *Chronicles*, p. 5; Noth, *ÜS*, pp. 171-80; Kellermann, *Nehemia*, pp. 69–73; Hartmut Gese, 'Zur Geschichte der Kultsänger am zweiten Tempel', in *Vom Sinai zum Zion: Alttestamentliche Beiträge zur biblischen Theologie* (BEvT, 64; Munich: Kaiser Verlag, 1974), pp. 147–58; Williamson, 'Post-Exilic Historiography', p. 194.

73. Cf. Philip R. Davies, *Scribes and Schools: The Canonisation of the Hebrew Scriptures* (Louisville: Westminster John Knox Press, 1998), pp. 74–75. For other probable functions of scribes, see Michael Fishbane, *Biblical Interpretation in Ancient Israel* (Oxford: Clarendon Press, 1985), esp. pp. 23–43, where he argues that ancient Israelite scribes were the custodians and tradents of the *traditum* (i.e., the received text) and were responsible for adding superscriptive titles and summary colophons as well as copying texts, and maintaining, transmitting and collating literary records.

74. Anthony J. Saldarini, 'Scribes', *ABD*, V, pp. 1012–16, esp. p. 1013.

75. Cf. Davies, *Scribes and Schools*, pp. 131–34.

76. There has been some scholarly debate over the meaning of סֹפֵר, which is used as a title for Ezra. Hans H. Schaeder, *Esra der Schreiber* (Tübingen: Mohr, 1930), maintained that סֹפֵר denotes an imperial official dispatched to rule, and thus that Ezra was the governor. This position, however, has been challenged by many scholars. Cf. K. Galling, 'Bagoas and Ezra', in *Studien zur Geschichte*

It shows that each cleric commonly had his own duty such as weighing the revenue (Ezra 8.30-33), teaching (Neh. 8.7-8), preaching (1 Chron. 28.2-10; 2 Chron. 25.2-7; 16.7-9), or *scribing*, etc.

From the unexpected and important role of elders in the accounts of rebuilding the temple in Ezra 5–6, it might alternatively be possible to surmise that the book originated among the elders. This group, however, would most likely not have possessed the sort of cultic knowledge displayed by E–N, and it is questionable whether the elders would have had access to the temple archives.

More generally, it is true that Williamson often says Ezra 1–6 was composed by someone of decidedly *pro*-priestly leanings and such caution may be appropriate. We have no knowledge, though, of any group of people who were biased toward the clergy and would have had access to the temple archives without actually belonging to a clerical group. In the light of this, it is not surprising that scholars have commonly understood Williamson's thesis simply as priestly, rather than pro-priestly, authorship of E–N.[77] Even Williamson himself does not distinguish between priestly and pro-priestly authorship.[78] In the end, if somebody is *very* pro-priestly, we might as well call him a priestly writer. For our purpose, it makes no differences whether or not he actually *was* a priest.

Insofar as we support the view that the writer probably emerged from clerical circles, then, we can follow Williamson some of the way. However, the priesthood was not the only constituent of the clerical population in post-exilic Judah.

2.3.2 *Levitical Authorship*
There has long been scholarly consensus that both Chronicles and E–N have a strong interest in the Levites. This position is still prevalent, among those who favour common authorship of Chronicles and E–N and attribute both works to the Chronicler, since he is usually regarded as having belonged to a Levitical group.[79]

Opponents of common authorship, however, have naturally tried to maximize the disparity between Chronicles and E–N in as many areas as possible, including their attitudes toward, and descriptions of, the Levites. For example, resting his case upon Adam Welch's thesis,[80] Williamson maintains that the Levites in Chronicles

---

Israels im persischen Zeitalter (Tübingen: Mohr, 1964), pp. 149–84; Talmon, 'Ezra and Nehemiah', pp. 317–28. See, in particular, Williamson, *Ezra and Nehemiah*, p. 70, who points out that Ezra's status at the Achaemenid court is not attested in any documents available and, moreover, that the title itself is not Persian in wording.

77. E.g., Gary N. Knoppers, 'Hierodules, Priests, or Janitors? The Levites in Chronicles and the History of the Israelite Priesthood', *JBL* 118 (1999), pp. 49–72, esp. p. 52 n. 13.

78. For example, Williamson, 'The Composition of Ezra i–vi', p. 27, identifies the author of Ezra 1–6 with one of the *priests* who did not go to Shechem to found the Samaritan community but remained in Jerusalem.

79. Cf. Torrey, *Ezra Studies*, p. 243; Curtis and Madsen, *Chronicles*, p. 5; von Rad, *Old Testament Theology*, I, pp. 347–54; Robert H. Pfeiffer, *Introduction to the Old Testament* (New York: Harper & Brothers Publishers, 1941), pp. 792–801; Kellermann, *Nehemia*, pp. 69–73.

80. Adam C. Welch, *Post-Exilic Judaism* (Edinburgh and London: William Blackwood & Sons Ltd, 1935), pp. 227–41. Cf. *idem*, *The Work of the Chronicler: Its Purpose and its Date* (London: Oxford University Press, 1939), pp. 55–80.

are described as a distinct group more prominently than in E–N and that, in Chronicles, other functions such as teaching (2 Chron. 17.8; 35.3), judging (2 Chron. 19.8, 11), and prophesying (2 Chron. 20.14), which are never mentioned in E–N, are attributed to the Levites.[81]

Leaving aside criticisms which might be made of such specific examples (such as the fact that a teaching function is actually attributed to the Levites in Neh. 8.9), the following points, at least, oblige us not to discard the traditional view that a concern for the Levites in E–N is as strong as in Chronicles:

In the Old Testament, the word לוי[82] occurs 292 times, as shown in Table 2.2 (again, the first number in brackets indicates the frequency of the word in each book and the second its occurrence per 10,000 words).[83]

Exodus (4–2)	Leviticus (4–3)	*Numbers (59–36)*
Deuteronomy (20–14)	Joshua (16–16)	Judges (7–7)
1 Samuel (1–1)	2 Samuel (1–1)	1 Kings (1–1)
Isaiah (1–1)	Jeremiah (3–1)	Ezekiel (8–4)
Malachi (1–11)	Psalms (1–1)	*Ezra (22–59)*
Nehemiah (43–83)	*1 Chronicles (35–33)*	*2 Chronicles (65–49)*

Table 2.2

From Table 2.2, it is apparent that the book of Chronicles contains the greatest number of occurrences of the word (100 times), followed by Ezra–Nehemiah (65 times)[84] and Numbers (59 times). When we take into account the size of each book, however, it is not in Chronicles that we find the greatest concentration of references, for that book is quite large.[85] Rather, E–N has the most relatively frequent

81. Williamson, *Israel*, p. 69.

82. The word לוים / לוי (to be subsequently represented by לוי) in the Old Testament is used to denote Levi, son of Jacob and Leah (e.g., Gen. 29.34; Exod. 1.2), one of the twelve tribes of Israel (e.g., Num. 1.49; 3.6), or a Levite/Levites (e.g., Deut. 31.25; 2 Sam. 15.24). Since our present interest is limited to Levites in contradistinction to priests, we will focus only on the biblical references with the third meaning. Thus, the word לוי hereafter, unless otherwise mentioned, connotes a Levite/ Levites who belonged to one of the two clerical orders of Israel. More specifically, the present book deals mainly with the exilic and post-exilic literature, and the *Zadokite* priests had obtained a monopoly at the Jerusalem temple and the priestly traditions since Zadok's support for Solomon in the struggle for succession to the throne of David until the end of the post-exilic period. Hence, in this book, לוי would, in most cases, be used as a term including the Levites as well as the Abiathar priests, often to be expressed as 'non-Zadokite Levites' for both in the following discussions.

83. These statistics are based on Andersen and Forbes, *The Vocabulary of the Old Testament*, p. 350. Andersen and Forbes may have made a small error here in their count of Nehemiah. According to my own study, the word occurs in Neh. 43 times, rather than 44. Their extra one might be due to adding either of the references to לוי in Neh. 10.40 or 12.23, where it is used as the meaning of Levi, son of Jacob and Leah. The figure 292, then, is my total count, not theirs.

84. Ezra 1.5; 2.40, 70; 3.8 (×2), 9, 10, 12; 6.16, 18, 20; 7.7, 13, 24; 8.20, 29, 30, 33; 9.1; 10.5, 15, 23; Neh. 3.17; 7.1, 43, 72; 8.7, 9, 11, 13; 9.4, 5; 10.1, 10, 29, 35, 38 (×2), 39 (×3); 11.3, 15, 16, 18, 20, 22, 36; 12.1, 8, 22, 24, 27, 30, 44 (×2), 47 (×2); 13.5, 10 (×2), 13, 22, 29, 30.

85. Below are the numbers of printed pages of the Revised Standard Version and those of verses of each book under consideration according to the *Masorah Finalis*.

occurrence of the word in the Old Testament with 71 occurrences per 10,000 words. Chronicles, though second in relative frequency, is significantly lower at 41 per 10,000, followed by Numbers (36/10,000) and Joshua (16/10,000).

In addition, it is also noteworthy that, in E–N, לוי occurs even more frequently in the 'authorial portions' attributed to the author himself, than in the 'raw material' produced independently of the author. According to my own reckoning, the word occurs 25 times in 507 verses of the raw material and, thus, once in about every 20 verses, while occurring 40 times in 178 verses of the authorial portions and, thus, more than once every 5 verses.[86] The extent of the authorial portions we use here may be debatable, but even if we consider the views of various scholars on the extent of the author's pure contribution, the result is similar and reinforces this conclusion. For example, the word occurs 24 times in 72 authorial verses reckoned by Rudolph and thus is used once per 3 verses,[87] and 23 times in 68 verses reckoned by Williamson, again about once every 3 verses.[88]

While we cannot yet say that E–N shows partiality to the Levites, we can, at least, assert that, since the author was directly responsible for the authorial portions with numerous references to the Levites, he had a very strong interest in them. This implies that it may be rash to jettison the possibility of Levitical authorship for E–N, and that we should consider it seriously.

Chronicles	58 / 1765
Numbers	39 / 1228
Ezra–Nehemiah	22 / 685

Curiously, Haran, who also counted them, supplies slightly different values for the number of verses in Chronicles and Ezra–Nehemiah, i.e., 1656 verses for Chronicles and 688 for Ezra–Nehemiah, though he also used the same Masorah. Cf. Haran, 'Book-Size and the Device of Catch-Lines', pp. 3–4.

86. The extent of the raw material taken here is as follows: (1) the lists: Ezra 1.9-11a; 2.1-67; 8.1-14; 10.18-44; Neh. 3.1-32; 7.5-71; 10.2-28; 11.4-19, 21-24, 26-35; 12.1b-26; (2) the decree and correspondence: Ezra 1.2-4; 4.8-22; 5.7-17; 6.6-12; 7.12-26; (3) the Ezra material: Ezra 7.27-28; 8.15-19, 21-25, 28-29, 31-32, 36; 9.1-11, 13-15; (4) the Nehemiah Memoir: Neh. 1–2; 3.33–7.4; 12.27-29, 31-32, 37-40; 13.4-31. Cf. Batten, *Ezra and Nehemiah*, pp. 14-24; Kellermann, *Nehemia*, pp. 4–56; Williamson, *Ezra, Nehemiah*, pp. xxiv–xxxiii. The remaining passage of the book may be categorized as the authorial portions: i.e., Ezra 1.1, 5-8, 11b; 2.68-70; 3.1–4.7; 4.23–5.6; 6.1-5, 13-22; 7.1-11; 8.20, 26-27, 30, 33-35; 9.12; 10.1-17; Neh. 7.72–10.1; 10.29-40; 11.1-3, 20, 25, 36; 12.1a, 30, 33-36; 12.41–13.3.

87. *Viz.*, Ezra 1.5; 3.8(×2), 9, 10, 12; 6.20; 7.7; Neh. 9.4, 5; 10.1, 29, 35, 38(×2), 39(×3); 11.20, 22; 12.44(×2), 47(×2). The passages that Rudolph regards as the author/editor's hand are Ezra 1.1-7, 11b, 3.1–4.5; 4.24; 6.19-22; 7.1-11; Neh. 9.3-5a; 10.1; 10.29–11.2; 11.20-25a; 12.44–13.3. Cf. Rudolph, *Esra und Nehemia*, pp. xxiii–xxiv.

88. Viz., Ezra 1.5; 3.8(×2), 9, 10, 12; 6.16, 18, 20; Neh. 9.4, 5; 10.1, 29, 35, 38(×2), 39(×3); 12.44[×2], 47[×2]. The authorial/editorial contribution, according to Williamson, *Ezra, Nehemiah*, pp. xxiv-xxxiii, is found in Ezra 1.1, 5-8; 3; 4.1-5; 4.23–5.5; 6.1-2, 13-22; 7.11, 27-28; Neh. 9.1-5; 10.1, 29-40; 12.44-47. Cf. VanderKam, 'Ezra–Nehemiah or Ezra and Nehemiah?', p. 63 n. 29.

Summary of Part I

Ancient tradition ascribed the composition of E–N to Ezra, but this attribution was successfully challenged by Leopold Zunz in 1832. Zunz presented the Chronicler as its author, and his view remained the consensus position for a long time, until the challenges by Sara Japhet and Hugh Williamson. These scholars have argued persuasively that E–N is independent of Chronicles in origin, but some commentators retain Zunz's position, while a few others regard Ezra and Nehemiah as two distinct works. Currently, therefore, scholarly views on the authorship of E–N can be divided into three groups: (1) E–N is part of the Chronicler's work, and was penned by the Chronicler; (2) E–N is a single work, separate from Chronicles; and (3) Chronicles, Ezra and Nehemiah are all different books with their own independent authors.

This complicated situation led us first to establish the relationships between Ezra, Nehemiah and Chronicles. Our examination of the arguments *for* the common authorship of Chronicles and E–N and *against* the unity of E–N has shown that they are unconvincing and that E–N should be treated not only as a work independent of Chronicles, but also as an internally unified composition rather than two separate works.

Establishing the scope of E–N brought us to a position where we could begin our examination of the authorship issue. Prior to this, our position on the compositional date of E–N was affirmed. Some scholars argue that E–N should be dated no earlier than the fourth century BCE, but the persuasive arguments in defence of Ezra's traditional date (458 BCE) and the lack of indication that the Persian rule has come to an end forced us to take the late fifth century BCE as the best date for the composition.

A subsequent survey of prior research showed us that E–N is most likely to have been composed all at once on the basis of the ideology of an author who accepted the political *status quo* and who emphasized the common people. We noted, however, that little attention has been paid to *who* composed E–N. Albright did study this and suggested Ezra's authorship, but his suggestion is very similar to the traditional view, which had already been refuted by Zunz. It is only Williamson who has been particularly concerned with the identity of the author, arguing for a *priestly* authorship of E–N. His arguments for this theory appear plausible, since it is obvious that E–N has a strong interest in cultic matters and is filled with sources preserved in temple archives. Certain peculiar features found in the book, however, obliged us to consider another possibility, that of *Levitical* authorship: the Levites were also a clerical group, and it is in E–N of all the Old Testament literature that לוי occurs most frequently, showing the author's interest in the Levites.

From the discussion so far, then, we conclude that *E–N as an independent single work is most likely to have originated in a priestly or Levitical group around the late fifth century BCE*. The only problem to be resolved is which clerical group composed E–N. In the following discussion, we will attempt to investigate whether priestly or Levitical authorship is the more plausible. Part II looks at the literary context and Part III at the historical context.

Part II

LITERARY CONTEXT

In Part I, we concluded that Ezra–Nehemiah originated in either a priestly or a Levitical group. The purpose of Part II is, in the literary context, to investigate which of these two groups is more likely to have written the book. We shall begin with an examination of the ways the Levites are described *vis-à-vis* the priests in Old Testament texts of the exilic and post-exilic periods (Chapter 3). We shall then compare these findings with a description of the Levites in E–N. Additionally, we shall analyse a few literary phrases in E–N in order to note their priestly or Levitical bias (Chapter 4).

Chapter 3

LEVITES IN OLD TESTAMENT TEXTS SINCE THE EXILE

Several texts from the Old Testament have been selected here for an examination of the *Levites* in the exilic and post-exilic periods.[1] The book of Ezekiel, the Priestly Sources (= P), and the book of Chronicles have all been chosen because they are generally believed to have been composed in one of these periods, and all show clearly the position of the Levites with respect to the priests.[2] Moreover, because they are generally thought of as works penned by either a priestly author or a Levitical author, they can be used to compare the priestly and Levitical attitudes toward the Levites.

We shall examine relevant issues of date and authorship with respect to those texts, but shall focus on the picture of the Levites in each work. Our findings can then be compared with the picture presented in E–N, in order to assess whether or not a Levitical or a priestly authorship is most likely for that text.

3.1 *Levites in Ezekiel*

3.1.1 *Status of Levites in Ezekiel*
It has unanimously been agreed that in Ezekiel the Levites are clearly distinguished from the priests in position and function.[3] This distinction is easily recognized by glancing at its references to the Levites. The Hebrew word לוי occurs eight times in the book.[4] Three of these occurrences do not speak of the relationship between the priests and the Levites. Two of these three occurrences appear in the form of הכהנים הלוים (literally, 'the priests, the Levites'), which in Ezekiel is synonymously used with the sons of Zadok, i.e., the Zadokite priests (Ezek. 43.19; 44.15) rather than having to do with the Levites *per se*. The third appears without mention of the priests and, therefore, does not show their relationship with the Levites (48.22).

---

1.   The period to which E–N directly relates is from 538 BCE to shortly after 433 BCE. Thus, it may be asked why we should examine the Levites in the *exilic* period, which seems irrelevant to E–N. However, it seems impossible to understand the Levites in the post-exilic era without understanding them in the exilic era, since the position of the Levites in these two eras is closely related.
2.   Of other Old Testament works which can be dated to those periods, only three books (i.e., Isa. 66.21; Jer. 33.18, 21, 22; Mal. 3.3) have references to 'Levites' under our definition (cf. note 82 in Chapter 2). The number of references is too small for us to draw useful conclusions.
3.   E.g., Raymond Abba, 'Priests and Levites in Ezekiel', *VT* 28 (1978), pp. 1–9, esp. p. 3; D. Kellermann, 'לוי', in *ThWAT*, Band IV, pp. 499–521, esp. pp. 513–14.
4.   *Viz.*, 43.19; 44.10, 15; 45.5; 48.11, 12, 13, 22.

In the remaining five occurrences of the word, however, the Levites are *always* described as *clerus minor* in their position and function relative to the priests. In 44.10, the Levites are sharply contrasted with the priests, who remained faithful, when the Levites, together with the people of Israel, went astray. In 45.5, the strip of land allotted to the Levites is expressly separated from that allotted to the priests, who were given the temple precinct as part of their allotment. This differentiation between the priests and the Levites is also made in 48.11, 12 and 13, where the priests alone are sanctified and, as a result, given the holy district (cf. 48.10-11). The Levites are allowed to minister at the sanctuary but only as gatekeepers, butchers, and handymen (cf. 44.10-14). That is, they have a ministry which has nothing to do with strictly priestly functions, while the Zadokite priests enjoy the exclusive privilege of entering the temple and offering the fat and blood on the altar (44.15-31).[5]

Therefore, we may conclude that Ezekiel clearly shows the Levites as inferior and subordinate to the priests. What remains unclear here, however, is the identity of the Levites. As shall be examined below, some scholars argue that they were originally the *priests* in the high places, whereas the Levites in Ezekiel are frequently contrasted with the *Zadokite* priests (cf. 43.19; 44.15; 48.11) and thus it looks as though the term לוי in Ezekiel may include both the non-Zadokite priests and the other remaining Levites.

Scholars have focused primarily on Ezekiel 44.6ff to examine this issue, since it is here that the Levites appear most conspicuously contrasted with the Zadokite priests.

3.1.2 *Views on the Identity of the Levites in Ezekiel*
(a) *J. Wellhausen*
It was Julius Wellhausen who first formulated one of the most influential theories of the Levites' identity in Ezekiel.[6] According to him, Ezekiel was the first writer who made explicit a distinction between the Zadokite priests and the Levites, even though such a distinction was prevalent and tacitly taken for granted in his time. Ezekiel, as one of the Zadokites, merely wanted to give moral sanction to the existing situation; this is reflected in Ezekiel 44.

More specifically, Wellhausen ascribes the historical separation of the priests and the Levites, and the consequent two-tier ranking of the priesthood, to Josiah's reform. After abolishing the high places in Judah, Josiah brought the priests from there to Jerusalem, but the provincial priests were deterred from ministering at the altar by the Jerusalemite priests. Deuteronomy urged them to stop by stipulating that all the Levites have the same right in ministering at the altar and in their portions as

---

5. Cf. G. Hölscher, *Hesekiel, der Dichter und das Buch* (BZAW, 39; Giessen: Alfred Töpelmann, 1924), p. 197; L.L. Grabbe, *Priests, Prophets, Diviners, Sages: A Socio-Historical Study of Religious Specialists in Ancient Israel* (Valley Forge: Trinity Press International, 1995), p. 47.

6. Julius Wellhausen, *Geschichte Israels* (Berlin: G. Reimer, 1878), which has been titled with *Prolegomena zur Geschichte Israels* since the second edition (1883). Its English translation, *Prolegomena to the History of Israel* (Edinburgh: Adam and Charles Black, 1885), was reprinted in 1994 (Atlanta: Scholars Press). For the reference to the priesthood in Ezekiel, see ET *Prolegomena* (1994), pp. 121–67, esp. pp. 123ff and 140ff.

the (Jerusalemite) priests do (Deut. 18.7-8),[7] but the regulations were not put into practice. Thus, the division between the Jerusalemite priests and the other clerical groups, whose descendants are the Levites, became established, and that situation lasted until Ezekiel's time. Wellhausen concluded that the passage in Ezekiel 44.6ff is referring back to Josiah's reform recorded in 2 Kings 23 and, therefore, the Levites in 44.10 represent the priests in the high places before the reform.

His theory has been accepted by some scholars,[8] but seriously challenged by others.[9] Among several objections to Wellhausen's view, it has been most strongly argued that the term גלולים ('idols'), to which the text indicates that the Levites turned (44.10), refers more to foreign gods and images than to the idols in the high places.[10] In the light of this, it seems improbable that the Ezekiel passage is related to the event reported in 2 Kings 23. Therefore, Wellhausen's thesis is hard to accept and scholars have advanced several alternatives to it, as will be examined below.

---

7.   There has been controversy surrounding the Levites in Deuteronomy. Opposing the view of Wellhausen, G. Ernest Wright, 'The Levites in Deuteronomy', *VT* 4 (1954), pp. 325–30, maintains that there was a *de facto* clerical distinction since the book distinguishes between altar-priests and client-Levites. His position is accepted by R. Abba, 'Priests and Levites in Deuteronomy', *VT* 27 (1977), pp. 257–67, who argues that Deut. 18.1-2 supplies a natural introduction to the two distinct provisions in the following verses (vv. 3-5 for priests and vv. 6-8 for Levites) and concludes that the terms *priests* and *Levites* in Deuteronomy are discriminately used: *Levites* connotes a subordinate order of cultic officials, whereas *priests* indicates the clergy ministering at the sanctuary. Ulrich Dahmen, *Leviten und Priester im Deuteronomium: Literarkritik und redaktionsgeschichtliche Studien* (BBB, 110; Bodenheim: Philo Verlag, 1996), also seems to favour this view since he observes that, in the basic text of Deuteronomy, the Levites were treated as a social group in special need of benevolence and the priests, by contrast, had clearly defined juridical and sacrificial roles at the central sanctuary. This view has been effectively challenged by J.A. Emerton, 'Priests and Levites in Deuteronomy', *VT* 12 (1962), pp. 129–38, however, who argues that Deuteronomy not only regards service at the altar as a right common to all Levites (Deut. 10.8; cf. 21.5), but it also sees priestly functions as conferred on the tribe of Levi as a whole (18.5; 33.8-10), and, therefore, there is no evidence for clerical distinctions. See also Moshe Weinfeld, *Deuteronomy 1–11: A New Translation with Introduction and Commentary* (AB, 5; Garden City, NY: Doubleday, 1991), p. 35.
8.   E.g., John W. Bowman, 'Ezekiel and the Zadokite Priesthood', *TGUOS* 16 (1955–56), pp. 1–14, esp. p. 2; H. Gese, *Der Verfassungsentwurf des Ezekiel (Kap. 40–48): Traditionsgeschichtlich Untersucht* (BHT, 25; Tübingen: Mohr-Siebeck, 1957), p. 121 n. 1; Roland de Vaux, *Ancient Israel: Its Life and Institutions* (London: Darton, Longman & Todd Ltd, 2nd edn, 1965), pp. 363–64; Walter Eichrodt, *Ezekiel* (OTL; Philadelphia: Westminster, 1970), pp. 564–65; Cody, *A History of Old Testament Priesthood* (Rome: Pontifical Biblical Institute, 1969), pp. 135–36; Nigel Allan, 'The Identity of the Jerusalem Priesthood during the Exile', *HeyJ* 23 (1982), pp. 259–69, esp. pp. 259–60. For more, see Iain M. Duguid, *Ezekiel and the Leaders of Israel* (Leiden: E.J. Brill, 1994), p. 58 n. 2.
9.   E.g., Moshe Greenberg, 'A New Approach to the History of the Israelite Priesthood', *JAOS* 70 (1950), pp. 41–47; Abba, 'Priests and Levites in Ezekiel', pp. 1–9; J.G. McConville, 'Priests and Levites in Ezekiel: A Crux in the Conclusion of Israel's History', *TynBul* 34 (1983), pp. 3–32; R.K. Duke, 'Punishment or Restoration: Another Look at the Levites of Ezekiel 44.6-16', *JSOT* 40 (1988), pp. 61–81; Duguid, *Ezekiel and the Leaders of Israel*, pp. 75–80; Stephen L. Cook, 'Inner-biblical Interpretation in Ezekiel 44 and the History of Israel's Priesthood', *JBL* 114 (1995), pp. 193–208, esp. pp. 194–96.
10.   Cf. M. Haran, *Temple and Temple-Service in Ancient Israel: An Inquiry into the Character of Cult Phenomena and the Historical Setting of the Priestly School* (Oxford: Clarendon Press, 1978), pp. 104–105; Duke, 'Punishment or Restoration', p. 78 n. 21.

(b) *Raymond Abba and Risto Nurmela*

Raymond Abba observes that the sin condemned in Ezekiel 44 was a *national* apostasy, because the whole people were involved in it (vv. 6ff).[11] He also observes that the passage extols the Zadokite priests' lack of involvement in this national apostasy (vv. 15ff). Accordingly, the apostasy cannot be referring to Judah's apostasy since the Zadokite priests were always involved in that. On the basis of these observations, Abba argues that the calf-worship initiated by Jeroboam I in Northern Israel (cf. 1 Kgs 12.28-32) may be the only case suitable for the context of Ezekiel 44. On balance, he concludes that 'Ezekiel's polemic is directed not against the dispossessed priests of the Judean high places, but against the priests who had taken part in this idolatrous worship in Northern Israel'.[12]

Risto Nurmela concurs with Abba in that he also believes the Levites in Ezekiel to have been those who officiated at the northern kingdom's cult.[13] He further claims that the idols (גלולים) in Ezekiel 44.10, 12 should be interpreted as pointing to the golden calves of Jeroboam I, and the Levites considered the northern priestly group of Bethel. His view is based on the observation that its context is dealing with the sin of the northern tribes; he believes that the phrase, 'the house of Israel' in 44.6 is a conventional phrase used by Ezekiel to imply the northern tribes.[14]

The views of Abba and Nurmela are open to criticism, however. The primary objection is that they have overlooked the crucial fact that *my sanctuary* (מקדשי) in 44.7, 8, 9 must surely mean the Jerusalem temple, not a sanctuary in the northern kingdom. This word is most likely being employed with the same meaning as in verses 15 and 16, where it definitely indicates the sanctuary in Jerusalem, since Jerusalem was the only place in which the Zadokite priests were in charge (v. 15). It should also be noted that, in Ezekiel, the expression מקדשי almost always denotes the sanctuary in Jerusalem (5.11; 8.6; 24.21; 25.3; 37.26, 28), while other sanctuaries outside of Jerusalem always appear in the plural form (מקדשים; 7.24; 28.18).

(c) *I.M. Duguid*

Another possible alternative to Wellhausen's view has been put forward by Iain Duguid, who has pointed out that 'there is no indication in the text that the Levites previously functioned as priests';[15] for, when seen in the light of verses 11b and 12, their ministry on behalf of the people before idols (v. 10) cannot be regarded as priestly work. Rather, the Levites must be 'a preexisting (lower) class of cultic personnel who went astray with the mass of the people after idols and performed cultic duties in the service of idolatrous cults'.[16] Furthermore, Duguid suggests two possibilities for the idolatrous cult to which the text refers: one is the cult which was

11.   Abba, 'Priests and Levites in Ezekiel', pp. 1–9.
12.   Abba, 'Priests and Levites in Ezekiel', p. 5.
13.   Risto Nurmela, *The Levites: Their Emergence as a Second-Class Priesthood* (Atlanta: Scholars Press, 1998), pp. 85–106.
14.   Nurmela, *The Levites*, p. 90.
15.   Duguid, *Ezekiel and the Leaders of Israel*, p. 79.
16.   Duguid, *Ezekiel and the Leaders of Israel*, p. 80.

observed during the last years immediately before Judah's destruction (cf. Jer. 7.16-18; 11.9-13); the other is the cult in Jerusalem, which continued after its destruction in 587 BCE.[17]

Neither of these two possibilities is adequate, however. If we adopt either of them, we are faced with the difficult situation of explaining how the Zadokite priests could be in charge of the sanctuary in Jerusalem (v. 15), when most of them had already been taken captive to Babylon (cf. 2 Kgs 24.14-15; Jer. 52.28) and the Jerusalem temple already lay in ruins. In addition, Ezekiel reports that the priests, too, were among those who went astray during the last years before the total destruction of Jerusalem (Ezek. 7.26; 22.26). The circumstances do not, therefore, suit the situation depicted in Ezekiel 44.

(d) *S.L. Cook*

Recently, there has been a new proposal by Stephen Cook, who approaches the issue from a different angle.[18] He first argues that when Ezekiel mentions the Zadokites' faithfulness at the time of betrayal (44.15), the text cannot be referring to an event in the monarchic period, for it is Ezekiel's general position that the temple priests cannot be exempted from his condemnation of that period (Ezek. 7.26; 8; 22.26). Further, Cook finds more compelling the view that the chapter was influenced by P rather than the reverse; Ezekiel 44 shows stricter regulations for joining the priesthood (only the Zadokite priests) than P (all of the Aaronite priests).[19]

In addition, Cook agrees with Jon Levenson in assuming that Ezekiel 44 uses a specific P wilderness tradition.[20] Because of this, Cook contends that the text makes direct reference to the story of Korah's rebellion recorded in P (Num. 16–18). In support of his thesis, he attempts to show the connection between both passages. For example, the references to the people of Israel and the Levites in Ezekiel 44, both of whom went astray, fit well with the story of Korah, which shows that Israel as a whole was involved in the rebellion (Num. 16.2, 22; cf. Num. 17.6 [Eng. 16.41]).[21] In sum, he argues that Ezekiel 44 drew on the story of Korah in Numbers 16–18, where the distinction between the clerical groups is clearly set out.[22]

However, Cook's argument has several significant flaws. First, his assumption that Ezekiel 44 postdates P is not grounded in scholarly consensus.[23] Second, while

---

17. Duguid, *Ezekiel and the Leaders of Israel*, p. 80. For the second possibility, see also Allan, 'The Identity of the Jerusalem Priesthood', pp. 262ff; and Elizabeth Achtemeier, *The Community and Message of Isaiah 56–66* (Minneapolis: Augsburg Publishing House, 1982), p. 23.

18. Cook, 'Innerbiblical Interpretation in Ezekiel 44'.

19. Cook, 'Innerbiblical Interpretation in Ezekiel 44', p. 196, says that 'this text [Ezek. 44] presupposes the restrictions in P and further tightens them'.

20. Cf. Jon D. Levenson, *Theology of the Program of Restoration of Ezekiel 40–48* (HSM, 10; Missoula: Scholars Press, 1976), pp. 134, 137.

21. Cook, 'Innerbiblical Interpretation in Ezekiel 44', p. 199. For more examples, see pp. 197–201.

22. Cook, 'Innerbiblical Interpretation in Ezekiel 44', pp. 201–204, contends that the purpose of employing the Numbers passage was so that the Ezekielian Zadokites could present Ezekiel 44 as 'a paradigm for understanding the Zadokites' future role after their exilic punishment'.

23. Cook's position can be supported by the argument that the so-called *Zadokite stratum* in

Ezekiel 44.7 speaks of 'my house', referring to the Jerusalem temple, no mention is made of the temple in the Korah story. Finally, he fails to address the question of the emergence of the Aaronite priests in Chronicles and E–N, whose dates coincide with the period *after* Ezekiel 40–48. In order to adhere to his view (P → Ezek. → Chronicles and E–N), one of the following two possibilities must be accepted: (1) that Chronicles and E–N used P's term for the priests (i.e., the Aaronites) and ignored Ezekiel's term (i.e., the Zadokites) and thus do not have any reference to the Zadokites; or (2) that the term for the priests underwent a double transition: i.e., the Aaronites in P to the Zadokites in Ezekiel and, then, the Zadokites in Ezekiel to the Aaronites in Chronicles and E–N. Neither possibility is plausible, however. It is doubtful whether Chronicles and E–N could have accepted P's common expression, since they were 'unwilling to acquiesce in any principle of Levitical inferiority with respect to the priests', which was characteristic of P.[24] The second possibility can also easily be replaced with the widely held view, which supposes only one transition: from the Zadokites in Ezekiel to the Aaronites in P, Chronicles, and E–N.[25] Cook's theory, therefore, while very ingenious, does not address problems raised by relative dating and the mention of the temple, thus making itself improbable and over-complicated.

3.1.3 *Levites in Ezekiel*
Since Wellhausen, then, there have been several attempts to determine who the Levites in Ezekiel 44 were. Wellhausen himself viewed them as the priests of the high places prior to Josiah's reform. Because of problems with his reading of the text, his thesis has yielded to several alternative theories. Abba and Nurmela correlate the Levites with the priestly group in Bethel, and Duguid regards them as second-class cultic personnel during the period shortly before or after the destruction of Jerusalem. Cook, on the other hand, denies that Ezekiel had a monarchic period referent in mind and interprets the passage in the light of the story of Korah's rebellion. None of these theories is persuasive, however, primarily because they fail to note that 'my sanctuary' in the text must refer to the *Jerusalem* sanctuary. Any comprehensive theory must stand on this ground.

Ezekiel 40–48, where Israel is addressed as *you* (plural) and priestly rights are confined to the Zadokites, was not written by Ezekiel, who lived during the exilic era, but should be placed in the post-exilic period, thus postdating P. See Welch, *Post-Exilic Judaism*, p. 237; Gese, *Der Verfassungsentwurf des Ezechiel*, pp. 111ff. But we take the more commonly accepted scholarly view that the book of Ezekiel as a whole was completed sometime during the exilic period. For the arguments in support of this view, see Pfeiffer, *Introduction*, pp. 553–54 and Duguid, *Ezekiel and the Leaders of Israel*, pp. 87–90. We will explore the dating of P in section 3.2.2 below. Suffice it to say, at this point, that the dating of P is debated and that Cook's position is not the consensus one.

24. Cody, *A History of Old Testament Priesthood*, p. 184.

25. Cody persuasively expounds the historical reason for this transition. According to him, the Zadokites in the exile accused the Levites of their sins in order to relieve their anger. When the age of restoration came, however, their anger diminished and they compromised, using the term Aaronites to include both the Levites and themselves. See Cody, *A History of Old Testament Priesthood*, p. 166.

The fact that מִקְדָּשִׁי ('my sanctuary') in Ezek. 44.7, 8, 9, 15, 16 indicates the Jerusalem temple serves as the starting point for exploring the identity of 'the Levites' in the text. From this fact we can, at least, claim that the place and date for the incident recorded in the text should be linked with the Jerusalem temple and a time before its destruction in 587 BCE. Another crucial clue is the designation of the priests as the sons of Zadok (44.15), for it leads us to think that a term antithetical to the Zadokite priests most necessarily includes the other priests, who lived mostly in the northern kingdom and did not belong to the Zadokites. These fundamental observations prompt us to hypothesize that the reference to foreigners in verse 7 probably points to the northern priests in Bethel,[26] and that the date for the incident referred to in the text may be the period after the destruction of the northern kingdom in 722 BCE. Some of the northern priestly group fled to Judah, and this refuge might have provided the first opportunity for the northern priests to encounter the Jerusalem priests since their split during the reign of Rehoboam. The northern priests presumably brought their own religious traditions and practices to Judah. As shown in Ezekiel 44.7ff, these northern practices were accepted by the people of Judah and the Levites, who felt sympathy with the northern priests, since both were marginalized from the priestly function and subordinate to the Jerusalemite priests. This situation embarrassed and threatened the Jerusalemite (Zadokite) priests, and they began to defend the sanctuary against the influx of northern customs by doing guard duty (44.15), which the Levites were originally responsible for, but did not perform.[27] Similarly, Ezekiel attacks the northern priests, who are described as having been allowed to enter the Jerusalem temple, by depicting them as foreigners uncircumcised in heart and flesh (44.7), and by regarding what they brought into the temple as idols (v. 10).

Why, then, are the Levites unexpectedly favoured again in the text by the promise that they will resume their duty as gatekeepers of the sanctuary (v. 14)? It should be borne in mind that Ezekiel 44 is in the middle of the section (Ezekiel 40–48) which is presenting a so-called blueprint for the new Jerusalem.[28] Therefore, the text is targeted to the future, in which the Levites will also have their shared roles in a new Jerusalem temple. Ezekiel here merely wanted to make a clear distinction between the Zadokite priests and the non-Zadokite Levites in terms of their future

---

26.   There is no consensus on the identity of the uncircumcised foreigners in this verse, although several possibilities have been put forward: e.g., 'the Gibeonites' in Joshua (König), 'the unfaithful priests' (Hengstenberg), 'nethinim and sons of Solomon's servants' (Abba), 'foreign temple guards' (Duguid), and 'the temple servants' (Nurmela), etc. Cf. Eduard König, 'The Priests and Levites in Ez 44.7-15', *ExpTim* 12 (1901), pp. 300–303, esp. p. 300; Ernst W. Hengstenberg, *Die Weissagung des Propheten Ezechiel, für solche die in der Schrift forschen erläutert* (Berlin, 1867/8), p. 268; Abba, 'Priests and Levites in Ezekiel', p. 3; Duguid, *Ezekiel and the Leaders of Israel*, p. 76; Nurmela, *The Levites*, p. 91.

27.   For the interpretation of שָׁמַר מִשְׁמֶרֶת as 'guard duty' in verse 15, see Jacob Milgrom, *Studies in Levitical Terminology*: I. *The Encroacher and the Levite; The Term 'Aboda* (Berkeley: University of California Press, 1970), pp. 8–11.

28.   E.g. Pfeiffer, *Introduction*, p. 554; Bernard W. Anderson, *Understanding the Old Testament* (Englewood Cliffs: Prentice-Hall, 4th edn, 1986) p. 445.

functions. Although there was a time when the Zadokites provisionally did guard duty of the sanctuary, this subordinate duty should be the Levites' role in the future temple, as articulated in 44.11-12. Simultaneously, Ezekiel does not forget to author-ize the Zadokite priests to minister in the sanctuary (v. 13). Viewed in this light, as Duguid rightly points out, Ezekiel 44 highlights the distinct separation between the clerical ranks by corroborating the position of the Levites as the *second* rank of temple clergy.[29]

In conclusion, though the career of Ezekiel is confined to the exilic period, this book shows the relationship of the Levites to the priests both in the late pre-exilic and exilic periods: i.e., the Levites' subordinate relationship to the priests in position and function. Also, if we accept the general view that Ezekiel, who was one of the Zadokite priests, was responsible for the book which bears his name, the fact that he describes the Levites as being demoted and *clerus minor* is of utmost signifi-cance, for it provides a crucial illustration of a priestly writer's attitude toward his opposing party, the Levites.

3.2 *Levites in the Priestly Sources*

3.2.1 *Two Features of the Priesthood in P*
Two features of the priesthood in P have been widely recognized: first, in P there is no reference to the *Zadokite* priests; instead, the *Aaronite* priests appear as the coun-terpart to the Levites (Exod. 28.1, 43; Num. 3.10; 18.1-7, etc.);[30] second, P strictly distinguishes between the priests and the Levites by treating the former favourably and depicting the latter as lower clergy, subordinate to the former.[31] For example, in the book of Leviticus, which is generally regarded as belonging to P,[32] reference to Levites occurs only 4 times, though their existence is taken for granted. This paucity of occurrences is contrasted with a huge number of references to the priests, which occur 194 times in the same book. This conspicuous contrast is also retained in the occurrence of the two words in all of P, where the word כהן occurs 250 times while לוי only 62 times.[33] Not only are the priests spoken of more frequently than the Levites; they are also described as more privileged in their clerical duties. They are entitled to minister in the sanctuary by offering sacrifice (Lev. 1–5), burning incense (Exod 30.7-8), keeping the lamps burning (Lev. 24.1-4; Num. 8.2), and setting out the showbread (Lev. 24.8-9), whereas the Levites are largely limited to guard duty, which entails physical labour.[34] The Levites are subordinated to the priests in their location at the sanctuary, too; the favoured east side of the camp is allotted to the

---

29. Duguid, *Ezekiel and the Leaders of Israel*, pp. 78–79.
30. See, for example, de Vaux, *Ancient Israel*, p. 365.
31. E.g., A.H.J. Gunneweg, *Leviten und Priester: Hauptlinien der Traditionsbildung und Geschichte des israelitisch-judischen Kultpersonals* (FRLANT, 89; Göttingen: Vandenhoeck & Ruprecht, 1965), p. 185.
32. Cf. Fohrer, *Introduction*, p. 180.
33. Cf. Andersen and Forbes, *The Vocabulary of the Old Testament*, pp. 341, 350.
34. Kellermann, 'לוי', pp. 514–15.

priests and the holy precincts of the tabernacle are their place of service, out of bounds to the Levites.[35]

3.2.2 *Date of P*
3.2.2.1 *Challenges to the Antiquity of P*
Conceiving of the P accounts as records of what really happened in the time and space to which they refer, some scholars used to argue that the emergence of the Aaronite priests, and their priority over the Levites, must have originated in the wilderness period.[36] Modern scholarship, however, has rejected this position, primarily with a documentary hypothesis, which we shall examine below, but also with a close reading of texts related to these issues. For example, John Spencer asks why, if Aaron and the Aaronites had existed since the pre-exilic period, references to them are absent in Ezekiel, which has a very strong interest in priests.[37] Blenkinsopp also asks 'why, if the Aaronites were in place from the beginning of Israel's existence, they and their eponym are so poorly attested in non-P writings to which a pre-exilic date can safely be attached'.[38] This situation has propelled scholars to question the historical reliability of the narratives contained in P and thus to explore the dating of P.

Recent scholarly efforts to explore the dating of P have primarily assumed a late date. Thus, since Wellhausen,[39] P has widely been accepted as the latest of the sources/traditions in the Pentateuch, being dated to the exilic or post-exilic period.[40] However, there have been a few challenges to this position, particularly by Yehezkel Kaufmann and his followers, who defend the antiquity of P and date it to the pre-exilic period.[41] The debate continues, but we are persuaded by the scholars who

35.   Philip Jenson, 'לוי' in *NIDOTTE*, II, pp. 772–78, esp. p. 773.

36.   E.g., Samuel I. Curtiss, *The Levitical Priests: A Contribution to the Criticism of the Pentateuch* (Edinburgh: T&T Clark, 1877), p. viii.

37.   John R. Spencer, 'Aaron', in *ABD*, I, pp. 1–6, esp. p. 1.

38.   J. Blenkinsopp, 'An Assessment of the Alleged Pre-Exilic Date of the Priestly Material in the Pentateuch', *ZAW* 108 (1996), pp. 495–518, esp. p. 501.

39.   Viz., Wellhausen, *Prolegomena*. There were forerunners, who supplied the grounds for Wellhausen's documentary hypothesis (J → E → D → P), such as W.M.L. de Wette, Johann George, Eduard Reuss, Karl-Heinrich Graf, Abraham Kuenen. Cf. Eissfeldt, *Introduction*, pp. 158–66; Blenkinsopp, 'Assessment', p. 496.

40.   Werner H. Schmidt, *Old Testament Introduction* (trans. M.J. O'Connell; New York: Crossroad, 1984), pp. 97–98, summarizes the reasons for assigning a late date to P: (1) the centralization of cult is called for in Deuteronomy (12.13ff), but is taken for granted in P ('in that book [Deuteronomy] the unity of the cultus is commanded; in the Priestly Code it is presupposed'; cf. Wellhausen, *Prolegomena*, p. 35); (2) the fact that P mentions the precise dating of feasts, the differentiation of types of sacrifice, and the divisions within the priesthood represents a late stage in the history of a cult; (3) in P, the concept of 'people' (עם) is replaced with that of 'community' (עדה), which indicates a situation in which certain members of the post-exilic community lost their civic independence; (4) P's emphasis on circumcision and sanctification of the Sabbath can be intelligible only in the conditions of the time in exile.

41.   Yehezkel Kaufmann, תולדות האמונה הישראלית (8 vols. ;Tel-Aviv: Bialik Institute-Dvir, 1937–56). מימי קדם עד סוף בית שני . This has been translated and abridged by M. Greenberg, *The Religion of Israel: From its Beginnings to the Babylonian Exile* (London: George Allen & Unwin

propose a late date and appear to respond effectively to the challenges presented by the proponents of an early dating of P.

A current representative of these scholars is Joseph Blenkinsopp, who has thoroughly examined the arguments of scholars who hold Kaufmann's position and concluded that they are unconvincing. For example, in contrast to Kaufmann, Blenkinsopp is convinced that P presupposes Deuteronomy since the idea of disposing the twelve tribes around the tent shrine reflects that of a central Israelite sanctuary rather than one of several local shrines.[42] Furthermore, he also points out the uselessness of attempts to distinguish between (Early) Biblical Hebrew and Late Biblical Hebrew and then favouring the antiquity of the Hebrew in P; for, in a situation where 'we still have a long way to go in elaborating a sound methodology and attaining a reasonable degree of assurance about our results', we are easily tempted to conclude the date of this or that text by preconceived ideas.[43]

Ltd, 1961). Kaufmann supports the antiquity of P in that, for example, P (Exod. 12.2-20) prescribes that the paschal sacrifice should be performed at home, which is similar to an ancient home sacrifice, while Deuteronomy forbids the paschal celebration 'in your gates' (*The Religion of Israel*, p. 179). Scholars who have followed Kaufmann's lead include: Avi Hurvitz, 'The Evidence of Language in Dating the Priestly Code: A Linguistic Study in Technical Idioms and Terminology', *RB* 91 (1974), pp. 24–56, who compares P with Ezekiel, E–N, Chronicles, and Mishnah and concludes that P's phrases and idioms are different from those of the exilic and post-exilic texts; Haran, *Temple and Temple-Service*, pp. 7–10, 140–48, 397; *idem*, 'Behind the Scenes of History: Determining the Date of the Priestly Source', *JBL* 100 (1981), pp. 321–33; who argues that P was composed in the period of King Hezekiah and that his reform was based upon P's regulation of the cult; Abba, 'Priests and Levites in Ezekiel', pp. 8–9, who places P in the pre-exilic period since the assertion that P presupposes Ezekiel cannot stand any longer; Ziony Zevit, 'Converging Lines of Evidence Bearing on the Date of P', *ZAW* 94 (1982), pp. 321–33, who maintains, on a linguistic analysis of P, that the *terminus ad quem* for P should be before 586 BCE; M. Weinfeld, 'Social and Cultic Institutions in the Priestly Source against their Ancient Near Eastern Background', in D. Krone, *Proceedings of the Eighth World Congress of Jewish Studies. Panel Sessions: Bible Studies and Hebrew Language* (Jerusalem: World Union of Jewish Studies, 1983), pp. 95–129, who finds similarities in social and cultic institutions between P and the Hittite texts and argues for an early date for P. For an assessment of most of the above views, see Blenkinsopp, 'Assessment', pp. 504–16. For more lists of scholars in favour of the thesis of the pre-exilic origin of P, see J.G. Vink, 'The Date and Origin of the Priestly Code in the Old Testament', in *The Priestly Code and Seven Other Studies* (*OTS*, XV; Leiden: E.J. Brill, 1969), pp. 10–11.

42.   Blenkinsopp, 'Assessment', p. 500. He also criticizes Kaufmann's ignorance of the fact that 'P's wilderness sanctuary is in the center of the camp (e.g., Num. 2.17), unlike the non-P account in which the oracle tent lies outside the camp (ex[*sic*] 33.7-11)'. For more arguments Blenkinsopp addresses, see, 'Assessment', pp. 500–504.

43.   Blenkinsopp, 'Assessment', p. 509. His position was critically examined by J. Milgrom, 'The Antiquity of the Priestly Source: A Reply to Joseph Blenkinsopp', *ZAW* 111 (1999), pp. 10–22, who pointed out that Blenkinsopp has misconstrued, for example, the priestly term, עבדה, which does appear in late texts referring to physical labour just as in P, but not in connection with the temple service, and thus should not be regarded as post-exilic (p. 11). After observing that the Holiness Code (=H; Lev. 17–27) fits well in a pre-exilic setting and that Deuteronomy, which is also pre-exilic, is dependent on H, and H borrowed from P (i.e., P → H → D), Milgrom concludes 'the entire priestly law corpus is pre-exilic' (p. 22). But I hesitate to accept his arguments since, as he confesses, his study did not include the priestly narrative, which is the main source for Blenkinsopp's arguments (Blenkinsopp, p. 496). In fact, as noted by George W. Anderson, *A Critical Introduction*

3.2.2.2 Exilic or Post-exilic?
If it is right that P was written in a period after the exile, then was it exilic or post-exilic? If it is exilic, then which is earlier, Ezekiel or P? These questions are important because the position of the Levites shown in P might reflect the religious atmosphere during the period when P was written.

There is a long-standing debate about this issue, and a huge number of proposals have been advanced. Scholarly attention has been drawn mainly to Wellhausen's view. According to him, P was completed in the post-exilic period, with the purpose of establishing the restoration community as a religious group.[44] Similar positions to this have been held by many scholars, such as J.G. Vink who concluded that P is to be linked up with Ezra's mission as dated to 398 BCE, and Ernst Sellin who noted that in Haggai, Zechariah and Malachi there is no hint of any awareness of P. P's influence has been detected only in Chronicles, which is generally assumed to have been written after the second half of the fourth century BCE.[45]

Another group of scholars have dated P to the exilic period, instead of the post-exilic. According to them, the finalization of P must have taken place during the exile,[46] because, for example, Second Isaiah, which is normally dated to 550 BCE, seems to have known P's creation story and Exodus narrative.[47] Also, because P lacks a narrative of the occupation of Canaan and ends with the people of Israel poised on the edge of the promised land, Deborah Rooke has contended that this reflects 'the position of the Babylonian exiles awaiting re-establishment in their own land, implying that P should be dated at a time during the exilic years when a new future seemed promised but was as yet unattained'.[48]

As regards a *terminus a quo* for P, it has generally been agreed that since Ezekiel did not know P, the latter must postdate the former (thus Ezek. → P),[49] and

---

to the Old Testament (London: Duckworth, 2nd edn, 1994), 'to show that any individual law or custom is of great antiquity is not decisive for the date of the entire source'. I am also not persuaded by Gordon Wenham, 'The Priority of P', *VT* 49 (1999), pp. 240–58, who argues that P was written earlier than J, because his argument is based only on the examination of the P material in Genesis.

44.   Wellhausen, *Prolegomena*, pp. 99–112.

45.   Vink, 'The Priestly Code', pp. 17, 143–44; Ernst Sellin and Georg Fohrer, *Introduction to the Old Testament* (Nashville: Abingdon Press, 1968), p. 185.

46.   E.g., A.S. Kapelrud, 'The Date of the Priestly Code (P)', *ASTI* III (1964), pp. 58–64; F.M. Cross, 'The Priestly Work', in *Canaanite Myth and Hebrew Epic* (Cambridge: Harvard University Press, 1973), pp. 293–325; Paul D. Hanson, *The People Called: The Growth of Community in the Bible* (San Francisco: Harper & Row, 1986), pp. 224–33; Deborah W. Rooke, *Zadok's Heirs: The Role and Development of the High Priesthood in Ancient Israel* (OTM; Oxford: Oxford University Press, 2000), pp. 11–13.

47.   Kapelrud, 'The Date of the Priestly Code (P)', pp. 59–62.

48.   Rooke, *Zadok's Heirs*, p. 12.

49.   In contrast, some scholars may argue that, since the date of Ezekiel is undeterminable, it is misleading to form a judgment on the basis of the relationship between the dates of Ezekiel and P. For example, it is necessary to place P prior to Ezekiel if we treat Ezekiel 40–48 (so-called, 'die Sadoqidenschicht') as an independent corpus from the rest of the book and date the composition of the whole book to the post-exilic period or even to the Maccabean period (e.g., Gese, *Der Verfassungsentwurf des Ezekiel*, pp. 65, 120–23; Gunneweg, *Leviten und Priester*, pp. 188–203;

therefore the earliest date for P should be after 571 BCE, when the last oracle of Ezekiel was declared (Ezek. 29.17).[50] Arvid Kapelrud provides us with a reason for the statement that Ezekiel was not aware of P: i.e., the creation story that Ezekiel knows (Ezek. 28.16) relies upon the ancient narratives of Genesis 2–3, which are generally accepted as the earlier levels of tradition, and has no trace of Genesis 1, which is part of P.[51] Another guideline for the *terminus a quo* of P is supplied by Rooke, who observes that P's detailed legislation is not found in the books of Samuel and Kings and concludes that it was not in force during the time these books were composed, i.e., *circa* 550 BCE.[52]

In the light of what has been examined so far, we have two quite plausible arguments: (1) P was composed before Second Isaiah (i.e., during the exilic period), as suggested by Kapelrud, and (2) P should be regarded as a product of the post-exilic period, as suggested by Vink and Sellin. This situation affirms Brevard Childs' suggestion that we should have to investigate fully the purpose and motivation behind the priestly source in order to solve this dilemma.[53] However, because this is not the place to examine the whole issue in detail, we intend to compromise over the issue of the date for P with Werner Schmidt, who argues that the basic priestly document (= P^G) arose during the exile, while its secondary expansion (= P^S) was added sometime during the post-exilic period.[54] His position is supported by Otto Eissfeldt, who underlined the connection between the final redaction of P and Ezra, and also by George Anderson, who paid attention to the fact that such a document as P is unlikely to be entirely the product of a single generation and proposed the dating of the process of codification of P to the post-exilic period.[55] This position treats P as being both exilic and post-exilic.

To sum up, the priestly source must be treated as spanning a period from the time immediately after Ezekiel through to Ezra, which is assumed to be 458 BCE.[56] On this basis, we may take the relationship between the priests and the Levites in P to reflect the religious situation in the period *circa* 571–458 BCE.

Zimmerli, *Ezekiel*, pp. 547–53; Cook, 'Innerbiblical Interpretation in Ezekiel 44', p. 196; the dating of Ezekiel to the Maccabean period was contended by George R. Berry, 'Priests and Levites', *JBL* 42 (1923), pp. 227–38, esp. p. 227). But, in the previous section, we have already articulated our position that we regard Ezekiel 40–48 as part of the work written during his lifetime. See n. 23 above.

50. For this 571 BCE date, see John W. Wevers, *Ezekiel* (NCB; Grand Rapids: Eerdmans, 1982), p. 162.

51. Kapelrud, 'The Date of the Priestly Code (P)', p. 63. He further concludes that P is a product completed between 585 and 550 BCE (p. 64). For a similar view, see Niels-Erik A. Andreasen, *The Old Testament Sabbath: A Tradition-Historical Investigation* (SBL, 7; Missoula, MT: SBL, 1972), p. 62.

52. Rooke, *Zadok's Heirs*, pp. 12–13.

53. Brevard S. Childs, *Introduction to the Old Testament as Scripture* (London: SCM Press, 1979), p. 123.

54. Schmidt, *Old Testament Introduction*, pp. 96–99.

55. Eissfeldt, *Introduction*, p. 208; Anderson, *A Critical Introduction to the Old Testament*, p. 48.

56. Cf. see section 2.1.

3.2.3 *Levites in P*

At the beginning of this section, we observed that the two most notable features of priesthood in P are: (1) the emergence of the term *Aaronites* and (2) the subordination of the Levites to the priests. The question remains as to what implications these features have, if P was penned in the exilic and post-exilic periods. More specifically, why does P employ the term 'Aaronites' in place of 'Zadokites'? It is also evident that, in P, the Levites are distinguished from the priests in very rigorous ways; for example, if they touch or even watch the holy things, they will die (Num. 4.15, 20). What, then, was the context of P that resulted in these strict regulations?

As far as the emergence of the Aaronite priests in P is concerned, numerous answers have been suggested. At one extreme, doubting the reliability of P and the Chronicler's statements concerning priestly matters, George Berry has actually denied the historical existence of the priests called Aaronites. He asserts that the reason the writer of P used the term 'Aaronites' was simply because he wished to give an ancient lineage to the priests in order to enhance the glory of the cult.[57] Wolf Baudissin, on the other hand, believes that the 'sons of Aaron' existed as a specific priestly group during the time before the exile.[58] Most scholars have agreed with Wellhausen, who aligns them with the Zadokite group, and argue that there was a compromise between the non-Zadokite Levitical group in Judah and the Zadokite group who had returned from Babylon.[59] What is not clear is the identity of the non-Zadokite Levitical group in Judah and why they desired to merge with the Zadokites under the name of 'sons of Aaron'.

Robert Kennett deals with this matter comprehensively.[60] In order to identify the 'sons of Aaron', he first asks who Aaron was. After careful investigation into the references to Aaron in the Old Testament, he concludes that Aaron was the originator of the cult of the golden calf at Bethel. If so, then how did Aaron, a non-Judean priest, come to be regarded as the head and source of the only orthodox priesthood in Jerusalem? Kennett answers this question by reviewing the religious history of Palestine since the middle of the eighth century BCE: (1) despite the destruction of the northern kingdom, some of Jehovah's devout worshippers still remained at Bethel and other cities; (2) these worshippers sent a petition to the king of Assyria to continue to worship and, as a result, the priests were allowed to reside at Bethel; (3) under Manasseh a strong reaction set in against the reformation of Hezekiah and many worshippers of Jehovah in Judah fled to Bethel for refuge, carrying with them the traditions of their Judean forefathers; (4) since most of the Jerusalem

---

57.   Berry, 'Priests and Levites', pp. 228, 234–35.

58.   Wolf W.G. Baudissin, 'Priests and Levites', *Hasting's Dictionary of the Bible*, vol. IV (New York: Charles Scribners' Sons, 1902), pp. 67–97, esp. p. 89.

59.   Scholars who concur are: W. Robertson Smith and Alfred Bertholet, 'Priest', in *Encyclopaedia Biblica*, III (New York: McMillan and Co., 1902), cols. 3837–47; H.G. Judge, 'Aaron, Zadok and Abiathar', *JTS* n.s. 7 (1956), pp. 70–74; John R. Bartlett, 'Zadok and His Successors at Jerusalem', *JTS* n.s. 19 (1968), pp. 1–18, esp. p. 16; de Vaux, *Ancient Israel*, pp. 395–96, etc. Cf. O'Brien, 'Priest and Levite in Malachi', pp. 36–40.

60.   Robert H. Kennett, 'The Origin of the Aaronite Priesthood', *JTS* 6 (1905), pp. 161–86. His view was favoured by Theophile J. Meek, 'Aaronites and Zadokites', *AJSL* 45 (1928–29), pp. 149–66, esp. pp. 155–56, and Francis S. North, 'Aaron's Rise in Prestige', *ZAW* 66 (1954), pp. 191–99.

priests were deported to Babylon, leaving few priests to minister at Jerusalem in the exilic period, the body of priests at Bethel flourished. Subsequently, the priests of Bethel became the priests of Jerusalem. The first priest of Jerusalem from Bethel might have been Jehozadak the father of Joshua, who had never been taken into Babylon. Thus, Joshua was of Bethel priestly lineage; and (5) when the sons of Zadok returned with Zerubbabel, they were compelled to accept Joshua as their head. News had travelled to Babylon that the sons of Aaron had been recognized as legitimate priests and, therefore, there was no room for the sons of Zadok, unless they consented to a merger with the guild of Aaron. Consequently, the title *sons of Aaron* came to take the place of the title *sons of Zadok*.

This theory has been attacked by many scholars, mainly because of its lack of evidence. For example, Abba points out that there is no reason to doubt that Joshua came back from Babylon with the other priests of Zadokite descent (Ezra 2.2, 36).[61] Thus, Kennett's radical and speculative proposal has been replaced with somewhat more moderate and convincing theories, which largely regard the designation 'sons of Aaron' as the outcome of a compromise or a conflict between two opposing clerical parties, though there are a variety of views on the identity of these parties, and the nature of this compromise or conflict.[62] Summarizing these theories, a picture of what happened to the clerical groups in Judah as well as in Babylon after the exile emerges as follows:

(1) While most of the Zadokite priests were taken captive into Babylon after the destruction of Jerusalem, those who were poor and/or those not regarded as a threat to Babylon were left behind (2 Kgs 24.14; 25.11; Jer. 39.9; 52.15-16, 24-27). Among these were the non-Zadokite Levites (i.e., the Levites plus the non-Zadokite priests) who had been marginalized and served largely in the local sanctuaries. The collapse of the Jerusalem temple did not deter those people faithful to Yahweh from performing their religious activities at Jerusalem though it lay in ruins (cf. Jer. 41.5-6; Lamentations; Zech. 7.1-7).[63] The Bethel priests suggested to the other non-Zadokite priests that they all designate themselves with the glorified title *sons of Aaron*. It is

61. R. Abba, 'Priests and Levites', *IDB* vol. 3, pp. 876–89, esp. p. 884. For another notable criticism, see de Vaux, *Ancient Israel*, p. 395, who says 'there is not a single fact to prove that the sanctuary of Bethel took on a new lease of life after the reform of Josiah, or that it was active during the Exile; and the connection between the cult practised at Bethel and the episode of Aaron's golden calf can be interpreted in a number of ways'.

62. E.g., Judge, 'Aaron, Zadok and Abiathar', pp. 70–74 and Welch, *Post-Exilic Judaism*, p. 239, argue that the term resulted from a compromise between *the Zadokites* and *the Levitical circle* which took place in Judah. De Vaux, *Ancient Israel*, pp. 395–96, and Abba, 'Priests and Levites', p. 885, believe that it was in Babylon that the Aaronite group was formed as a compromise, between *priestly* families. The view that the designation reflects a conflict or a compromise within priestly families is shared by Norman K. Gottwald, *The Hebrew Bible: A Socio-Literary Introduction* (Philadelphia: Fortress Press, 1985), p. 461, and Bartlett, 'Zadok and His Successors at Jerusalem', p. 16. Cf. O'Brien, 'Priest and Levite in Malachi', pp. 36–40.

63. E. Janssen, *Juda in der Exilszeit* (FRLANT, 69; Göttingen: Vandenhoeck und Ruprecht, 1956); de Vaux, *Ancient Israel*, p. 387; P.D. Hanson, *The Dawn of Apocalyptic* (Philadelphia: Fortress Press, 1979), p. 91.

likely that the suggestion was accepted since they needed a designation for themselves in contradistinction to 'sons of Zadok'. Thus, the title 'sons of Aaron' came into use.

(2)   When the Zadokite priests returned to Jerusalem after the exile,[64] they came into unavoidable conflict with the priests who had stayed on in Judah and had identified themselves as the sons of Aaron because the Zadokite priests naturally desired to resume their hegemony over the priestly duty in Jerusalem. This struggle between the two priestly groups may be reflected in the account of the death of Nadab and Abihu, Aaron's sons, who offered unauthorized fire before Yahweh (Lev. 10). It is commonly agreed that this account was written by the priestly writer responsible for P to warn the priests, who were connected with the Bethel priesthood and who are here represented by Nadab and Abihu, not to grasp the full priestly office.[65] As can be seen from the story of Nadab and Abihu, the struggle concluded with the victory of the Zadokite camp.[66] After resuming control over the temple, the Zadokite priests did not jettison the noble title, but enjoyed being called the sons of Aaron.

(3)   A further conflict occurred between the (Zadokite) priests and the Levites. In post-exilic times, the Levites who had resided in Judah rejected the subordinate position which had been taken for granted in the pre-exilic period. Similarly, those Levites returning from Babylon, hoping that their position in Judah would be higher than in Babylon, also objected to the hierarchical clerical system. The account of the revolt of Korah (Num. 16), who may represent the disgruntled Levites, possibly reflects the atmosphere of conflict between the priests and the Levites. Some scholars have pointed out that the priestly writer loses his balance in treating traditions related to Korah. According to them, other Old Testament texts assess Korah favourably,[67] or describe Korah's story differently.[68] These texts imply that the account of Korah's revolt in Numbers 16 was reworked by the priestly writer to intentionally degrade the descendants of Korah, who might be representing the Levites opposing the Zadokite priests. Contrasted with the large numbers in other desert-wandering traditions, the small number of followers of Korah

64.   For the statement that the priests from Babylon mostly belonged to the Zadokites, see de Vaux, *Ancient Israel*, p. 388.

65.   Cf. M. Noth, *Das dritte Buch Mose. Levitikus* (ATD, 5; Göttingen: Vandenhoeck & Ruprecht, 1962), pp. 69–70; Walter Kornfeld, *Levitikus* (NEB; Würzburg: Echter Verlag, 1983), p. 41; Richard D. Nelson, *Raising up a Faithful Priest: Community and Priesthood in Biblical Theology* (Louisville, Westminster/John Knox Press, 1993), p. 5; Nurmela, *The Levites*, pp. 119–24.

66.   The fact that the Zadokites gained the victory can be corroborated in Ezra 10.18-22 and Neh. 11.10-14, which show that the entire priesthood in Jerusalem was taken by four Zadokite families returning from Babylon at the time of Ezra and Nehemiah.

67.   E.g., Pss. 42, 44–49, 84–85, 87–88, which are ascribed to the sons of Korah, and 2 Chron. 20.19, which says 'some Levites from the Kohathites and the Korahites stood up and praised Yahweh, the God of Israel, with very loud voice'.

68.   E.g., Deut. 11.6 and Ps. 106.17, which mention the incident recorded in Numbers 16, but have no reference to the rebellion of Korah.

(250; Num. 16.35) indicates that this account is alluding to a rebellion which transpired during the time of the priestly writer.[69] Accordingly, this account lucidly illustrates P's penchant for prescribing the position of the Levites as *clerus minor*, which is similar to that of Ezekiel.

On the basis of the above discussion, we may conclude that:

First, the subordination of the Levites to the priests shown in P occurred *circa* 570–458 BCE.

Secondly, during this period there were major conflicts between the Zadokite priests and the non-Zadokite priests, on the one hand, and between the Zadokite priests and the Levites, on the other. The priestly writer describes the attempts to challenge the Zadokite prerogative as unholy and unforgivable, and thus emphasizes the clear difference between them and the non-Zadokite Levites.

Lastly, in this respect the priestly writer is in line with Ezekiel, who regards the Levites as subordinates to the priests rather than as their partners and co-workers.

3.3. *Levites in Chronicles*

3.3.1 *Irreconcilable Features of the Priesthood in Chronicles*

It has widely been held that the Levites in Chronicles are not as downgraded as in Ezekiel and the priestly sources, and rather remarkable importance is ascribed to them.[70] In Chronicles the Levites are not only frequently referred to, but also favourably described. The word לוי occurs 100 times in the book, and thus on average 1.54 times per chapter.[71] Since the average occurrence per chapter in the Old Testament is 0.31,[72] it may be said that Chronicles is one of the books in which the word occurs very frequently. It is especially noteworthy that its frequent occurrence in Chronicles is sharply contrasted with its rare occurrence (only 3 times) in 1 Sam–2 Kings, which were among the Chronicler's major sources. For example, the account of bringing the ark to Jerusalem in 1 Chron. 15–16 mentions the Levites a number of times, and does not confine their duties merely to porters but depicts them even as ministers (16.4). On the other hand, its parallel in 2 Samuel 6.12-20 has *no* mention of the Levites.[73] In addition to this passage, there are numerous

---

69. Nurmela, *The Levites*, pp. 124–34.

70. E.g., A.C. Welch, *The Work of the Chronicler: Its Purpose and its Date* (London: Oxford University Press, 1939), p. 77; Fishbane, *Biblical Interpretation in Ancient Israel*, pp. 137–38, 154–59; P.D. Hanson, '1 Chronicles 15–16 and the Chronicler's Views on the Levites', in M. Fishbane *et al.* (ed.), *Sha'arei Talmon: Studies in the Bible, Qumran, and the Ancient Near East. Presented to S. Talmon* (Winona Lake: Eisenbrauns, 1992), pp. 74ff; Kellermann, 'לוי', pp. 515–16.

71. See Table 2.2 on page 46.

72. Namely, 292 (occurrences of לוי) divided by 929 (the number of chapters in the Old Testament) equals 0.314.

73. Many scholars make a specific note of this. See particularly Welch, 'The Chronicler and the Levites', in *The Work of the Chronicler*, pp. 55–80 and Cody, *A History of Old Testament Priesthood*, p. 183.

other texts in Chronicles which favour the Levites (e.g., 2 Chron. 20.19-23; 23; 29.5-36; 34.8-14; 36.14). For instance, 2 Chron. 29.34b states 'for the Levites were more upright in heart than the priests in sanctifying themselves', and it appears not to be by chance that the Levites are absent in the indictment for the fall of Judah to the Babylonians (2 Chron. 36.14, 'All the leading priests and the people likewise were exceedingly unfaithful...').[74]

However, these facts do not mean it can be assumed that Chronicles as a whole can be treated as a Levitically-centred book and that the Levites in the book are always favourably described and promoted. Interestingly, in Chronicles, the word כהן also occurs very frequently (108 times). In addition, several texts insist on the same proper priestly position as is found in Ezekiel and P.[75] For example, 1 Chron 23.26ff highlights the Levitical duties in subordination to the priestly ones, by describing the Levites as assistants of the priests (vv. 28-29).[76] Thus, these texts may reflect the priestly tradition which emphasizes the superiority of the priests over the Levites in status and function and, consequently, appear to contradict the verses which attribute astonishing importance to the Levites.

This inconsistency within the book raises the question of what we can say about the Levites in Chronicles? Can we assert that they are described favourably, unlike Ezekiel and P, or does the book simply follow the priestly-centred attitude toward the Levites? How can we unravel the puzzling double description of the Levites in Chronicles?

3.3.2 *Two Theories*
3.3.2.1 *One-hand Hypothesis*

The majority of scholars have sought to circumvent this difficulty by maintaining that Chronicles was composed of two main literary layers, each of which had its own independent origin. According to them, one of the layers may have originated in a priestly group, and the other in a Levitical group; since the book was edited by someone who opposed the bias of one of the layers, it was unavoidable that an ambivalent attitude would emerge. Some of these scholars claim that Chronicles was penned by a priestly writer and later added to by a Levitical reviser.[77] Others argue, mainly on the basis of 1 Chron. 23–27, that the Chronicler, who had a pro-Levitical tendency, was responsible for the primary layer and that a reviser, who belonged to the priestly line, was responsible for the secondary one.[78] Both of these views presuppose two different irreconcilable literary layers, while differing in their understanding of the order in which these layers were composed.

---

74. Cf. Hanson, 'I Chronicles 15–16', pp. 74–75; Japhet, *I & II Chronicles*, p. 1070.

75. E.g., 1 Chron. 6.33-34, 49; 16.39; 23.26-32; 2 Chron. 5.5 [cf. 1 Kgs 8.4]; 19.11; 35.3.

76. According to Williamson, *1 and 2 Chronicles*, p. 162, this expression is 'a way of suppressing, rather than exalting, their [Levitical] status'.

77. E.g., Johann W. Rothstein and Johannes Hänel, *Kommentar zum ersten Buch der Chronik* (KAT, 18/2; Leipzig: A. Deichert, 1927), p. xliv; Noth, *ÜS*, pp. 110–23; Rudolph, *Chronikbücher*, pp. 1–5; Rudolf Mosis, *Untersuchungen zur Theologie des chronistischen Geschichtswerkes* (Freiburg: Herder, 1973), pp. 44–45.

78. E.g., Welch, *Post-Exilic Judaism*, pp. 172–84 and 217–44; Williamson, *1 and 2 Chronicles*, pp. 28-31; De Vries, *I and II Chronicles*, pp. 191–96.

Recently, this widely held two-layer hypothesis has been challenged by Gary Knoppers.[79] He argues that, in Chronicles, there exist no especially pro-Levitical texts, nor can any later adaptation in its composition be detected. Rather, the Chronicler maintains a conciliatory posture toward the two parties, a crucial aspect of the goal of his writing. He was responsible for the book as a whole, thus allowing us to call Knopper's view the 'one-hand hypothesis'. All that we can find from the book, insists Knoppers, is a gesture of cooperation and complementarity, not of competition and hierarchy, and a basic kinship between the Levites and the Aaronites (1 Chron. 23.32).[80]

First, Knoppers strongly argues that the word ליד in 1 Chron. 23.28, which has commonly been thought to show the subordination of the Levites to the priests, should be reinterpreted. According to him, if the Chronicler had intended to communicate subordination, he would have written על־יד, as he does on many other occasions (e.g., 1 Chron. 25.2, 3, 6; 26.28; 29.8; 2 Chron. 12.10; 17.5, 8, 16; 21.16; 26.11, 13; 31.15; 34.10, 17).[81] The word ליד in the Hebrew Bible consistently denotes *proximity* (1 Sam. 19.3; Ps. 140.6; Prov. 8.3; Neh. 11.24; 1 Chron. 18.17) and hence the right interpretation for it should be 'at the side of' or 'alongside' not 'subordinate'. In consequence, 1 Chron. 23.28-32, which includes the verse under consideration, no longer stands as a pro-priestly text. This conclusion leads people to doubt the existence of Chronicles' pro-priestly texts, which support the two-layer hypothesis.

Secondly, Knoppers further asserts that there are a number of texts in Chronicles which present a collateral understanding of the relationship between the priests and the Levites (1 Chron. 9.10-34; 28.12-13, 21; 2 Chron. 5.4-14; 7.4-6; 11.13-17; 13.9-12; 23.1-11; 29.3-30; 31.2-21; 34.8-13; 35.1-19).[82] Thus, in his opinion, it may be an oversimplification to claim that the Chronicler's work reflects either Zadokite dominance or Levitical ascendancy during the post-exilic period. Instead, the conciliatory posture of the Chronicler is plainly found in every corner of the book.[83]

Lastly, Knoppers recognizes that there is no firm evidence to insist that the Chronicler holds to an absolute equality between the priests and the Levites, but emphasizes that the author considerably relaxes the hierarchical distinction which is frequently found in Ezekiel and the priestly sources.[84] He believes that this tendency is due to the Chronicler's purpose of conciliation.

Knoppers's arguments do not convince, however, for several reasons:

---

79. Knoppers, 'Hierodules, Priests, or Janitors?', pp. 49–72.
80. Knoppers, 'Hierodules, Priests, or Janitors?', p. 70.
81. Knoppers, 'Hierodules, Priests, or Janitors?', p. 59.
82. Knoppers, 'Hierodules, Priests, or Janitors?', pp. 71–72. This position may be supported by Hanson, 'I Chronicles 15–16', p. 71, who has argued that the references to the priests and their relation to the Levites in Chronicles demonstrate the harmonious social realities of its time (1 Chron. 13.2; 23.2; 28.12; 2 Chron. 5.5; 7.6; 8.14-15; 17.7-9; 19.8-11; 29.4; 30.15-16, 21, 25, 27; 31.4, 9; 34.30; 35.1-9).
83. Knoppers, 'Hierodules, Priests, or Janitors?', p. 71.
84. Knoppers, 'Hierodules, Priests, or Janitors?', pp. 70–71.

First, Knoppers argues that ליד denotes *proximity* and, in order to communicate subordination, על־יד is needed.[85] It is true that ליד signifies proximity in some of the verses he cites (1 Sam. 19.3; Ps. 140.6; Prov. 8.3) but, in the others (Exod. 21.13; Neh. 11.24; 1 Chron. 18.17), the word is used with diverse meanings: for example, in Exodus 21.13, it has the concept of power ('God delivered *into his hand*'); in Neh. 11.24, it is most appropriately rendered as subordination ('Pethahiah… was the king's *deputy* in all matters concerning the people'); and in 1 Chron. 18.17, it denotes subordination ('David's sons were the chief officials *in the service of* the king'). Similarly, while על־יד usually contains a sense of subordination, it does not always do so: for example, the word in 2 Chron. 21.16 obviously means proximity rather than subordination ('the Arabs who are *near* the Cushites').[86] As noted, ליד and על־יד have various meanings depending on the context. Consequently, there does exist a strong possibility that ליד in 1 Chron. 23.28 may indicate subordination.

Secondly, some of the texts presented by Knoppers as collateral evidence fail to show a harmonious portrait of the two clerical orders. For instance, he seems to read הכהנים הלוים in 2 Chron. 5.5 as 'the priests *and* the Levites' by emending it to הכהנים והלוים, but this emendation is little favoured.[87] This verse rather demonstrates that the priestly prerogative of transferring the ark into the *inner* sanctuary (קדש הקדשים) is *not* to be shared *at all* by the Levites. 2 Chron. 23.6 also reveals a distinction between priests and Levites ('except the priests and the *attendant* Levites'); and 2 Chron. 8.14 may possibly be understood likewise ('the Levites for their duties to praise and *attend* the priests').[88]

Finally, the fact that Chronicles acknowledges the superior status of the priests without emphasizing it does not necessarily mean that Chronicles' descriptions were reconciliation-oriented; there are, as pointed out earlier, numerous texts biased toward Levites or priests.

In sum, it is hard to accept the one-hand hypothesis, mainly represented by Knoppers, who attacks the view that the Chronicler was a follower of either the Deuteronomic (= pro-Levitical) or the priestly (= pro-priestly) traditions, and who maintains that the appointment of the Levites is 'to be at the side of [not assist] the sons of Aaron' (1 Chron. 23.28).[89] If the Chronicler had really intended this, he could have included more conciliatory descriptions and left out various priestly or Levitically inclined texts.

3.3.2.2 *Two-layer Hypothesis*
The weakness of the one-hand theory leads us to find the two-layer theory more convincing. This judgment can be bolstered by the following arguments which support the idea that Chronicles is composed of at least two literary layers and that

---

85. He seems to quote the verses cited for his argument from BDB (cf. BDB, p. 391).

86. Cf. Japhet, *I & II Chronicles*, p. 814.

87. The majority of scholars find this emendation unsatisfactory: e.g., von Rad, *Das Geschichtsbild des chronistischen Werkes*, pp. 87–88; Ackroyd, *I & II Chronicles, Ezra, Nehemiah*, p. 110; Williamson, *1 and 2 Chronicles*, p. 214.

88. R.B. Dillard, *2 Chronicles* (WBC, 15; Waco, TX: Word Books, 1986), p. 60.

89. Cf. Knoppers, 'Hierodules, Priests, or Janitors?', pp. 68–72.

they are irreconcilable to each other in their fundamental attitudes toward the clerical parties.

First, in his literary analysis of 1 Chron. 5–6, Antti Laato demonstrates that these chapters preserve traces of an old tradition, and that this tradition was subsequently modified and then used by the Chronicler to legitimate the organization of the cultic personnel of his own time.[90] His argument is persuasive in the light of: (1) the differences in Korah's genealogy between 6.7-13 and 6.19-23; (2) the confusion of the name Elkanah in 6.10-11, which indicates a later addition that was prompted by a desire to forge genealogical connections between Samuel and the Levitical families; and (3) the insertion of the line from Joel (or Samuel) to Zoph (or Elkanah) (6.18-20) into the cultic genealogy of the time of David (6.16-18), to claim that Samuel in fact belonged to the tribe of Levi.[91]

Secondly, it is normally agreed that 1 Chron. 15–16 also consists of two compositional layers for the following reason: 15.4-10 and 15.16-24 represent secondary elaborations of 15.11 and of 16.4-6, 37-42 respectively. If 15.4-10 is not secondary, verse 11, a parallel verse, is superfluous and 15.16-24 breaks the narrative connection between verse 15 and verse 25.[92]

Lastly, it is evident that there are two main strands of material in 1 Chron. 23–27: on the one hand, as articulated in 23.3-6a, these five chapters were originally written to list the four categories of the Levites and they are subsequently listed in 23.6b-13a, 15-24; 25.1-6; 26.1-3, 9-11, 19, 20-32. On the other hand, the remaining texts of those chapters are intrusive or uneven, showing that they were later added for particular reasons.[93]

If Chronicles contains two layers, another question may be raised: which one came first?

Hanson argues, on the basis of an analysis of 1 Chron. 15–16, that the original sources show a pro-priestly inclination and were composed by the original Chronicler with a propagandistic intent during the period of the rebuilding of the second temple led by the Zadokites. The secondary sources were added later out of a huge effort to bring reconciliation into a community which had threatened to destroy itself through bitter infighting. That is to say, the Chronicler added new history,

---

90.   Antti Laato, 'The Levitical Genealogies in 1 Chronicles 5–6 and the Formation of Levitical Ideology in Post-exilic Judah', *JSOT* 62 (1994), pp. 77–99.

91.   Cf. Laato, 'The Levitical Genealogies', pp. 80–82.

92.   Williamson, *1 and 2 Chronicles*, p. 121. See also Hanson, '1 Chronicles 15–16', pp. 70–73, who pursues the ulterior motive behind such elaborations. According to Hanson, the writer wished to secure the Levitical pedigree of the priestly families mentioned in 15.11 by specifically identifying their patronymics with the earliest descendants of Levi. This pro-Levitical tendency is detected also in 15.16-24, in which four more names of Levites, appointed by David as musicians and gatekeepers, are added on the basis of 16.5. A patronymic element is added as well to each of the three groups' names, thereby establishing each within a line of descent leading to the three sons of Levi (Heman to Kohath, Asaph to Gershom, and Ethan to Merari). In contrast, in 16.4-6, 37-42, the original layer of 15.16-24, priests and Levites are mentioned alongside each other and conciliatorily allotted to their roles after the ark had been installed.

93.   For a more detailed discussion, see Williamson, 'The Origins of the Twenty-four Priestly Courses', pp. 251–68.

displaying the important role of the Levitical families, to the original material.[94] On the other hand, Williamson argues that the original material of Chronicles was authored by the Chronicler, who had a pro-Levitical tendency, and the secondary material was added by a pro-priestly reviser under the impact of the institution of the system of twenty-four courses, which consistently appears only in the secondary material.[95]

It does not matter which group was responsible for the first or second layer. What is significant at this stage is that one layer was penned by a Levitical group and the other by a priestly group. This assertion dovetails with the irreconcilable features of the priesthood in Chronicles noted in the beginning of this section; namely, that those texts which show a strong interest in the Levites and take a harmonious posture between the clerical parties were written by an author who belonged to the Levitical group, whereas the others, clinging to a clerical hierarchy, were probably composed by someone belonging to the priestly line.

3.3.3 *Levites in Chronicles*

On this basis, we can briefly summarize the place of the Levites in Chronicles: Chronicles presents two different descriptions of the Levites – pro-Levitical and pro-priestly. It is impossible to harmonize these descriptions adequately. This dilemma, however, can be overcome by a literary analysis of the book, which points to two different literary layers, each of which was penned by a different religious group.

The literary layer composed by the Levitical group (= Chron.-L) describes the Levites favourably and promotes them to the status of the priests. The harmonious description of the religious orders also belongs to this layer since it is almost impossible to suppose that a priestly author was responsible for the relaxation of clerical differences. The other literary layer composed by the priestly group (= Chron.-P) describes the Levites as *clerus minor*, just as in other priestly works (Ezekiel and P). Chronicles preserves these two opposing descriptions of the Levites.

3.4 *Conclusion*

So far, we have examined the portrait of the Levites in Ezekiel, P, and Chronicles. The examination may be summarized as follows:

First, these three texts provide a picture of the Levites from the period immediately before the exile to approximately the fourth century BCE.[96] More specifically,

---

94.   Hanson, 'I Chronicles 15–16', p. 75.

95.   Williamson, 'The Origins of the Twenty-four Priestly Courses', pp. 265–68. Cf. Laato, 'The Levitical Genealogies', pp. 77–99, who does not clearly mention who was responsible for each layer, even though he seems to maintain that the second layer originated in the pro-Levitical group and the third from the pro-priestly group.

96.   For this date of Chronicles, see Williamson, *Israel*, pp. 83–86; *1 and 2 Chronicles*, pp. 15–16; Japhet, *I & II Chronicles*, pp. 23–28. We have not discussed the dates of each literary layer, which is another big issue to study but, for the present purpose, this dating may be acceptable.

Ezekiel reveals the status of the Levites from the late monarchic period to 571 BCE; P, *circa* 570–458; and Chronicles, the post-exilic period. Since E–N was composed during this period, the study of the Levites in these other books complements our study of the Levites in E–N.

Secondly, the authorship of Ezekiel and P is easily ascribed to priests, while Chronicles preserves two different literary layers, one ascribed to priests and the other ascribed to Levites, the opposing religious party.

Finally, the priestly-penned texts, among which Ezekiel, P, and Chron.-P are to be included, emphasize the distinction between the priests and the Levites in their status and function, describing the Levites as *clerus minor*. In contrast, the Levitically-penned text, i.e., part of Chronicles (= Chron.-L), relaxes the clerical disparity, presents the Levites as co-workers with the priests, and generally elevates the status of the Levites.

Chapter 4

LEVITES IN EZRA–NEHEMIAH

In the preceding chapter, we saw that a pro-priestly author tends to highlight sub-ordination of the Levites to the priests by describing the former as *clerus minor*. A pro-Levitical author, by contrast, is inclined to favour them by replacing the accounts which emphasize disparity between the clerical groups, with others that confer important roles on the Levites in certain matters (e.g., 1 Chron. 15) or depict them as co-workers of the priests (e.g., 2 Chron. 17.8; 19.8).

The initial purpose of this chapter is to examine how the Levites are described in E–N in the light of those observations. From that examination, we may hope to determine the work's own viewpoint, and thereby establish whether or not it does indeed appear to be pro-Levitical. We shall go on then to look at the use in the work of certain expressions which appear to have connections with the Levites.

4.1 *Literary Analysis of the Texts*

4.1.1 *'Priestly' Texts in Ezra–Nehemiah*
Are there any texts of priestly origin in E–N? In the light of our conclusions in the last chapter, we may say that priestly-penned texts commonly emphasize the inferior status of the Levites to the priests and contain descriptions of their feuding relationship.

As we saw, the book has sixty-five occurrences of the word לוי.[1] Interestingly, a perusal of these texts mentioning the Levites allows us to point to, at most, four cases (Ezra 9.1; 10.15, 23; Neh. 12.47) where there are features which might be indicative of pro-priestly authorship, while the other texts have little to do with the subordination of the Levites or partiality to the priests. Of these four texts, Ezra 9.1 and 10.23 appear to regard the Levites somewhat negatively because they took foreign wives. It should be observed, however, that the very same criticism is also directed at the priests in each context (Ezra 9.1; 10.18-22). In these cases, therefore, no real bias toward the priests is expressed. In the case of Neh. 12.47, a superficial reading shows a hierarchical relationship between the clergy, since it says that the Levites should set some of their portions apart for the sons of Aaron. However, this does not necessarily mean Levitical subordination to the priests. If it did, we would also have to say that the singers and gatekeepers were inferior to the Levites since they set apart portions for the Levites (12.47a). However, nowhere

---

1. For all of the occurrences of לוי in E–N, see note 84 in Chapter 2.

else is this idea corroborated in E–N. Rather, this practice should be understood as an ancient tradition, which is attested in Numbers 18.

The last text is Ezra 10.15 (RSV, 'Only Jonathan the son of Asahel and Jahzeiah the son of Tikvah opposed this, and Meshullam and Shabbethai the Levite supported them'). Its overall meaning is obscure, but it has normally been viewed in the following three ways:

(1) Carl Keil argues that the verse lists those who were in opposition to Ezra. His argument is rooted in his interpretation that אך, at the beginning of the verse, is a *linking* word which points to what ensued after the proposal made in the preceding verses (Ezra 10.12-14), that the separation from foreign wives should be done more slowly. He also takes the meaning of עמד על as 'stood up for', i.e., 'supported' rather than 'opposed' and, thus, regards the four people in the verse as taking sides with the community opposing Ezra's plan.[2] This would make Shabbethai the Levite one of the opponents of Ezra.[3]

(2) The second view is represented by Charles Fensham. Convinced by Bruno Pelaia's view that עמד על should mean 'opposed to',[4] he holds that its object זאת ('this') must refer to the proposal of the representatives of the congregation and, thus, Jonathan and Jahzeiah are in support of Ezra. Meshullam and Shabbethai are not in support, however, since the text says עזרם and the plural suffix to עזר is best taken to indicate the proposals of the congregation and the 'ו' before Meshullam can be regarded as an adversative. Therefore, according to Fensham also, Shabbethai was an opponent of Ezra's reform.[5]

These two views both regard Shabbethai and Meshullam as opponents of Ezra. If so, it is significant that Shabbethai, one of the opponents, is here designated as a *Levite*, which serves as a direct contrast to the designation of Ezra as a *priest* (Ezra 10.10), a title never given to him in the preceding passages (Ezra 10.1, 2, 5, 6). On this basis, it can be maintained that the designation of Shabbethai as a Levite is deliberately given to show that the Levites at that time were among the major opponents of the *priestly-centred* reform and this verse, therefore, adumbrates a tension between the priests and the Levites.

(3) However, those two views have certain weaknesses in the light of a third view, associated especially with Batten and Williamson.

Batten first points out that the particle אך in Ezra 10.15 is *restrictive* rather than continuative and, therefore, shows a contrast with the preceding passage.[6] He then notes that the preposition for עמד in verse 14 is different from that in verse 15, which indicates that the author intended a different

2.   Keil, *Ezra, Nehemiah, and Esther*, p. 131. This position has also been presented by Frank Michaeli in *Les livres des Chroniques, d'Esdras et de Nehemie* (Commentaire de l'AT 16; Neuchâtel: Delachaux & Niestle, 1967).

3.   Richard J. Coggins, *Ezra and Nehemiah* , p. 64.

4.   Bruno M. Pelaia, *Esdra e Neemia* (La Sacra Bibbia; Turin, Roma: Marieti, 1960), p. 119.

5.   Fensham, *Ezra and Nehemiah*, p. 141.

6.   Batten, *Ezra and Nehemiah*, p. 346.

meaning for each. Since עמד ל in verse 14 means 'act for', עמד על in verse 15 must express opposition to the proposal and support for Ezra.[7]

Williamson argues that this same conclusion also applies to the second half of verse 15, since the third-person *masculine* plural suffix on עזרם cannot denote the proposal, which is referred to here as זאת (a *feminine* singular suffix), but rather indicates its antecedent as Jonathan and Jahzeiah. Williamson finds support for his view in the fact that Shabbethai and Meshullam were in a positive position to support Ezra's plan rigorously since they were presumably exempted from the accusation of foreign marriage (cf. Ezra 8.16; 10.23). He notes also that it is possible to link them with the Levites who were supporters of Ezra in Neh. 8.4 and 7, though the name of Meshullam was very common.[8] Consequently, this verse lists those who oppose the proposal and support Ezra's reform. If so, it is notable that Shabbethai the Levite is described as a *supporter* of Ezra, which means that he is depicted as a co-worker of Ezra, the priest.

In conclusion, we may say that there is no description in E–N of the Levites as *clerus minor* nor any hint of their feuding relationship with the priests. At no point, therefore, does E–N share the attitude toward Levites characteristic of pro-priestly literature in this period.

4.1.2 *'Levitical' Texts in Ezra–Nehemiah*

If there are no texts which show a 'priestly' attitude toward the Levites, are there any which demonstrate a specially pro-Levitical perspective? We now turn our attention to the portrait of the Levites in the book as a whole.

The word לוי occurs 65 times in E–N. The references can be categorized according to the term's occurrence in relation to terms describing the priests: (1) references where לוי occurs in apposition to כהן; (2) references where לוי occurs with כהן contextually, but not alongside; and (3) references where לוי occurs independently of כהן.

Categories	References in E–N
Occurring *in Apposition* (25 occurrences)	Ezra 1.5; 2.70; 3.8, 12; 6.16, 20; 7.7, 13, 24; 8.29, 30; 9.1; 10.5; Neh. 7.72; 8.13; 10.1, 29, 35; 11.3, 20; 12.1, 30, 44 (×2); 13.30
Occurring *Contextually Together* (31 occurrences)	Ezra 2.40; 3.8, 9, 10; 6.18; 8.33; 10.23; Neh. 3.17; 7.43; 8.7, 9, 11; 10.10, 38 (×2), 39(×3); 11.15, 16, 18, 22, 36; 12.8, 22, 24, 47 (×2); 13.5, 13, 29
Occurring *without Priests* (9 occurrences)	Ezra 8.20; 10.15; Neh. 7.1; 9.4, 5; 12.27; 13.10 (×2), 22

Table 4.1

7.   According to Batten, *Ezra and Nehemiah*, p. 346, in its late usage, עמד על normally means 'stood against' (e.g., Lev. 19.16; 1 Chron. 21.1; 2 Chron. 20.23; Dan. 8.25; 11.14).

8.   Williamson, *Ezra, Nehemiah*, pp. 156–57.

As shown, almost all the references to Levites (56 out of 65 occurrences) appear in apposition to, or contextually with, the priests. Noting that the book has a tendency to place them closely, let us now undertake a thorough examination of these texts.

4.1.2.1 *Priests and Levites in Apposition*

One of E–N's literary features in its use of לוי is that the word very frequently occurs alongside כהן in the form of הכהנים והלוים ('the priests and the Levites'),[9] or in very similar forms.[10] This side-by-side expression of the cultic officials has been understood in several ways,[11] but is normally accepted as demonstrating Levitical *equality*, not inferiority, *vis-à-vis* the priests.[12] This position can be verified by the following observations:

(1) It is noteworthy that this phrase usually appears when all of Israel is addressed.[13] E–N occasionally uses the simple expression עם ישראל ('the people of Israel') to refer to all Israel (e.g., Ezra 2.2; 5.12), but it frequently also adds other clans of people. In these cases, we might expect to see two groups of people, i.e., *priests* (representing clerical groups) and *laity*, because this is often found in other passages of the Old Testament (e.g., Exod. 19.24; Lev. 16.33; Jer. 28.1; 31.14; Zech. 7.5). E–N does use this combination in Ezra 7.16; 8.15 and Neh. 9.32. But in these texts, it is not the author who is speaking of all Israel. In the case of the Ezra 7.16 text, this is located in the middle of the Artaxerxes' edict, which is thought to have remained intact in the present book,[14] and thus shows the way *Persians* addressed all of Israel, rather than the author's style. Ezra 8.15 is also ruled out for the same reason because it is clearly part of Ezra's own material, rather than an authorial portion. Neh. 9.32 lists sinners in the context of repenting for their disobedience against God (Neh. 9.34), and it is rather remarkable that the Levites are not mentioned in the list and seem to be intentionally exempted from the list of the sinners. Hence, these three verses (Ezra 7.16; 8.15; Neh. 9.32), which speak of priests and the people, not Levites, should not be taken as evidence to show the author's way of addressing all of Israel.

On the other hand, all of Israel is never expressed in the form of *people and Levites*, but in all places where priests are one of the major groups representing the

---

9. Ezra 1.5; 2.70; 3.8, 12; 6.16, 20; 7.7, 13, 24; 8.29, 30; 9.1; Neh. 7.72; 8.13; 11.3; 12.1, 30, 44 (×2); 13.30.

10. For example, in an asyndeton, הכהנים הלוים, as in Ezra 10.5; Neh. 10.29, 35; 11.20, or in its reverted form לוינו כהנינו in Neh. 10.1. For a detailed discussion about these forms, see section 4.2.3.

11. For example, as a term which is different from the expression characteristic of Deuteronomy הכהנים הלוים ('the Levitical priests') and distinguishes between the priests and the Levites. Thus, Haran, *Temples and Temple-Service*, p. 63, sees it as occurring within the framework of the *priestly* doctrine. Nurmela, *The Levites*, p. 166, regards it as a technical term, which demonstrates that the Levites are not the priests. In contrast, Gunneweg, *Leviten und Priester*, pp. 207–208, stresses its similarity to the Deuteronomistic expression הכהנים הלוים.

12. E.g., Welch, *The Work of the Chronicler*, p. 77; Cody, *A History of Old Testament Priesthood*, pp. 184–85.

13. Cf. Ezra 1.5; 2.70; 3.8, 12; 6.16; 7.7, 13, 24; 9.1; 10.5; Neh. 7.72; 8.13; 10.1, 29, 35; 11.3, 20.

14. Cf. U. Kellermann, 'Erwägungen zum Esragesetz', *ZAW* 80 (1968), pp. 373–85.

people, the Levites are also present. Williamson explains this practice as demonstrating 'the regular sociological division of the people in the Persian period'.[15] He fails, though, to trace the reason why the three regular components for the whole of Israel (i.e., priests, Levites, and the laity) are not found in other works of the same period, such as Haggai, Zechariah, and Malachi. It is, however, of utmost significance to note that this expression is only used in E–N and in the portions of Chronicles for which the Levites are widely regarded as having been responsible (e.g., 2 Chron. 34.30; 35.8). Therefore, it is not a term which was prevalent in a special period but it is a technical term which reflects the author's own penchant for recognizing the social entity of the Levites, instead of ignoring it, and further treating the Levites as partners of the priests.

(2) The remaining texts using the phrase הכהנים והלוים (Ezra 6.20; 8.29, 30; Neh. 12.1, 30, 44 [×2]; 13.30) also contain no indication of Levitical subordination to the priests but, rather, show an effort to promote Levitical parity with the priests. (a) We will begin by examining Ezra 6.20. This text is problematic because, if we translate the Masoretic text as it stands, another branch of the priests, which is never attested elsewhere in the book, appears in the second half of the verse.[16] Scholars have, therefore, on the basis of 1 Esdr. 7.11, omitted והכהנים ('the priests and') and taken לוים ('the Levites') as the subject of the whole verse[17] or got around the difficulty by inserting 'the Levites' as the subject of וישחטו, thus translating it '…the Levites slaughtered…' (NIV).

This widely held view was challenged by Williamson, who objects to the proposal of the NIV and, by separating הכהנים from הלוים, regards the priests alone as the only subject of הטהרו ('they purified'). Accordingly, he offers this translation: 'for the priests had purified themselves, and the Levites were all pure to a man, and they slaughtered the Passover for all the exiles, and for their brothers the priests, and for themselves'. He adds that this translation does not produce any grammatical problems.[18]

His argument is far from compelling, however. First, by not taking הכהנים והלוים ('the priests and the Levites') as one unit, he translates כאחד as 'to a man', when it is elsewhere, without exception, best rendered as 'together' in E–N (Ezra 2.64 [Neh. 7.66]; 3.9). Secondly, grammatically speaking, his translation, especially the translation which separates הכהנים from הלוים, is possible, but the appropriateness of his translation in this context is a different matter. If grammar were the only norm for meaning, one could translate, for example, the first half of Ezra 1.5 as 'then rose up the heads of the families of Judah and Benjamin and the priests, and the Levites [rather than, of Judah and Benjamin, and the priests and the Levites],

---

15. Williamson, *Ezra, Nehemiah*, p. 15.

16. Namely, 'For *the priests* and the Levites had purified themselves together; all of them were clean. So they killed the passover lamb for all the returned exiles, for *their fellow priests*, and for themselves' (RSV).

17. Cf. Rudolph, *Esra und Nehemia*, p. 64; Gunneweg, *Esra*, p. 115; Blenkinsopp, *Ezra–Nehemiah*, p. 131.

18. Williamson, *Ezra, Nehemiah*, pp. 69, 72.

every one whose spirit God had stirred…',[19] which, though grammatically correct, is adopted by no one.[20]

Because of this, the commonly accepted view that the original text lacked the words והכהנים ('the priests and'), seems more acceptable; but supporters have not properly expounded why this later addition was made.[21] This difficulty, however, may be diminished if we assume that the original text was biased toward the Levites as seen in their taking the initiative for celebrating the Passover. This partiality for the Levites was presumably judged as unsuitable by the redactor and he, valuing literary harmony and cooperation between the clerical groups more than syntactical consistency, might have added the two words (והכהנים).

This is not the place to address the whole issue of redactional intent, but suffice it to say that this reference to the Levites does not reveal their subordination to the priests but, in contrast, proves that this text was originally pro-Levitical and was later altered to be less so by adding 'the priests'.

(b) Ezra 8.29, 30 can also be cited as describing the Levites favourably rather than as inferior to the priests. The clerical groups mentioned in verse 29 are different from those in verse 30; the latter speaks of those who are nominated to carry the freewill offering for the temple from Babylon to Jerusalem, and the former of those who were supposed to receive it in Jerusalem. At any rate, what is significant here is the fact that the Levites are included, together with the priests, in these crucial missions: i.e., the Levites, together with the other clerical group, faithfully fulfil the mission given in Ezra 8.29 (see vv. 33-34), and *both* they and the priests play an important role in receiving the goods in Ezra 8.30.

Ezra 8.30, in particular, shows the author's interest in the Levites and their cooperative relationship with the priests. The verse is out of context since it refers to the Levites while the initial verse of this text (v. 24) lacks any reference to the Levites. This points to the possibility that לוי in verse 30 was added on account of that interest.

It might be objected, of course, that the two religious groups in verse 30 are virtually identical with those listed in verse 24. Following 1 Esdras and emending לשרביה חשביה to ושרביה וחשביה, some scholars argue, indeed, that Sherebiah and Hashabiah should not be regarded as priests, and thus that Ezra 8.24 has twelve priests and twelve Levites. Their argument is supported by the fact that those two individuals are called Levites in verses 18-19,[22] and so the text mentions 'twelve priests for oversight and an equal number of Levites for carrying'.[23]

---

19. 'ויקומו ראשי האבות ליהודה ובנימן והכהנים והלוים לכל העיר האלהים את־רוחו'

20. Although it seems trivial, it is also of note that if the Masoretes had intended to separate the sentences as Williamson does, the Athnah (+) would have been placed between הכהנים and והלוים.

21. Most supporters note the awkwardness of the text in the second half of the verse and merely presume a later addition by redactors or copyists, without giving any explanation for this addition. See the references in note 17 above.

22. Cf. Batten, *Ezra and Nehemiah*, p. 323; Rudolph, *Esra und Nehemia*, pp. 82–83; Williamson, *Ezra, Nehemiah*, p. 114.

23. Brockington, *Ezra, Nehemiah and Esther*, p. 87. Cf. Myers, *Ezra–Nehemiah*, p. 71; Fensham, *Ezra and Nehemiah*, p. 118.

That interpretation of the text does not affect our position that verse 30 shows an equal treatment of the clerical orders, but it is, anyway, hard to accept since it is based principally on an unsupported emendation of Ezra 8.24, and while Sherebiah and Hashabiah are most likely to be the names of Levites (e.g., Neh. 9.4-5; 10.11-12; 11.15), they not always so (Neh. 12.21). Even if we read the text with no emendation, the notion that the Levites are favourably described in 8.30 is not shaken, but rather reinforced. When 8.24 is read as it stands, it would appear to mean 'then I set apart twelve of the leading priests, *namely* Sherebiah, Hashabiah, and ten of their kinsmen with them'.[24] That is, the ל before Sherebiah here is an indicator of apposition, the use of which is well attested in other texts (e.g., Lev. 5.3; 1 Chron. 13.1; Ezek. 44.9) as well as in E–N (e.g., Ezra 1.5; 2.6, 16, 36, 40; 8.24; Neh. 8.9). Verse 24, indeed, has no mention of the Levites.[25] Why, then, does ללוי appear unexpectedly in the subsequent verse 30? If our interpretation is correct, it is possible that ללוי in verse 30 was added by the author, who intended to show the cooperation between the cultic orders in this crucial mission.

It is highly likely, therefore, that 8.30 should also be taken as demonstrating the favourable status of the Levites, rather than any subordination of the Levites to the priests: even if this proposed identification of an addition is not accepted, the alternative hardly suggests strong subordination.

(c) The remaining references to the phrase הכהנים והלוים (Neh. 12.1, 30, 44 [×2]; 13.30) also support our position. The Levites are treated as being on a par with the priests in the list of those returning with Zerubbabel in Neh. 12.1[26] and in the account of the preparation for the wall-dedication ceremony in 12.30, where the purification of the people, the gate and the wall was performed by the Levites as well as the priests. This latter text is significant in that, originally, the priests alone were privileged to do the work (Lev. 16; Num. 19) and even to cleanse the Levites (Num. 8.6). Again, in Neh. 12.44, the priests and the Levites are both described as objects of Judah's delight and recipients of gifts. Lastly, the Levites are equally given tasks with the priests in the service of the cult (13.30).

In summary, where Levites appear in apposition to the priests in E–N, they are described as fellow-workers without any real hint of a hierarchical difference.[27]

4.1.2.2 *Priests and Levites Contextually Together*
Although ללוי does not occur directly in apposition with priests elsewhere, the two are found in the same context together in numerous other texts.[28] Of these, two texts (Ezra 10.23; Neh. 12.47), on the face of it, seem to point to subordination of

---

24. This is also the way most of the modern versions of the Bible translate (e.g., ASV, RSV, NKJV, NRSV).

25. For a detailed description of ל as an apposition, see P. Joüon, *Grammaire*, §125l; GKC, §117n.

26. See n. 31 below.

27. For a discussion about five texts where Levites occur in the form of an asyndeton, i.e., הכהנים הלוים (Ezra 10.5; Neh. 10.1, 29, 35; 11.20), see section 4.2.3.

28. Viz., Ezra 2.40; 3.8, 9, 10; 6.18; 8.33; 10.23; Neh. 3.17; 7.43; 8.7, 9, 11; 10.10, 38(×2), 39(×3); 11.15, 16, 18, 22, 36; 12.8, 22, 24, 47(×2); 13.5, 13, 29.

Levites but, as discussed earlier,[29] they do not show a negative attitude specifically toward the Levites. All of the remaining references also demonstrate that the Levites are favoured and are described as working together with the priests.

First, many of the references to the Levites appear in lists of social groups (Ezra 2.40; Neh. 3.17; 7.43; 10.10; 11.15, 16, 18, 22, 36; 12.8, 22, 24). This is significant since, despite their small number *vis-à-vis* other cultic personnel,[30] the Levites are recognized as one of the social components without showing any disparity with the priests, whereas some of the lists often miss out other personnel (e.g., the signatories to the pledge in Neh. 10.1-28).[31]

Secondly, the Levites also appear to have been treated favourably by the stipulation of the tithe (Neh. 10.38, 39; 13.5). In this case, it is obvious that these texts reflect Numbers 18.26-32, which prescribes the Levites' inheritance and their tithe obligations to the priests, differing a little in that they give the Levites privilege to *levy*[32] the tithe rather than depending on the voluntary contribution of the people, and relax the tithe obligation to the priests (Neh. 10.39-40; cf. Num 18.28).

Finally, the Levites are described as cooperating with priests in all crucial work.[33] For instance, in Ezra's account of the rebuilding of the second temple (Ezra 3.8ff), the author focuses on the equal sharing of roles between the priests and the Levites, whereas 1 Kings 6, concerning the building of the first temple, focuses

---

29. Cf. section 4.1.1.

30. E.g., the Levites who returned with Zerubbabel, only numbered 74 – a striking contrast to 4289 for the priests, 128 for the singers, 139 for the gatekeepers, and 392 for the Nethinim and the children of Solomon's servants (Ezra 2). Ezra strove to gather Levites, but was only able to muster 38 (Ezra 8.15-18).

31. The major lists in E–N use 292 verses and constitute 42.6% of E–N (685 verses). Apart from the list of returned vessels (Ezra 1.9-11a), they are primarily made up of personal names. People in the lists may be categorized into four classes: (a) priests (b) Levites (c) other temple personnel (singers, gatekeepers, temple servants, sons of Solomon's servants), and (d) laity (listed with heads of families or the men of the people of Israel). The scope of the groups that each list contains is as follows:

- List of returned exiles (Ezra 2.1-67) → (a)(b)(c)(d)
- List of Ezra's companions (Ezra 8.1-14) → (a)(d)
- List of men who separated from foreign wives (Ezra 10.18-44) → (a)(b)(c)(d)
- List of builders of the wall (Neh. 3.1-32) → (a)(b)(c)(d)
- Repeated list of returned exiles (Neh. 7.5-71) → (a)(b)(c)(d)
- List of signatories to the pledge (Neh. 10.2-28) → (a)(b)(d)
- List of settlers and settlements (Neh. 11.4-19, 21-24, 26-35) → (a)(b)(c)(d)
- List of cultic personnel (Neh. 12.1b-26) → (a)(b)

It is again quite notable that except for the list of Ezra's companions (Ezra 8.1-14), the Levites are in every list. It is of little significance that the list of Ezra's companions omits the Levites, since its primary focus is on the heads of the families who went up with Ezra (8.1). Priests, too, are mentioned only very briefly, in a much shorter form than in other lists.

32. For the translation of עשׂר as 'to collect or levy', see Keil, *Ezra, Nehemiah, and Esther*, pp. 255–56, and other modern commentaries.

33. Namely, the rebuilding of the temple (Ezra 3.8, 9, 10), its dedication ceremony (Ezra 6.18), the work of receiving and weighing the offerings (Ezra 8.33), the reading of the law (Neh. 8.7, 9, 11), the charge of the storerooms (Neh. 13.13), and the cultic duty (Neh. 13.29).

largely on its material or shape, and shows no interest in the workers or their relationship. This Levitical cooperation is also highlighted in the account of the reading of the law in Neh. 8.[34]

In conclusion, both the texts showing Levites in apposition to the priests and the texts containing both Levites and priests in context support the position that the Levites are described favourably and as co-workers with priests in E–N.

4.1.2.3 *Levites in Texts without Priests*

In the remaining nine references to לוי in E–N, the word is used with no mention of the priests (Ezra 8.20; 10.15; Neh. 7.1; 9.4, 5; 12.27; 13.10 [×2], 22) and therefore does not elucidate the relationship between the clergy. It is notable, however, that in these texts, the Levites are portrayed favourably in other ways.

(1) Ezra 8.20 is the only text in the Old Testament which mentions the origin of the Nethinim as attendants of the Levites prescribed by David, and thus offers a clue to their promoted status.

(2) As explored earlier,[35] Ezra 10.15 describes Shabbethai the Levite as cooperating with Ezra's reform, not opposing it.

(3) In Neh. 7.1, the Levites are appointed as custodians of the gates of the new wall. In fact, there is general consensus that והמשררים והלוים ('and the musicians and the Levites') are late additions since they had nothing to do with the security of the city.[36] Regarding the reason for the addition, there have been several proposals which usually maintain that the author's addition crept in from 7.43ff, where the three groups of people in the text (the Levites, the singers, the gatekeepers) subsequently appear together,[37] or from 13.22, which stipulates that the Levites keep the gates on the Sabbath.[38] Further analysis is needed to decide which is more convincing but, at this point and for our purpose, it is sufficient to say that the Levites are positively presented by the author in his additions.

(4) Neh. 9.4 and 5 depict the Levites leading the great confession.

(5) In Neh. 12.27, the Levites are not ignored but sought out for participation in the dedication ceremony of the wall.

(6) Neh. 13.10ff describes a rebuke given to those who had neglected to bring the portions owed to the Levites.

(7) In Neh. 13.22, the Levites are chosen to guard the gates on the Sabbath.

---

34. A detailed discussion on this will take place in section 5.2.2.

35. See section 4.1.1.

36. E.g., Rudolph, *Esra und Nehemia*, p. 138; Myers, *Ezra–Nehemiah*, p. 141; Clines, *Ezra, Nehemiah, Esther*, p. 178. Opposed to this view, a few scholars argue that the gatekeepers asked the musicians and the Levites for their assistance in order to perform the protection of the city more effectively in an emergency situation and, thus, there was no later gloss or addition in the text. For this view, see Williamson, *Ezra, Nehemiah*, p. 270, where he follows Ryle (*Ezra and Nehemiah*, pp. ix–v). It is somewhat odd, however, that so many people were needed to watch the gates (v. 3).

37. E.g., Fensham, *Ezra and Nehemiah*, p. 209.

38. Brockington, *Ezra, Nehemiah and Esther*, p. 127.

In all these texts, where Levites are specified without mentioning the priests, they are presented in a positive light.

4.1.3 *Conclusion*

Our conclusions, from the examination of the Levites in E–N, may be summed up as follows:

> First, as discussed earlier (cf. section 2.3.2), לוי occurs more frequently in E–N than in any other book in the Old Testament. Its numerous occurrences are congregated particularly in the authorial portions. This shows that the author had a strong interest in the Levites.
>
> Secondly, there are no texts which may be regarded as priestly-authored since nowhere in E–N are the Levites certainly described as *clerus minor* or negatively.
>
> Lastly, לוי in E–N can be categorized by these types of occurrence: (1) priests and Levites in apposition; (2) Levites and priests contextually together; and (3) Levites in texts without priests. An analysis of each category consistently favours the conclusion that, in E–N, the Levites are described favourably, usually as co-workers with the priests.

Our analysis has shown that the description of Levites in E–N is similar to their description in Levitically-penned texts, and is in direct contrast with their portrayal in priestly-penned texts. In the light of this, we conclude that the author of E–N was pro-Levitical, and most likely belonged to a Levitical group.

4.2 *Additional Evidence – Levitical Terms*

We concluded in the preceding section that E–N was most likely composed by a person who belonged to a Levitical group. This conclusion was based on an examination of its literary style, which favours and elevates the Levites and is similar to those portions of Chronicles whose authorship is ascribed to a Levitical group, and which forms a striking contrast with the style of priestly-penned texts portraying the Levites as *clerus minor*. This section attempts to corroborate this conclusion by adding further noteworthy, though admittedly inconclusive, evidence.

E–N has several terms which are thought to have come from Levitical groups. Three of these will be discussed here: (1) the mouth of *Jeremiah*; (2) Judah and *Benjamin*; and (3) הכהנים הלוים.

4.2.1 *The Mouth of Jeremiah*

E–N begins with a decree issued by Cyrus, king of Persia (Ezra 1.1-4). According to the biblical account, he was stirred up by the Lord and, as a result, permitted the Jewish exiles in his territory to return to Jerusalem and build the house of God. The author interprets this epochal event as an accomplishment of the word of the Lord by the mouth of *Jeremiah* (v. 1). This has led commentators to link this word of the Lord to certain Jeremiah passages such as 25.11-12 and 29.10, which speak of seventy years and the return to Jerusalem.[39] This link has been based on the presupposition that 2 Chron. 36.21, which mentions seventy years, is part of the subsequent passage (2 Chron. 36.22-23) and that it parallels the Ezra text.[40]

This widely held view has been challenged, however, since the Jeremiah passages cited above have no mention of the building of the temple, which is one of the most crucial components of Cyrus's decree.[41] Besides, there is no reference to seventy years in the Ezra text. What is more, as is generally accepted, 2 Chron. 36.22-23 is most likely derived from the Ezra text, and not vice versa.[42] It is thus a misunderstanding to place it under the umbrella of 2 Chron. 36.21.

This situation has led scholars to note a few Isaiah passages which refer to the 'stirring up' of Cyrus to restore the people of God and to the 'building of the temple' (Isa. 41.2, 25; 44.28; 45.1, 13, etc.). Because Ezra 1.1 designates Jeremiah, not Isaiah, as the prophet through whom the word was spoken, they maintain either that there was textual corruption from the original reading, which had Isaiah, to the present text which has Jeremiah,[43] or that Jeremiah was perceived to have been responsible for Isaiah 40–55.[44] Williamson pinpoints the absurdity of these two explanations: there is no external evidence for the first argument whatsoever and, for the second, Isaiah 40–55 has always been linked with Isaiah 1–39 and there is no possibility of misunderstanding Isaiah 40–55 as Jeremiah's work.[45]

Therefore, we face a dilemma. On the one hand, it seems clear that the word of the Lord in Ezra 1.1 originated in the prophetic words of Isaiah. On the other hand, the text itself ascribes them not to Isaiah but to *Jeremiah*. This incongruity has forced most scholars to suggest that the present text conflated the passages of Isaiah (Isa. 41; 44; 45) with those of Jeremiah (Jer. 25; 29).[46] Williamson also agrees with the conflation theory, but he conflates the Isaiah passages with Jeremiah 51 instead of 25 and 29.[47]

This conflation theory seems to offer the best solution to the dilemma of incongruity between the text and stated author thus far, but it still does not satisfactorily answer the question of why *Jeremiah*, not Isaiah, was chosen by the author as the originator of the prophetic words in Ezra 1.

---

39. E.g., Keil, *Ezra, Nehemiah, and Esther*, p. 20; Raymond A. Bowman, 'Introduction and Exegesis to the Book of Ezra and the Book of Nehemiah', *The Interpreter's Bible*, 3 (Nashville: Abingdon Press, 1954), pp. 551–819, esp. p. 570; Fensham, *Ezra and Nehemiah*, pp. 42–43; Grabbe, *Ezra–Nehemiah*, p. 11.

40. Cf. Williamson, *Ezra, Nehemiah*, p. 9.

41. For a useful discussion of the purpose of the decree, see M. Noth, *The History of Israel* (London: Adam & Charles Black, 2nd edn, 1960), p. 308.

42. Cf. Williamson, *Israel*, p. 9; Japhet, *I & II Chronicles*, p. 1076.

43. Cf. Batten, *Ezra and Nehemiah*, pp. 56–57; Williamson, *Ezra, Nehemiah*, p. 10.

44. Bernhard Duhm, *Das Buch Jeremia* (Tübingen and Leipzig: Mohr, 1901), p. ix.

45. Williamson, *Ezra, Nehemiah*, p. 10; *idem*, *The Book Called Isaiah: Deutero-Isaiah's Role in Composition and Redaction* (Oxford: Oxford University Press, 1994), especially Chapter 5, where he says that the compiler of Isaiah 1–39 was also responsible for 40–55.

46. E.g., Brockington, *Ezra, Nehemiah and Esther*, p. 48; Ackroyd, *I & II Chronicles, Ezra, Nehemiah*, p. 213; McConville, *Ezra, Nehemiah and Esther*, p. 7; Throntveit, *Ezra- Nehemiah*, p. 14.

47. Williamson, *Ezra, Nehemiah*, p. 10.

Some would insist upon the compositional connection between Chronicles and E–N. This would provide a more convincing explanation for the emergence of Jeremiah in Ezra 1.1; that is, the author chose Jeremiah alone in order to keep consistency with the preceding verse (2 Chron. 36.21). But we must reject this theory in the light of our conclusion in Chapter 1 that E–N was not part of a greater whole by the Chronicler.

In an attempt to solve this problem, it is possible to argue that Jeremiah was *deliberately* chosen by the author of Ezra, as the originator of the prophetic words. As Eskenazi points out, Ezra 1.1-4 is a crucial unit in that it states the objective of the book.[48] Thus, it is unlikely that the author would be careless or designate the originator of the prophetic words in this text by accident.

If so, which authorship – priestly or Levitical – provides a more plausible explanation for such a deliberate choice of Jeremiah?

In reply, it may be useful, first of all, to probe Jeremiah's background. According to Jeremiah 1.1, he was one of the priests of Anathoth, in the land of Benjamin.[49] According to biblical accounts, Anathoth was the town to which Abiathar, the last priest of Eli's family, was exiled by Solomon for taking part in the plot to make Adonijah king (1 Kgs 2.26-27). It is thus normally thought of as a *Levitical* refuge city.[50] Because Jeremiah was of disenfranchised priestly descent in Anathoth, and it is commonly held that he was a descendant of Abiathar,[51] it is possible that he was associated in some way with the Levitical groups.[52] This is, perhaps, attested in Jeremiah's utterances against the temple, which had been monopolized by the opposing party, i.e., the *Zadokite* priests (Jer. 7.14; 26.2).[53] It may also be worth noting that there is a close connection between Jeremiah and Deuteronomy in terms of similarities in language and theology,[54] and that Deuteronomy has a strong interest in the Levites.[55]

---

48. Eskenazi, *Age of Prose*, pp. 37–45.

49. This biblical testimony has been strongly defended by J. Bright, *Jeremiah* (AB, 21; Garden City, NY: Doubleday, 1965), pp. lxxvii–lxxviii, who says that the priests living in Anathoth might be related by kinship.

50. Hanson, *The Dawn of Apocalyptic*, p. 224.

51. See, for example, E. Achtemeier, *Deuteronomy, Jeremiah* (Proclamation Commentaries: The Old Testament for Preaching; Philadelphia: Fortress Press, 1978), p. 56; Robert R. Wilson, *Prophecy and Society in Ancient Israel* (Philadelphia: Fortress Press, 1980); Bright, *Jeremiah*, p. lxxvi.

52. It should be borne in mind that our working definition of Levites in this book has been both Levites in contradistinction to priests, and the Abiathar priests. See Chapter 2 n. 82.

53. Cf. de Vaux, *Ancient Israel*, p. 376; Hanson, *The Dawn of Apocalyptic*, pp. 224–25.

54. E.g., the pattern of 'Kinderfrage' or the emphasis on the faithfulness to the covenant. See S. Mowinckel, *Zur Komposition des Buches Jeremia* (Oslo: Jacob Dybwad, 1914); Wilson, *Prophecy and Society in Ancient Israel*, p. 236; Achtemeier, *Deuteronomy, Jeremiah*, p. 53; R.P. Carroll, *From Chaos to Covenant-Prophecy in the Book of Jeremiah* (New York: Crossroad, 1981).

55. See especially von Rad, *Studies in Deuteronomy*; G.E. Wright, 'Deuteronomy', in *The Interpreter's Bible*, 2 (Nashville: Abingdon Press, 1954), p. 326. Mary Douglas also observes the discrepancy between the doctrine of defilement in Ezra and in the priestly texts, Leviticus and Numbers. She also points out that E–N follows, in several points, Deuteronomy which is, with respect to the responsibilities of the Levites and the Day of Atonement, in contrast with these

Taking into account all these points, there is no obvious reason for a priestly author to have chosen Jeremiah, who might have been little favoured among the Zadokites, as the originator of the prophetic word in Ezra 1.1. By contrast, if we accept that the author of E–N had pro-Levitical inclinations or belonged to a Levitical group, it would be most understandable for him to choose Jeremiah instead of Isaiah in this crucially important verse. This evidence is admittedly slight, but it does add something to the argument for Levitical authorship.

4.2.2 *Judah and Benjamin*

We suggested above that the deliberate choice of Jeremiah as the originator of the prophetic word in Ezra 1 might have been motivated by the author's pro-Levitical inclinations. If this conclusion is sound, as shall be examined below, an unexpected use of בנימן ('Benjamin') in E–N, which geographically includes Anathoth, hometown of Jeremiah, thus implicitly but repeatedly delivering a Levitical concept, could also serve as corroborative evidence in favour of Levitical authorship.

Of course, the emergence of the word in the book *per se* does not necessarily confirm its connection to Jeremiah or Levitical authorship since it often occurs in other books where such a connection is not detected. Yet, attention should be paid to the word here, for it is used distinctively in E–N.

בנימן occurs ten times in E–N: seven times referring to the tribe of Benjamin (Ezra 1.5; 4.1; 10.9; Neh. 11.4, 7, 31, 36) and three times as a personal name (Ezra 10.32; Neh. 3.23; 12.34). Interestingly, when it refers to the tribe, it is always found either in apposition to the tribe of Judah (Ezra 1.5; 4.1; 10.9; Neh. 11.4)[56] or contextually with the tribe of Judah (Neh. 11.7, 31; cf. 11.4, 25). In other words, except for its use as a personal name, it appears with Judah in *every* case in order to express the whole of Israel. This expression in E–N seems to suggest that the post-exilic Israel was composed of two tribes – Judah and Benjamin – and has led some scholars to define Israel in the post-exilic period with 'Judah and Benjamin'.[57]

This understanding, however, overlooks more common expressions used in E–N for the whole of Israel: i.e., the whole of Israel is more frequently expressed by 'the people of Judah' or 'Judah and Jerusalem' (Ezra 2.1; 4.6; 5.1, 8; 7.14; 9.9; Neh. 2.5; 5.14; 6.7, 17, 18, etc.).[58] For example, all areas of Northern Israel as well as Judah (Ezra 2.21-35) are commonly represented simply by the phrase 'Jerusalem and Judah' (2.1) rather than the combination of two tribes, 'Judah and Benjamin'. Thus, this practice means that Judah *alone* was enough to represent the whole

---

priestly books. For a more detailed discussion, see Mary Douglas, 'Responding to Ezra: The Priests and the Foreign Wives', *Biblical Interpretation* 10 (2002), pp. 1–23.

   56.   Ezra   1.5, ראשי האבות ליהודה ובנימן ('the heads of the families of Judah and Benjamin')

                4.1, צרי יהודה ובנימן ('the enemies of Judah and Benjamin')

               10.9, אנשי־יהודה ובנימן ('the men of Judah and Benjamin')

     Neh. 11.4, מבני יהודה ומבני בנימן ('some of the descendants of Judah and of Benjamin').

   57.   See von Rad, *Das Geschichtsbild des Chronistischen Werkes*, p. 24; Williamson, *Israel*, pp. 87–140.

   58.   Or, 'the priests and the Levites and the people'. For a discussion about this expression for the whole Israel, see section 4.1.2.1.

people of Israel. It could be claimed, therefore, that בנימן in the phrase יהודה ובנימן ('Judah and Benjamin') is not necessarily needed to convey the intended meaning.

Why, then, does E–N have another way of describing the whole of Israel by the two tribes? It is hard to answer the question, but a literary analysis of the references cited as 'Judah and Benjamin' provides a clue, since many of them belong to the authorial portions (Ezra 1.5; 4.1; 10.9; Neh. 11.36).[59] Therefore, it may not be unfair to say that בנימן was deliberately added alongside Judah by the author for some specific purpose.[60] This habit of the authors cannot be understood properly in terms of priestly authorship. Presumably, such an expression (i.e., יהודה ובנימן) was strange to the priests who had lived a life centred on Judah and Jerusalem. By contrast, if we accept Levitical authorship for E–N, such an expression is comprehensible. By means of putting the word 'Benjamin' after Judah, the author may have intended that readers treat Benjamin, representing Levitical cities, as the partner tribe of Judah, representing priestly groups. Again, this evidence is slight, but a Levitical connection may once more be the best explanation for a curious characteristic of the text.

4.2.3 הכהנים הלוים

Finally, we may focus on whether the use of the phrase, הכהנים הלוים supports or opposes Levitical authorship.

הכהנים הלוים is not rare in the Old Testament. Mostly, this phrase can be translated as the *Levitical priests* and is used as a substitute term for the priests.[61] This phrase also occurs five times in E–N (Ezra 10.5; Neh. 10.1, 29, 35; 11.20) but, in *every* case, the Levites are recognized in modern translations as a separate entity. Thus, the two entities are always translated together as *the priests and the Levites*. In fact, as examined in section 4.1.2.1, the phrase with a conjunction (הכהנים והלוים) is more frequently used in E–N than הכהנים הלוים, but few scholars have questioned why two different forms are used for the same meaning. It seems to me that the author was discontent with the practice of that time which used both הכהנים and הלוים, as in the form of הכהנים הלוים, merely to refer to the priests alone. He thus challenged this practice by deliberately using the asyndetic phrase for 'the priests and the Levites', thus showing the author's Levitically-biased contention that the Levites should be recognized as a social entity on its own in any phrase which contained the word לוי.[62]

---

59. For the extent of the authorial portions of E–N, see Chapter 2 n. 86.

60. Against this reasoning, some may argue that the phrase appears in other texts which are not suspected of deliberate addition by an author (1 Kgs 12.21, 23; 1 Chron. 9.3; 12.16; 2 Chron. 11.1, 3, 10, 12, 23; 14.7; 15.2, 8, 9; 17.7; 25.5; 31.1; 34.9, etc.). However, it should be mentioned that in most cases the word בנימן in the verses cited is used merely to mean 'Benjamin' as an independent tribe, distinct from other tribes, rather than being verbosely added.

61. E.g., Deut. 17.9, 18; 18.1; 24.8; 27.9; Josh. 3.3; 8.33; 2 Chron. 23.18; Jer. 33.18, 21; Ezek. 43.19; 44.15.

62. Because some of these texts in E–N (Ezra 10.5; Neh. 10.1, 29, 35; 11.20) have variants reading הכהנים והלוים ('the priests and the Levites'), scholars have argued that 'ו' was included in the original text, but dropped for stylistic reasons (e.g., Kropat, *Die Syntax des Autors der Chronik*, pp. 62–63). Neh. 10.29 and 11.20 have no variant readings, however. Nurmela offers another

Of further interest is that, of the references in E–N to the asyndetic phrase, Neh. 10.1 has its inverted form, which places כהנים behind לוים (לוינו כהניו) and thus is very rare in the Old Testament. This verse serves to introduce the subsequent section in 10.2-28, where the names of signatories are listed in the following order: the governor (התרשתא; v. 1a); the priests (vv. 1b-9); the Levites (vv. 10-14); and the chiefs of the people (ראשי העם; vv. 15-28). It is significant that the introduction in verse 1 describes the list as follows: שרינו ('our princes'), לוינו כהנינו ('our Levites and our priests'). The word-order (לוינו כהנינו) is unparalleled with that of the names in its following section. We cannot supply the exact reason for the inverted order,[63] but it is, at least, intriguing to note that the only other time this inverted and asyndetic form occurs in the Old Testament is in the book of Jeremiah (33.18), which was pro-Levitical.[64]

Summary of Part II

In this part, we have examined the authorship of E–N from the literary evidence, first by comparing the descriptions of the Levites in Old Testament texts of the exilic and post-exilic periods with that of E–N; and secondly, by examining some peculiar phrases which denote their priestly or Levitical bias.

From an examination of the texts under comparison, the conclusions we have reached are as follows:

(1)   Ezekiel and P originated in priestly circles. In these works, the Levites are almost always described as *clerus minor* in their position and function in relation to the priests.

(2)   In the case of Chronicles, there are irreconcilable descriptions of the clergy, because some passages ascribe remarkable importance to the Levites, while others highlight the subordination of the Levites to the priests. Hence, we see here an inconsistency within the book in the descriptions of the Levites: pro-Levitical on the one hand and pro-priestly on the other. Scholars have elucidated this dilemma, in my judgment rightly, by arguing that the book

---

possibility for the deletion of 'ו' before הלוים. According to him, it was caused by later redactors, who mistakenly replaced the original Chronicles expression (הכהנים והלוים) with the Deuteronomistic one (הכהנים הלוים) (Nurmela, *The Levites*, p. 166). This view, however, can be accepted only when we suppose that the redactors were very inattentive and were confused with this important phrase as many as five times, which, in my view, is beyond credibility. Therefore, I agree with Cody, who found this peculiar expression hard to understand and ascribed it to the author's general tendency to add והלוים to any mention of priests.

63.   Most scholars say, without giving sufficient attention to the inverted order 'Levites and priests', that this unparalleled order just shows the literary independence of the document in Neh. 10. For example, see Williamson, *Ezra, Nehemiah*, p. 332.

64.   The order where the Levites precede the priests is also found in 2 Chron. 19.8 and 30.21. It is of note that these two references are immediately preceded by Levitical sermons, thus being located in the middle of Levitically-penned texts. Cf. von Rad, 'The Levitical Sermons', pp. 267–80, where he ascribes to the Levitical sermon 1 Chron. 28.2-10; 2 Chron. 15.2-7; 16.7-9; 19.6; 20.15-17; 25.7; 30.6-9; 32.7-8.

has two different literary layers, each of which was penned by different religious groups. The layer which the Levitical group composed (Chron.-L), describes the Levites favourably and promotes them to the status of the priests, whereas the other layer, composed by the priestly group (Chron.-P), describes the Levites as *clerus minor*, just as in other priestly works.

(3) To sum up, the priestly-penned texts, to which Ezekiel, P and Chron-P belong, emphasize the distinction between the priests and the Levites in their status and function, describing the Levites as *clerus minor*. In contrast, the Levitically-penned text, i.e., part of Chronicles (Chron.-L), relaxes the clerical disparity, presents the Levites as co-workers with the priests, and generally elevates the status of the Levites.

(4) How does E–N describe the Levites? Those who favour Williamson's theory of priestly authorship would anticipate the descriptions of the Levites to be similar to those drawn in the priestly-penned texts. However, it is noteworthy that, of 65 references in E–N, the Levites are *nowhere* described as *clerus minor*. Rather, in all references to לוי, in my view, they are consistently favoured and presented as co-workers with the priests. This description of Levites in E–N is similar to their descriptions in Levitically-penned texts, and is in direct contrast to their portraits in priestly-penned texts. In the light of these findings, we have suggested that the author of E–N belonged most likely to a Levitical group.

(5) Lastly, we attempted to give supporting, though slight, evidence for Levitical authorship. E–N highlights 'Jeremiah', unexpectedly uses the word 'Benjamin', and has a peculiar form, הכהנים הלוים. According to our exploration, Jeremiah and Benjamin are attached to the town, Anathoth, which was a Levitical refuge city, thus enhancing the possibility of Levitical authorship. Similarly, הכהנים הלוים, an asyndeton, was thought to reflect the author's intention to highlight the Levites as a social entity distinct from the priests but equal to them.

From these findings and evidence, therefore, we are able to conclude that Levitical authorship for E–N is a highly probable thesis.

Part III

HISTORICAL CONTEXT

In Part II we examined the literary evidence for authorship and concluded that this pointed to a Levitical origin for E–N. In this part we turn our attention to the *historical* context for additional evidence of authorship.

In order to do this, one would ideally begin by reconstructing the history of the post-exilic period and then probe, in the light of the reconstructed history, which group, priestly or Levitical, was in the best position to produce the book.

However, in this case, we are confronted with several major obstacles to such an approach. The post-exilic period we are concerned with has commonly been regarded as one of the most difficult periods for historical reconstruction, mainly because of the questionable reliability of the few primary sources which exist. The situation is well described by Lester Grabbe:

> It is not really until after 200 BCE that we begin to find a reasonably reliable sequence of events and even some detailed data. Our knowledge of the Persian and Ptolemaic periods still has enormous gaps, and a good deal of what is presented in standard histories represents more wishful thinking than carefully documented historical reconstruction. We have some religious literature from these periods – or allegedly from them – but primary historical sources are few and far between.[1]

There are, indeed, both biblical and extra-biblical sources from the Persian period. However, given their restricted scope, the extra-biblical sources such as the Elephantine papyri, the Samaritan papyri and the various archaeological findings provide, at best, only a skeleton of the history of the era rather than a complete picture.[2] In the

---

1.   L.L. Grabbe, 'The History of Israel: The Persian and Hellenistic Periods', in A.D.H. Mayes (ed.), *Text in Context: Essays by Members of the Society for Old Testament Study* (Oxford: Oxford University Press, 2000), pp. 403–27, esp. p. 403. See also Francis I. Anderson, 'Who Built the Temple?', *ABR* 6 (1958), pp. 1–35, esp. pp. 5–6; Maxwell J. Miller, and John H. Hayes, *A History of Ancient Israel and Judah* (Philadelphia: The Westminster Press, 1986), p. 437.

2.   Grabbe, 'The Persian and Hellenistic Periods', pp. 404–405. For studies of the recent archaeological findings of that period, see Ephraim Stern, *Material Culture of the Land of the Bible in the Persian Period 538–332 B.C.* (Jerusalem: Israel Exploration Society; Warminster: Aris & Phillips, 1982); Yaakov Meshorer, *Ancient Jewish Coinage*. I. *Persian Period through Hasmonaeans*; II. *Herod the Great through Bar Kochba* (New York: Amphora, 1982); D.P. Barag, 'Some Notes on a Silver Coin of Johanan the High Priest', *BA* 48 (1985), pp. 166–68; *idem*, 'A Silver Coin of Yohanan the High Priest and the Coinage of Judah in the Fourth Century B.C.', *Israel Numismatic Journal* 9 (1986–87), pp. 4–21; Helga Weippert, *Palästina in vorhellenistischer Zeit* (HdA, Vorderasien 2, Band 1; Munich: Beck, 1988).

case of the biblical sources, which include E–N, there is a similar lack of any broad perspective, while serious questions have been raised about their historical reliability.[3] Even the Nehemiah Memoir, which has traditionally been accepted as the most reliable contemporary source, has not been free from that suspicion.[4]

In view of this situation, despite numerous attempts to reconstruct the Jewish history of that period, little consensus about several key historical issues has been reached,[5] and no one theory dominates.[6]

3. For example, Ezra 6 is directly followed by Ezra 7, allowing a gap of more than half a century and giving no mention of what happened during the periods in-between. This silence most likely resulted from a lack of sources available to the author. Cf. H.G.M. Williamson, 'Judah and the Jews', in M. Brosius *et al.* (eds.), *Studies in Persian History: Essays in Memory of David M. Lewis* (Leiden: Nederlands Instituut voor het Nabije Oosten, 1998), pp. 145–63, esp. p. 160. The question of the unreliability of the sources has been focused largely on the book of *Ezra*: Torrey, *Composition*, pp. 57–63 and Garbini, *History and Ideology in Ancient Israel*, pp. 151–69, both conceive of the Ezra narratives as a forgery by the Chronicler; Kellermann, 'Erwägungen zum Esragesetz', pp. 373–85, finds reliable historical information only in the edict of Artaxerxes in Ezra 7.12-26 and treats the other parts of the book simply as the Chronicler's propaganda; Gunneweg, 'Zur Interpretation der Bücher Esra-Nehemia', pp. 146–61, esp. pp. 150–51; *idem, Esra*, pp. 85–111, 141, doubts the genuineness of the Aramaic sources and the Ezra material; L.L. Grabbe, 'Reconstructing History from the Book of Ezra', in P.R. Davies (ed.), *Second Temple Studies*; I. *Persian Period* (JSOTSup, 117; Sheffield: JSOT Press, 1991), pp. 98–106; *idem*, 'What was Ezra's Mission?', in Eskenazi *et al.* (eds.), *Second Temple Studies*, II, pp. 286–99, also disputes the authenticity of the sources preserved in the book of Ezra and maintains that we should no longer write the history of Judah on the basis of that book; David Janzen, 'The "Mission" of Ezra and the Persian-Period Temple Community', *JBL* 119 (2000), pp. 619–43, thinks that the authenticity of Artaxerxes' letter in Ezra 7.12-26 is in great doubt, while the Ezra narrative is likely to be reliable. For views of scholars who have attempted to defend the reliability of most, though not all, of the sources, see especially Williamson, 'Exile and After', pp. 240–46, 256–59.

4. Clines, 'The Nehemiah Memoir', pp. 124–64, seriously challenges the inclination to use 'the evidence of the Nehemiah Memoir as a touchstone for historicity' (p. 125). He argues that we should make a distinction between literary description and historical fact.

5. For example, according to Widengren, 'The Persian Period', pp. 503–15, the following main historical issues are left unresolved: (1) the chronological order of Ezra and Nehemiah; (2) the administrative relationship of Judah and Samaria; (3) the Samaritan schism and the construction of the Samaritan temple; and (4) the identity of Ezra's law-book. Recently, another big historical issue has been raised by Joel P. Weinberg, *The Citizen-Temple Community* (trans. D. Smith-Christopher; JSOTSup, 151; Sheffield: JSOT Press, 1992). He formulates a hypothesis that the Jewish community in Judah during the Persian period was a *Bürger-Tempel-Gemeinde* ('Citizen-Temple-Community') as an independent socio-political unit. For a discussion of this hypothesis, see especially Blenkinsopp, 'Temple and Society in Achaemenid Judah', in Davies (ed.), *Second Temple Studies*, I, pp. 22–53; Williamson, 'Judah and the Jews'; *idem*, 'Exile and After', pp. 246-52.

6. For example, Talmon, 'Ezra and Nehemiah', pp. 322–28, has ambitiously attempted, on the basis of E–N, to reconstruct post-exilic Jewish history in chronological order. Scholars, however, disagree on numerous details. For example, while Talmon suggests that Ezra 2.1-67 is a list of only returning exiles under Zerubbabel and Jeshua, other scholars argue that the list reflects the membership of the Judean community in 458 BC (Weinberg's view), or that it shows not only the exiles returned (vv. 3-20), but also those who remained in the land (vv. 21-35) (Japhet's view). Cf. Weinberg, *The Citizen-Temple Community*, pp. 34–48; S. Japhet, 'People and Land in the Restoration Period', in G. Strecker (ed.), *Das Land Israel in biblischer Zeit* (Göttingen: Vandenhoeck & Ruprecht, 1983), pp. 103–25, esp. pp. 114–16. Talmon also argues that Ezra 4.7-23 probably refers

If any general reconstruction of the early post-exilic period is possible, and that seems doubtful, it is far beyond the scope of this book. The many problems mean, of course, that almost any detailed conclusions are necessarily somewhat provisional and tentative. It is possible to avoid some of the worst pitfalls, however, by focusing upon the political ideologies expressed in E–N, and attempting to correlate them with the more certain facts of the era. In Chapter 5 we shall examine, therefore, the attitudes of E–N toward the Persian empire, on the one hand, and the Jewish community, on the other. These two 'clues', which have attracted a certain amount of scholarly attention in the context of other discussions, will be applied to the issue of authorship in Chapter 6. There I shall attempt to show that, on the basis of the evidence available, the Levites are the group most likely to have been responsible for those attitudes.

Given the limitations of the evidence, any account of this issue must involve some degree of speculative reconstruction, and we can generally speak only of probabilities, rather than certainties. Nevertheless, it does seem clear that the historical evidence points the same way as the literary – toward a Levitical origin for E–N.

---

to events which transpired in the days of Nehemiah and should be placed after Neh. 5.7 or 5.9 and, noting its misplacement, he relocates Neh. 10.1-40 to a time shortly after the dedication ceremony of the wall (12.27-43) dated 435 BC. Others, however, associate 'the Jews who came up from you to us' in Ezra 4.12 with Ezra's caravan (e.g., Williamson, *Ezra and Nehemiah*, p. 75) and thus regard the event recorded in 4.7-23 as an event in which Ezra, not Nehemiah, was involved (e.g., Rudolph, *Esra und Nehemia*, pp. 44–45). Again, since Neh. 10 shows close connection with the subject matter of Neh. 13.4-31, most scholars have proposed that Neh. 10 should chronologically be placed after Neh 13, the episodes of which took place at the earliest in 432 BCE. Cf. Williamson, *Ezra, Nehemiah*, pp. 330–31.

Chapter 5

Two Clues

5.1 *Achaemenid Imperial Policy and Ezra–Nehemiah*

5.1.1 *Introduction*

It is widely recognized that, after having conquered the Neo-Babylonian empire in 539 BCE, and become the new master of the ancient Near East, Persia immediately invested energy in gaining political stability in those countries which had previously been colonized by Babylon but were now to be absorbed into its territory.[1] While removing any potential factors in the colonies which might contribute to rebellion, the new empire also had to ensure a strong hierarchical relationship between sovereign and subject.

The political stabilization of the colonies *per se* was not the final goal of Persian imperialism. Its ultimate aim was, on the basis of the stability gained, to maximize Persia's own national interest, and to increase imperial income. In pursuit of this purpose, the Persian government mapped out an imperial policy toward the colonized countries, which, as pointed out by Jon Berquist, underwent slight shifts in detail according to the empire's political objectives in any given context,[2] but was consistently maintained during their entire rule.[3]

We shall begin by summarizing the mechanisms used by the Achaemenids for control of their colonies, and especially of Yehud. Since Yehud never escaped from the influence of this policy and E–N is a work produced in the imperial context, one would expect to find Achaemenid imperial policy reflected in the book. We shall then examine the attitude of the author of E–N toward this policy in order to explicate his political perspective.

5.1.2 *Achaemenid Imperial Mechanisms of Control*

Among recent studies, those done by Kenneth Hoglund and Jon Berquist may provide a particularly useful understanding of Achaemenid imperial policy.[4] While

---

1. Cf. Jon L. Berquist, *Judaism in Persia's Shadow: A Social and Historical Approach* (Minneapolis: Fortress Press, 1995), pp. 23–44.

2. For example, Darius may have supported the rebuilding of the Jerusalem temple because it was regarded as a way to achieve more benefit from Yehud, but this policy of funding local cults was suddenly cancelled when Xerxes urgently needed funds to fuel his imperial army in their long-standing battle against the Greeks. Cf. Berquist, *Judaism in Persia's Shadow*, pp. 91–94, 141.

3. Berquist, *Judaism in Persian's Shadow*, pp. 23–44; Grabbe, *Judaism from Cyrus to Hadrian* (London: SCM Press, 1994), pp. 79–83, 115.

4. Kenneth Hoglund, 'The Achaemenid Context', in Davies (ed.), *Second Temple Studies*. I,

Hoglund focuses on the political and economic aspects of the imperial mechanism, Berquist largely elaborates on its ideological aspects.[5] These studies have gained acceptance by many scholars.[6] I will, therefore, briefly summarize the imperial mechanisms for control which they outline.[7] Not all of these mechanisms, of course, are directly relevant to E–N, but they give a flavour of the broader political world within which the post-exilic community was established.

(a) Migration and Grouping: comparing Achaemenid imperial policy with those of earlier empires, one of its most radical new characteristics was the policy of migration, under which Persia moved populations in the imperial core to colonial peripheries.[8] For this policy, Persia was indebted paradoxically to Babylon which, by contrast, had centralized subject populations toward its imperial core. Babylon's policy of centralization had resulted in a collapse of the economy in the boundary areas of the empire, and weakened its defensive strength, finally bringing about its downfall. In response, Cyrus permitted deportees, such as the Jewish exiles, to migrate back to their original lands, and the policy further involved the grouping of populations in the occupied areas according to their 'ethnic' backgrounds.[9] This

---

pp. 54–72; Berquist, *Judaism in Persia's Shadow*. See also Mohammad A. Dandamaev, *La Politique religieuse des Achéménides*; ET *A Political History of the Achaemenid Empire* (trans. W.J. Vogelsang; Leiden: E.J. Brill, 1989); Christopher Tuplin, *Achaemenid Studies* (Stuttgart: Franz Steiner Verlag Stuttgart, 1996), pp. 9–79; Schaper, *Priester und Leviten*, pp. 130–61.

5.   Cf. Hoglund, 'The Achaemenid Context', pp. 54–72, where he summarizes Persian imperial mechanisms of control over colonies in four areas: realization, commercialization, militarization, and ethnic collectivization; Berquist, *Judaism in Persia's Shadow*, esp. pp. 131–46, where he argues that 'through intensification, governors, law, and ritual, Persia maintained a firm control over the Yehudite colony' (p. 144).

6.   E.g., John M. Halligan, 'By Way of a Response to Hoglund and Smith', in Davies (ed.), *Second Temple Studies*, I, pp. 146–53; Samuel E. Balentine, *The Torah's Vision of Worship* (Minneapolis: Fortress Press, 1999), pp. 47–57; Williamson, 'Exile and After', pp. 255, 259–60; Carter, *The Emergence of Yehud in the Persian Period*, pp. 42–46, *et passim*; Paula M. McNutt, *Reconstructing the Society of Ancient Israel* (London: SPCK Press, 1999), pp. 188–212.

7.   Mechanisms which are not directly related to E–N (e.g., dissemination of creation stories) will not be summarized. See also n. 28 below.

8.   For the relationship between the imperial *core* and the colonial *periphery*, see Berquist, *Judaism in Persian's Shadow*, pp. 241–55, where, relying on other related theorists on empires, he defines the former as 'the locations of greatest power and privilege, whether measured in terms of politics, economy, military, or ideology' (p. 246). Designating the latter as colonies or secondary states, he explains them as the places which 'lack sufficient authority to govern themselves' and their populations (p. 244), and in which 'trade was scarce, taxation meant the removal of local resources rather than the accumulation of them, and there was no control over military might' (p. 246).

9.   Hoglund, 'The Achaemenid Context', pp. 65–68. See also Schaper, *Priester und Leviten*, p. 241. One may point out the inadequacy of the term 'ethnic', because it is uncertain whether people were *ethnically* perceived in those days. Needless to say, the identity of the people was often confused. For instance, many of the people living in Judah had been mixed up with other peoples and, as a result, their children had already lost their original ethnic identity. In addition, what Persia was probably concerned about was grouping itself for effective ruling rather than the way people were grouped. I appreciate the problem with this controversial term. Yet, I do not change the term Hoglund uses; for, whatever the original criterion for grouping was, it is obvious that when Ezra and Nehemiah applied this policy to the Judean community they presupposed ethnic groupings, as

was carried out by the imperial administration, which undertook the reorganization of dependent communities into corporate units.[10]

Both facets of the policy were designed to benefit the empire itself. Cyrus wanted to secure a loyal element in the subject population of each region, and to obtain a military buffer on the fringes of his empire.[11] In addition, the presence of the return-ees in each colony was expected to provide a check on the existing local authori-ties.[12] Ethnic grouping contributed to these general aims, and offered more effective ways to administer, tax, and regulate the colonized people.

(b) Commercialization: another mechanism Persia employed as a means of con-trol was to encourage international commerce. There is much evidence of intense commercial activity between countries in the Achaemenid period. According to Hoglund, for example, ceramics made in Athens and a special type of jar prevalent along the Levantine coast have been excavated almost everywhere in Yehud.[13] As with migration of ethnic groups, this policy was also intended primarily for Persia's own benefit. By fostering international commerce, Persia could not only levy taxes on trade and commerce, but could also subsume the traditional economic system of each country into a larger, interdependent economic system that would eventually engender 'the perspective that economic well-being relied on continued allegiance to the empire'.[14]

(c) Militarization: a need to fortify the imperial borders led the Persians to garri-son their troops in strategically important places – along the *Via Maris* early in the imperial period, for instance, and throughout the Levantine region by the mid-fifth century BCE.[15] It can readily be assumed that this militarization was intended for

---

can be seen in the narratives which overtly allude to the ethnic separation of the people of Israel from other peoples such as the Ammonites and the Moabites (cf. Ezra 9.1; Neh. 13.23-24).

10.   Note, for example, a group of Paeonians who lived as an ethnically separate community almost fourteen years after their deportation by Darius (Herodotus, *Histories*, 5.15, 5.98) and the Persepolis Fortification Tablets, which show that 'there are monthly rations issued to several different ethnic groups inhabiting small villages'. See Hoglund, 'The Achaemenid Context', p. 66. Cf. R.T. Hallock, *Persepolis Fortification Tablets* (Oriental Institute Publications, 92; Chicago: University of Chicago Press, 1969), pp. 306–308.

11.   This policy of migration may, in part, demonstrate Persia's moderate and generous stance. Cf. Bright, *A History of Israel*, p. 362. However, most scholars argue that permission for the return was given because it suited the purposes of the empire. Cf. Amélie Kuhrt, 'The Cyrus Cylinder and Achaemenid Imperial Policy', *JSOT* 25 (1983), pp. 83–97. See also A.H.J. Gunneweg, *Geschichte Israels bis Bar Kochba* (Stuttgart: W. Kohlhammer, 1972), p. 137; Pierre Briant, 'Villages et communautés villageoises d'Asie achéménide et hellénistique', *JESHO* 18 (1975), pp. 165–88; Miller and Hayes, *A History of Ancient Israel and Judah*, pp. 443–45; Berquist, *Judaism in Persia's Shadow*, p. 141.

12.   Cf. Balentine, *The Torah's Vision of Worship*, p. 47.

13.   Hoglund, 'The Achaemenid Context', pp. 60–62

14.   Hoglund, 'The Achaemenid Context', p. 62. Cf. Shmuel N. Eisenstadt, *The Political Systems of Empires* (New York: Free Press of Glencoe, 1963), p. 33.

15.   E.g., ever since Cambyses invaded Egypt in 526/5 BCE, the Persian army had been stationed in Yehud. When Persian hegemony in the Judean territory was severely challenged by the Greeks who supported the Egyptian revolt in the mid fifth century BCE, the Persians took strong measures to secure imperial control by fortifying some areas. Cf. Miller and Hayes, *A History of Ancient*

imperial, rather than local, benefit. As a matter of fact, most of the forts set up at that time were located on the major trade routes, suggesting that, through them, the Persians could effectively tax and control travel. We can assume that the Persians portrayed these forts to the local populations as a defence against any threat from outside enemies; but it is also clear that the local populations were obliged to support them, thus placing both financial and physical burdens upon the colonies.[16]

(d) Realization: archaeological surveys suggest that a process of 'realization', which decentralized the population outward to non-urban areas was at work in Judean territory.[17] Hoglund notes that the regions surrounding Judah showed a remarkable decrease in the number of settlements from the Iron II period to the Persian period; in contrast, Judah underwent a 25 per cent increase, during the same time period. Of the new settlements, 65 per cent had been unoccupied in the immediately preceding period, and 24 per cent had had no prior occupation at any period of Jewish history. This process occurred at the end of the sixth century BCE, when the first group of people began returning from Babylon to Judah, and probably reflects a deliberate process encouraged by Persia.[18] The policy was presumably intended to increase potential sources of tribute by developing the rural country-side.[19]

(e) Appointment of pro-Persian Governors: the empire believed that an effective and safe way to ensure imperial influence in conquered areas would be to work through the ruling class of each colony.[20] The Persians, correspondingly, appointed compliant agents from these classes, and we may presume that the nominated rulers, in order to maintain their status, pledged loyalty to the Persian kings.[21]

(f) The Codification of Law: in addition to the mechanisms for socio-economic control, outlined above, the empire also used symbolic mechanisms for ideological control.[22] They needed to provide ideological justification for the current political

---

Israel and Judah, p. 447; Hoglund, 'The Achaemenid Context', pp. 62–64; *idem, Achaemenid Imperial Administration in Syria-Palestine and the Missions of Ezra and Nehemiah* (SBLDS, 125; Atlanta: Scholars Press, 1992). For a more detailed discussion, see section 5.1.3.3 below.

16. Hoglund, 'The Achaemenid Context', pp. 63f; Grabbe, *Judaism*, p. 115.

17. Cf. M. Kochavi (ed.), *Judaea, Samaria, and the Golan: Archaeological Survey 1967–1968* (Jerusalem: The Survey of Israel [Hebrew], 1972).

18. Hoglund, 'The Achaemenid Context', pp. 57–60. One may suspect here that the increase in the number of settlements in Judah probably reflects a decline of urban economy or food shortages. This view, however, cannot provide the reason for why, then, the same phenomenon did not occur in other neighbouring countries.

19. Hoglund, 'The Achaemenid Context', p. 59.

20. Cf. Berquist, *Judaism in Persia's Shadow*, pp. 132–36.

21. Explaining this policy, Berquist furthermore argues that 'there is no revolt or attempted rebellion by the Yehudites throughout the two centuries of Persian hegemony' (Berquist, *Judaism in Persia's Shadow*, p. 144). This view seems a bit exaggerated. As Smith-Christopher points out, if so, why was the Persian military army continuously stationed in Yehud? Cf. Daniel L. Smith-Christopher, 'Book Review of J.L. Berquist, *Judaism in Persia's Shadow: A Social and Historical Approach*', *The Journal of Religion* 77 (1997), pp. 656–58.

22. Apart from this policy (the codification of law), another mechanism for ideological control may have been to encourage creation stories to be disseminated so that colonized people could conceptualize the world as divinely ordered and accept the current status quo (Cf. Berquist,

and social structure in order to eradicate any possibility of rebellion, especially in the face of taxation, and to maintain strong control over their colonies.[23] One way they did this was to encourage colonies to codify their own legal traditions, a codification which, however, was virtually under Persian supervision and eventually came to serve as a means to deter the colonies from having independent administrative practices.[24]

(g) Support for the Construction of Temples: Persia also seems to have encouraged the occupied nations under imperial rule to construct temples. The best-known example, the Jerusalem temple, was funded by the imperial treasury according to biblical sources (cf. Ezra 6.4, 8-9; 7.15, 20-22; 8.25, 33).[25] This seemingly generous policy was, however, just another attempt to provide an effective infrastructure, which could collect and administer both religious and secular taxes,[26] as well as conscripting labour. Thus the temple, while a significant national institution for the people, was for the Persians a further source of income.[27]

Judaism in Persia's Shadow, pp. 134–35, 139; Balentine, *The Torah's Vision of Worship*, pp. 48–50). I have not discussed this in detail because it is hardly found in E–N.

23.   Berquist, *Judaism in Persia's Shadow*, pp. 137–41; Cf. Balentine, *The Torah's Vision of Worship*, p. 47.

24.   This process was advanced primarily by Darius I, who attempted to standardize law throughout the colonies. Berquist, *Judaism in Persia's Shadow*, p. 138. See also Albert T. Olmstead, *History of the Persian Empire* (Chicago: University of Chicago Press, 1948), pp. 119–34; Gösta W. Ahlström, *The History of Ancient Palestine from the Palaeolithic Period to Alexander's Conquest* (JSOTSup, 146; Sheffield: JSOT Press, 1993), p. 842, where examples of Darius's efforts for the codifications in Babylon and Egypt are provided. For such a dual system of laws in the Persian empire, i.e., 'the 'king's law' applicable everywhere, and local laws which were codified by order of the king', see Richard N. Frye, *The History of Ancient Iran* (Munich: C.H. Beckische, 1984), p. 119. Williamson, 'Judah and the Jews', p. 161, also supports this argument by presenting the 'Passover Papyrus' from Elephantine as evidence.

25.   For other examples of Persian support for local temples, see Blenkinsopp, 'Temple and Society in Achaemenid Judah', pp. 24–26.

26.   Viz., the tithe which corresponds to approximately a tenth of the income of tax-payers for the *holy* tax; and מדה or מנדה ('tribute tax'; Ezra 4.13, 20; 6.8; 7.24; Neh. 5.4), בלו ('poll tax'; Ezra 4.13, 20; 7.24), and הלך ('land tax'; Ezra 4.13, 20; 7.24) for the *secular* tax. See J. Schaper, 'The Jerusalem Temple as an Instrument of the Achaemenid Fiscal Administration', *VT* 45 (1995), pp. 528–39. Cf. C.C. Torrey, 'The Foundry of the Second Temple at Jerusalem', *JBL* 55 (1936), pp. 247–60; M.A. Dandamayev, and V.G. Lukonin, *The Culture and Social Institution of Ancient Iran* (trans. P.L. Kohl; Cambridge: Cambridge University Press, 1989), pp. 36–62; J. Eph'al, 'Syria-Palestine under Achaemenid Rule', *Cambridge Ancient History IV* (Cambridge: Cambridge University Press, 2nd edn, 1988), pp. 158–59.

27.   According to Schaper, it is a well-attested fact that there was a special official – a *fiscal agent* of the central government – called יוצר in Yehud (Zech. 11.13) or *gitepatum* in Persia, whose task was to collect and administer the tax income of both the temple and the state. Babylon also had a similar official, called *rēš šarri bēl piqitti*, who controlled the inflow and the distribution of taxes received by a given temple. This suggests that such an official was prevalent in the ANE countries. See J. Schaper, 'The Jerusalem Temple as an Instrument of the Achaemenid Fiscal Administration', pp. 528–39; *idem*, 'The Temple Treasury Committee in the Times of Nehemiah and Ezra', *VT* 47 (1997), pp. 200–206; *idem*, *Priester und Leviten*, pp. 130–61. See also Berquist, *Judaism in Persia's Shadow*, pp. 140–42; Balentine, *The Torah's Vision of Worship*, pp. 52–57. Balentine says that it was the responsibility of the priesthood to advance the empire's economic and political

(h) Rituals: finally, in addition to political and ideological mechanisms, the empire implemented rituals which were designed to help them control the empire. Building on David Kertzer's theory,[28] Berquist presents an example of this policy: the tour or procession of the empire, which was organized to impress the emperor's grandeur upon the governed people and which ultimately impelled them to accept the imperial rule, not only with intellectual assent but also with emotional ardour.[29] The legal introduction of the Sabbath to Yehud is another example of this policy, for observance of it would provide an opportunity for the Yehudites to give thanks to the powers that conferred the time for rest as well as an opportunity to access the temple, with its required tax dues.[30]

In summary, the new Persian empire promulgated a number of new policies, which were essentially self-interested. There is little hint of any altruistic policy that would profit only the subject nations, although in practice, of course, the interests of the empire and its subjects might often coincide. The measures practised in Yehud, such as permission for the Jews to return and rebuild the temple, were likely to be regarded, at first, as Persian benevolence. This outlook is likely to have been encouraged by the excellent 'heart-and-mind' propaganda promulgated by the empire, as can be seen in the famous Cyrus cylinder.[31] As time passed, however, the people certainly came to know the ulterior motivations behind those mechanisms.

There is a general agreement that E–N was written after Persian policies had been in effect for some time, and when any initial glamour is likely to have dissipated. Therefore, an examination of the attitude of E–N's author toward the imperial policy might well show whether or not he was sponsored by, or received patronage from, the empire. The initial excitement caused by the collapse of Babylon, which inspired strongly pro-Persian sentiments in, for example, Second Isaiah, is likely to have given rise to greater realism by this point. We may assume, therefore, without undue cynicism, that writers expressing strong loyalty to Persia are likely themselves to have had some stake in the success of the empire.

---

objectives from the local temple (p. 52). Furthermore, he notes three functions of the temple as a mechanism for social control: an administrative centre, a religious centre, and the locus of regional power (pp. 53–55). For a recent thorough study of the temple in the post-exilic period which would oppose our position, see Peter R. Bedford, *Temple Restoration in Early Achaemenid Judah* (Leiden: Brill, 2001).

28. David Kertzer, *Ritual, Politics, and Power* (New Haven/London: Yale University Press, 1988), where he attempts to explain how effectively ritual can be used politically: for example, enhancing a sense of solidarity through performing rituals.

29. Cf. Berquist, *Judaism in Persia's Shadow*, pp. 142–43, where he says 'Through establishing occasional physical presence in most corners of the governed territory, the emperor takes advantage of opportunities for visible presence and for associated rituals to impress upon the citizens the emperor's grandeur and the essential rightness of imperial rule' (p. 142).

30. Berquist, *Judaism in Persia's Shadow*, p. 54. See also D.J.A. Clines, 'The Ten Commandments, Reading from Left to Right', in *Interested Parties: The Ideology of Writers and Readers of the Hebrew Bible* (JSOTSup, 205; Sheffield: JSOT Press, 1995), pp. 26–45, esp. 32–40, where he argues that the Sabbath serves the ruling class of Israel to control and manipulate the common people.

31. See *ANET*, pp. 315–16.

5.1.3 *The Attitude of E–N's Author toward Imperial Policy*

It seems highly probable that the Persian authorities would have had to confront major objections from some Jews to those policies implemented in Yehud which most obviously served imperial, rather than local, interests. Particular objections might have been raised by those who sought the restoration of a Davidic kingdom and political independence, and who therefore resisted the imposition of Persian government, or by those who were reluctant to share their privileges and land with returned exiles, and who therefore saw the migration polices as a threat to their own interests.[32] For other Jews, however, Persian policy offered significant benefits and new privileges. It was to their advantage, therefore, to persuade the Jewish people as a whole to accept the reality of their situation, and that they were banned from controlling their own destiny.[33]

What attitude, then, does E–N's author maintain toward Persian policy? In order to bring this question into focus, we may ask more specifically what attitude the author displays toward the *decrees* issued by Persian kings and preserved in his book. Those decrees are a concrete manifestation of imperial policy, and E–N is, after all, comprised largely of accounts showing how they were executed. The book has three substantial decrees: one by Cyrus, concerning the return of the exiles and rebuilding of the temple (Ezra 1.2-4; cf. 6.3-5), and two by Artaxerxes, one relating to the mission of Ezra in 458 BCE (Ezra 7.12-26)[34] and the other to the mission of Nehemiah in 445 BCE (cf. Neh. 2.7-10). E–N can, in fact, usefully be divided into three sections, each dealing with the execution of one of these decrees:

(1) Ezra 1–6 deals with Cyrus's decree and its fulfilment;
(2) Ezra 7–10 and Neh. 8–10 report on Ezra's activity in relation to the first decree of Artaxerxes;[35]
(3) Neh. 1–7 and 11–13 focus on Nehemiah's work in relation to the second decree of Artaxerxes.

We now turn our attention to the author's attitude toward the imperial policies as reflected in each of these three sections.

---

32.   Namely, those who had messianic vision, fuelled, perhaps, by Haggai (Hag. 2.20-23; cf. Sir. 49.11), or those who had a close relationship with neighbouring countries, as alluded to in E–N (e.g., Neh. 6.17-19; 13.23-24).

33.   Cf. Bustenay Oded, *Mass Deportations and Deportees in the Neo-Assyrian Empire* (Wiesbaden: L. Reichert, 1979), pp. 46–48; Hoglund, 'The Achaemenid Context', p. 65. Both characterize the returning Jews as a *dependent population* since they were given a territory to inhabit and till on the condition that they remained loyal to the empire.

34.   For this date of Ezra see a discussion in section 2.1.

35.   In fact, the name of Ezra is not referred to in Neh. 9–10 and it is commonly held that it is only Neh. 8 that originated in the Ezra source and that the other chapters have their own independent origins. But all of them will be dealt with here together, since it is also obvious that these three chapters have been carefully arranged to be read as a unit and comprise a consecutive narrative which began with Ezra's reading of the law. For a more detailed discussion about the relationship between these chapters, see section 5.2.2.1.

5.1.3.1 *Ezra 1–6*

Cyrus's decree, as represented in Ezra 1.2-4 (cf. 6.3-5), permitted the return of the exiles to Judah and the rebuilding of the temple in Jerusalem.[36] The biblical accounts subsequent to this decree give an orderly report of the process of implementing it: the return under Sheshbazzar (ch. 1); the list of returned exiles (ch. 2); the temple rebuilding planned and disturbed (chs. 3–4); and the restoration of the temple (chs. 5–6).

On the reasonable assumption that the land to be occupied by the returning migrants was in use, and that some religious provision had continued to exist in Palestine, it is clear that some of the resident population stood to lose income or status as a result of this decree. If E–N was penned from the perspective of this group of people, it might be expected that the book would preserve their objections but, interestingly, it has *little* mention of them. Instead, Cyrus's decree is treated favourably, and is regarded, indeed, as having a divine, not human, origin: Cyrus is spoken of as an agent chosen by God for this task (1.1). Interestingly, it is also described as having been warmly welcomed, not only by the whole Jewish people (1.5), but also by their neighbours, who are said to have supported the temple rebuilding willingly (1.6). The number of the returnees recorded in the list in Ezra 2 is unusually large (42,360; cf. Ezra 2.2, 64)[37] and thus doubt has been cast on whether it indicates the actual number of the returned exiles who came back with Zerubbabel.[38] This has given rise to a number of proposals about the purpose or nature of the list in Ezra 2.[39] What is clear, however, is that the author intentionally

---

36. Suspicion has been cast on the authenticity of the decree of Cyrus in 1.2-4 mainly because (1) it is written in the local language, Hebrew, which Cyrus might not have known, and (2) in the decree Cyrus calls himself the 'king of Persia', which is unusual. On the other hand, the authenticity of the memorandum of Cyrus in 6.3-5 has widely been accepted. Since 6.3-5 does not refer to the return, one may question whether it is appropriate to choose to examine the author's attitude toward imperial policy in the decree of Cyrus on the basis of 1.2-4. Cf. for further discussion exploring the lack of authenticity of the decree in 1.2-4, see Schaeder, *Esra der Schreiber*, p. 29; Rudolph, *Esra und Nehemia*, p. 3; S. Mowinckel, *Studien zu dem Buche Ezra-Nehemia III: Die Ezrageschichte und das Gesetz Moses* (SUNVAO. II. Hist.-Filos. Klasse. Ny Serie. No. 7, Oslo; 1965), p. 8; R. de Vaux, *Bible et Orient* (Paris: Cerf, 1967), p. 87; Noth, *The History of Israel*, p. 308. However, we find the argument which defends the authenticity of the decree, quite compelling. For discussions defending its authenticity persuasively, see E.J. Bickerman, 'The Edict of Cyrus in Ezra 1', in *Studies in Jewish and Christian History: Part One* (Leiden: Brill, 1976), pp. 72–108; F.I. Anderson, 'Who Built the Second Temple?', pp. 1–35; Williamson, *Ezra and Nehemiah*, pp. 33–34.

37. Cf. Albright, *Biblical Period*, p. 87, where he argues that the entire population in Yehud did not exceed 20,000 in 522 BCE.

38. Cf. Coggins, *Ezra and Nehemiah*, p. 17, says that such a mass return is unlikely. Ackroyd, *I & II Chronicles, Ezra, Nehemiah*, p. 221, also points out that the mention of the coin, Daric (v. 69), which was in use from the time of Darius, implies that the list was made later for certain reasons. For a similar position to Ackroyd, see Williamson, 'Eschatology in Chronicles', pp. 123–25.

39. E.g., 'a fiction' (Torrey, *Composition*, pp. 39ff); 'a census of the population of Judah from the time of Nehemiah' (Albright, *Biblical Period*, pp. 87, 110–11); 'sources for deciding the right of the returnees to land' (Albrecht Alt, 'Die Rolle Samarias bei der Entstehung des Judentums', in *Kleine Schriften zur Geschichte des Volkes Israel* [Munich: Beck, 1953], pp. 316–37, esp. pp. 334–35); 'a Persian tax list' (Hölscher, 'Die Bücher Esra und Nehemia', in E. Kautzsch *et al.* [eds.],

placed the list immediately after the account of the decree, in order to demonstrate that this large group of people returned to their homes as a result of the decree. In fact, the same list is also found in Neh. 7, which is commonly regarded as the original location for the list.[40] The repetition of the list here in Ezra 2 is strictly speaking, therefore, redundant and unnecessary, but it can be understood as an expression of the author's gratitude to Persia for the decree.

A second aspect of the policy preserved in Cyrus's decree is the decentralization and realization of the population in Yehud. This aspect is also alluded to in E–N. For example, the reference to 'his own city (לעירו) to which every returnee went back' (Ezra 2.1) is best understood in terms of the general Persian policy outlined earlier. Most of the returnees had never lived in the land. How and why, then, should they go back to their ancestral home towns? Hoglund persuasively argues that Ezra 2.1 must reflect an enforced reorganization and redistribution of the land occupied by the resident population, returning or assigning land to the new migrants.[41] Ezra 2.70 (= Neh. 7.72) may be a further allusion to the operation of this policy in Yehud.[42] In all likelihood, the policy would have been resented by the 'remainees', who had lived in their home towns for at least a couple of generations after the collapse of Judah in 587 BCE, and now had to share them with the newcomers, or move out to other places. What is of note here is that, in E–N, there is no mention of any complaints against this policy. Rather, the texts appear unhesitatingly to accept the resettlement system initiated by Persia.

Finally, what attitude does E–N exhibit toward the rebuilding of the temple, a third aspect of Cyrus's decree (Ezra 1.2-4; 6.3-5; cf. chs. 3–6)? As noted earlier, the rebuilding of the temple was encouraged because it was expected to provide Persia with political and economic, as well as ideological, gains from Yehud. When it was later judged that the temple might no longer suit this purpose, indeed, the empire was ready to cancel the permission, as can be clearly seen in Ezra 4, which describes the subsequent ban on rebuilding the temple. The work was apparently initiated at the wish of the Persian king, not by any request from the Jewish people,

---

Die heilige Schrift des Alten Testaments [Tübingen, Mohr, 1923], pp. 491–562, esp. pp. 503–504); 'names of those who obtained the Persian permission to participate in the building work of the temple' (Galling, 'The Gōlā List', pp. 149–58); and 'later compilation to combine the remainees and the returnees' (Japhet, 'People and Land in the Restoration Period', pp. 112–13). Cf. Clines, *Ezra, Nehemiah, Esther*, p. 44.

40. Conversely, some scholars have suggested that the original location of the list was in Ezra 2 rather than in Neh. 7. See Hölscher, 'Die Bucher Esra und Nehemia', pp. 491–562; Noth, *ÜS*, pp. 128–29; Mowinckel, *Studien I*, pp. 29–45; Pohlmann, *Studien zum dritten Esra*, pp. 57–64; Blenkinsopp, *Ezra–Nehemiah*, pp. 43–44. This view, however, has been quite convincingly rejected. See K. Galling, 'Die Liste der aus dem Exil Heimgekehrten', in *Studien zur Geschichte Israels im persischen Zeitalter*, pp. 89–108; Rudolph, *Esra und Nehemia*, pp. 11–15; Johannes Theis, *Geschichtliche und literarkritische Fragen in Esra 1–6* (Munich, 1910), pp. 60–67; Williamson, 'The Composition of Ezra i–vi', pp. 2–8; *idem*, 'The Problem with First Esdras', pp. 205–208.

41. Cf. Hoglund, 'The Achaemenid Context', pp. 59–60.

42. 'The priests, the Levites, and some of the people, the singers, the gatekeepers, and the temple servants dwelt in their cities, and all Israel in their cities.'

and the Persians were prepared to reverse their original permission. One would expect that a Jewish writer might consequently condemn the Persians, either for permitting the rebuilding, or, subsequently, for withdrawing permission. E–N, however, at no point condemns the Persians for their decisions. Indeed, it seems intentionally to minimize Persia's responsibility by imputing the ban to the adversaries of Judah and Benjamin (Ezra 4.1). The expression 'adversaries' in Ezra 4.1 is curious, inasmuch as the individuals concerned had originally approached the Jews to *support* their building work (Ezra 4.2).[43] The term may, perhaps, have been used by the author to shift the responsibility for the ban on to others, and to exculpate the Persians.

It is possible that the absence of any criticism with regard to the return and the redistribution of the land merely indicates that Persian policy coincided with the interests of the writer of E–N. That no resentment toward the authorities is expressed for permitting or for banning the temple is more significant, however. If the author is not simply afraid to criticize the Persians, and that seems unlikely, given his trenchant views, we may interpret this as an actively pro-Persian position, in which the empire escapes criticism whether its decrees correspond to the writer's own wishes or not.

5.1.3.2 *Ezra 7–10 and Nehemiah 8–10*

The second unit is comprised of Ezra 7–10 and Neh. 8–10, which deal with the first decree of Artaxerxes. In this, the king commissions Ezra as an imperial official, and the subsequent narrative describes Ezra's activity in Yehud to implement the tasks for which he has been commissioned. Judging from the biblical accounts of what Ezra did as a commissioned official in Yehud, he seems to have devoted himself to applying two particular aspects of imperial policy: one was the separation of the Jewish men from foreign wives, related to the policy of ethnic grouping (Ezra 9–10); the other was the teaching of the law, related to the policies of codifying law and, perhaps, conducting rituals (Neh. 8–10).

Hoglund has demonstrated that Persia's policy of ethnic grouping was at work in Yehud. He notes the recurring expression, 'the assembly of the exile' (קהל הגולה) in E–N, and argues that, because this expression still occurs many decades after the first return from Babylon (Ezra 9.4; 10.6, etc.), the imperial bureaucracy must have treated Jews as a collective unit, not an entity definable by a territorial or political referent. Intermarriage which was apparently prevalent in Yehud during the post-exilic period, was undesirable to the Persians, as it might lead to a confusion of ownership of one ethnic group's possessions with those of another, and thereby inconvenience the imperial officials – for example, in taxing property.[44]

Hoglund's interpretation may be a little forced, and there is little evidence that Persia implemented such rigorous segregation elsewhere in the empire. Some might argue, indeed, that the reform was motivated more by Ezra's devout zeal, and his

---

43. Cf. Holmgren, *Ezra & Nehemiah*, p. 28.
44. Cf. Hoglund, 'The Achaemenid Context', p. 67. He finds an example of this in the multiple property settlements of the Mibtahiah archives from Elephantine.

own interpretation of traditional Jewish law; this interpretation is not an ancient one, but is certainly in keeping with what we know of Jewish understandings and preoccupations in the period.[45] However, it is commonly agreed that Ezra 9–10, which deals with intermarriage, is an account of Ezra's activity in the first year of his return.[46] It is reasonable to think, then, that such early actions were associated in some way with the tasks for which he was commissioned, rather than independent enterprises unconnected to his role as an imperial official. This means that the reform carried out in Ezra 9–10 should be considered part of the implementation of Ezra's assigned tasks, although it may have involved an interpretation of Persian policy which was strongly informed by other ideological factors.

Since Ezra's request to expel foreign spouses was very radical and somewhat impractical, one might expect that there would have been opposition. This opposition can be inferred, indeed, from Ezra 10.12-14, which mentions a suggestion made by the congregation that the separation from pagan wives should be deferred and undertaken only progressively. But the subsequent story shows that their proposal was rejected[47] and immediate separation was enforced (Ezra 10.14, 16ff). The author of E–N never criticizes the imperial politics latent behind such a policy: one might say that this is an instance where imperial policy was seen to cohere with, and provide a vehicle for, the religious ideology of both Ezra and E–N.

Ezra's other assignment was to teach the law to the Jews. The extent and nature of the law which Ezra brought have been widely debated, but it is widely agreed that it had something to do with the Pentateuch, whether in part or in whole.[48] Some argue, on the basis of a few Ezra texts (Ezra 7.25-26), that Ezra's mission, mandated by Artaxerxes, was to consolidate the (Pentateuchal) law which had previously been authorized by Darius and which contained ideology perceived as favourable to Persian rule.[49] If so, the law which Ezra brought had two aspects: it included an internal synthesis of traditional laws on the one hand, and an aspect of imperial control on the other.[50] The presence of the second aspect might have given the Jews

---

45. Cf. Shaye J.D. Cohen, 'From the Bible to the Talmud: The Prohibition of Intermarriage', *HAR* 7 (1983), pp. 15–39. See also Schaper, *Priester und Leviten*, pp. 251f, who argues that 'Esra … war nach Jerusalem gekommen, nicht um – wie Nehemia – ein altes Gesetz auszulegen und anzuwenden, sondern um ein neues Gesetz zu verkünden'.

46. Cf. Williamson, *Ezra, Nehemiah*, pp. xxviii–xxxii.

47. Cf. section 4.1.1.

48. Most of those who accept the documentary hypothesis of the Pentateuch have identified the book either with P or with the whole Pentateuch. Cf. U. Kellermann, 'Erwägungen zum Esragesetz', pp. 374–76. Others see the book as a form of the Deuteronomic code. Cf. Kellermann, 'Erwägungen zum Esragesetz', pp. 372–85. Some deny any direct connection between Ezra's book and the present Pentateuch: e.g., Cornelis Houtman, 'Ezra and the Law', *OTS* 21 (1981), pp. 91–115 and Rolf Rendtorff, 'Esra und das "Gesetz"', *ZAW* 96 (1984), pp. 165–84. A few think Ezra's law consisted of both D and P. See Williamson, *Ezra, Nehemiah*, pp. xxxvii–xxxix.

49. Berquist, *Judaism in Persia's Shadow*, p. 102. Cf. Balentine, *The Torah's Vision of Worship*, pp. 50–52; Frank Crüsemann, *Die Tora: Theologie und Sozialgeschichte des alttestamentlichen Gesetzes* (Munich: Chr Kaiser Verlag, 1992), ET *The Torah: Theology and Social History of Old Testament Law* (trans. Allan W. Mahnke; Minneapolis: Fortress Press, 1996), pp. 349–65.

50. E.g., the creation story. See note 28 above.

room to condemn Ezra from an orthodox perspective. No condemnation is portrayed, however, and the whole people are described as keenly interested in the law (Neh. 8).[51] Indeed, they repent and renew their covenant to God because of it (Neh. 9–10).

Ezra 7–10 and Neh. 8, therefore, differ from Ezra 1–6 in displaying instances where Persian interests coincide with a particular religious ideology that has its roots in Deuteronomistic thought. What we find here is not simply approval of Persian policy, but an exploitation of that policy, which integrates internal reform with official imperial business.

5.1.3.3 Nehemiah 1–7 and 11–13

The last unit of the book is based on the activity of Nehemiah under the authorization of Artaxerxes (cf. Neh. 2.7-10). As a governor of the empire, Nehemiah undertook several tasks, including that of building the wall of Jerusalem, the story of which comprises the bulk of this unit (Neh. 1–6; 12.27-43). According to the biblical accounts, Nehemiah volunteered for this task (cf. Neh. 1–2). It may be undeniable that Nehemiah had a strong desire for the restoration of the Jewish community, but there is also no doubt that the mission of Nehemiah was politically designed. Most scholars believe that his mission to Yehud was designed to tighten imperial control after the revolt of Megabyzos, the satrap of Beyond the River, around the middle of the fifth century BCE and to guarantee the loyalty of the province.[52]

The widely held theory that the Megabyzos revolt caused Nehemiah's visit to Judah has been dismissed by Hoglund, however, who finds no clear evidence for that revolt in the historical sources.[53] Rather, he believes that Nehemiah was sent to fortify Jerusalem in 458 BCE in preparation for a likely threat from the Greeks; he compares the case of the Egyptian revolt *circa* 464–454 BCE.[54] In addition to both Greek literary and Persian imperial archaeological evidence, Hoglund finds some supporting evidence in E–N, noting that the quick shift in Artaxerxes' policy, from a ban on the fortification of Jerusalem (Ezra 4.7-23) to support of it, is suggestive of an urgent situation.[55] Moreover, he sees the fortification as evidence that Jerusalem was strategically chosen as a defensive centre for militarizing the province.[56]

---

51. Reading of the law is described as being initiated by the people, not by Ezra (v. 1) and the whole people are described as devoting themselves to listening and learning the law (vv. 3-12). For more details, see section 5.2.2 below.

52. For this traditional view, see Olmstead, *History of the Persian Empire*, pp. 312–13; Noth, *The History of Israel*, p. 318; Galling, 'Bagoas and Esra', pp. 149–84.

53. Hoglund, *Achaemenid Imperial Administration*, pp. 97–164.

54. Hoglund, *Achaemenid Imperial Administration*, pp. 165–226. See also Kellermann, *Nehemia*, pp. 154ff.

55. According to Neh. 6.15, the work was completed in fifty-two days. This short time for such a major task may be somewhat exaggerated (Josephus thinks it took two years and four months. Cf. *Ant.* XI.5.8), but it demonstrates that the work was done hurriedly and probably with Persian support.

56. Hoglund, *Achaemenid Imperial Administration*, pp. 209–10, observes a military aspect in the building work of the Jerusalem wall from a study of בירה, which was used to refer to a military

If Hoglund's thesis is correct, we may well conclude that Nehemiah was sent in his capacity as a Persian representative especially to implement a policy of militarization.

For all that some may have been keen to re-fortify Jerusalem, this mission probably inconvenienced the local people. It would have been their responsibility to support the imperial troops, and the military preparations would have led to a heavier burden from taxation, as alluded to in Neh. 5.4. The residents might well also have had to put up with problems caused by local garrisons of imperial soldiers.[57] Again, though, no mention is made in E–N of any complaints about the policy. The distress of the people narrated in Neh. 5 is depicted as caused by their Jewish brethren (v. 1) and by the nobles and rulers (v. 7), although it surely resulted mainly from the heavy tax burden levied to maintain the imperial troops garrisoned in Yehud.

Of course, most of this section is comprised of the Nehemiah Memoir, and is thus the work of a Persian official.[58] We might, therefore, expect a pro-Persian slant. The author of E–N, however, was free to choose and arrange his sources, as can be seen in other places,[59] and there is no opposition to the policy of militarization in the authorial material here. Both selection and composition seem to reflect a positive attitude toward Persian policy.

This section also reveals the author's attitude toward the governors appointed by Persia. Their positions obliged them to perform tasks which were primarily geared to Persian interests. As officials of the empire, they were naturally loyal to Persia and favoured the imperial mechanisms for control over Yehud. Nehemiah, thus, responded to the problem of heavy imperial taxation by rebuking the local nobles, and suggesting they stop exacting interest (cf. Neh. 5.6-12), rather than by asking the Persian government to alleviate the burden. He also apparently supported the Persian consolidation of an economic system subordinate to the empire. The account of foreign merchants in E–N, though quite short (Neh. 13.16), indicates that he had little concern about any negative consequences that commercialization would bring

---

installation in some ANE texts and thus has the sense of a fortress or citadel. For a similar position, see also I.J. Gelb *et al.* (eds.), *The Assyrian Dictionary of the Oriental Institute of the University of Chicago*, II (Gluckstadt: J.J. Augustin, 1965), p. 281; Meyers, 'The Persian Period and the Judean Restoration: From Zerubbabel to Nehemiah', in P.D. Miller, *et al.* (eds.), *Essays in Honor of Frank Moore Cross: Ancient Israelite Religion* (Philadelphia: Fortress Press, 1987), pp. 509–21, esp. p. 516.

57.   Such problems are timeless. For the case of American troops in modern Far Eastern countries, see, for example, 'Maehyang-ri Residents to Protest at US Embassy', *The Korea Times*, 9 January 2002; 'South Koreans Call for Closure of U.S. Firing Range', *Anti Imperial League*, 7 June 2000. For an example in Achaemenid times, note the tense relationship between the garrison and the local population depicted in the Elephantine letters (cf. *ANET*, pp. 491–92).

58.   For the extent of the Nehemiah Memoir, see note 86 in Chapter 2.

59.   For example, Neh. 8 was originally placed between Ezra 8 and Ezra 9. See Torrey, *Composition*, pp. 29–34. For a detailed discussion, see section 5.2.2.1. Williamson also argues that there must once have been more extensive sources in the hands of the author than the book reveals now, all of which were not chosen by him. Cf. Williamson, *Ezra and Nehemiah*, p. 15; *idem, Ezra, Nehemiah*, p. 309.

into Judean society. Instead, he took the current economic system for granted, and his concern in the following narratives (Neh. 13.17ff) lies purely in forcing the nobles of Judah to observe the Sabbath.

5.1.4 *Conclusion*

We have seen, then, that the Persians adopted a number of measures which were designed to stabilize their empire and enhance its profitability. E–N illustrates the application of some of these measures in the province of Yehud. In doing so, it incorporates imperial decrees, and a lengthy memoir attributed to a Persian official. It never focuses on the drawbacks, and where negative consequences are mentioned, they are never portrayed in such a way as to attach blame to the Persians. To be sure, this is sometimes, perhaps, because Persian policy was congruent with, or even facilitated reforms based on, a Jewish religious ideology to which E–N is sympathetic. At certain points, though, most notably in Ezra 4, the desire to exculpate Persia goes beyond any simple sharing of aims. In its response to Persian policy, therefore, E–N appears to approve of the complicated historical relationship between the empire and the returning Jews, with all the mutual benefit and interdependence which it involved. The work goes further, though, by seeming to demonstrate approval of the Persian empire itself.

5.2 *Ideology in Ezra–Nehemiah*

5.2.1 *Introduction*

In the preceding section, we gained a clue for resolving the authorship issue of E–N: the work is strongly pro-Persian, has an interest in the implementation of Persian policy, and is quite likely, therefore, to have been written by someone who, in their turn, enjoyed Persian support.

A further clue may be found in the ideology of E–N. The ideology presented in a book is of course an expression of the author's thought influenced by the historical context, and potentially provides a window into the *Sitz im Leben* of the author, as well as further data on which to base our decision regarding the identity of the author.

Like other literature in the Old Testament, E–N possesses a variety of thematic or ideological features. Some of these shed little light on our problem. For example, it is obvious that emphases on God's steadfast love toward his people and the legitimacy of the Jewish community are among the main themes of the book.[60] However, in the light of our question – priestly or Levitical authorship? – these themes are too general to be attributed to a specified clerical group and, thus, are of little value.

We will focus, therefore, on ideological motifs that are apparently peculiar to one or other of the two clerical groups. I have chosen to concentrate on Neh. 8–10,

---

60. Cf. Kidner, *Ezra & Nehemiah*, pp. 20–23; McConville, *Ezra, Nehemiah and Esther*, p. 4; Holmgren, *Ezra & Nehemiah*, p. xiii; Clines, *Ezra, Nehemiah, Esther*, pp. 25–26; Williamson, *Ezra, Nehemiah*, p. li.

where the ideology of the author is most explicit, and to use it as a cross-section of the work as a whole.

5.2.2 *Nehemiah 8–10, A Case Study*
5.2.2.1 *Characteristics of Nehemiah 8–10*
Most scholars agree that the ideology of the author of E–N is most clearly detected in Neh. 8–10, not least because, despite their being of independent origin, these three chapters are combined as one unit in the final form of the book for a special purpose apparently related to the author's ideology.[61] Some would disagree with this contention,[62] but a close reading of these chapters provides overwhelming support. A discussion of the composition is, therefore, in order before we turn to examine the ideology.

In the case of Neh. 8, few doubt that it originally belonged with Ezra 7–10.[63] The dating system in Neh. 8 fits with Ezra 7–10,[64] and Ezra is one of the central figures in Neh. 8 even though it is located in the middle of the Nehemiah narrative, whereas the single reference to Nehemiah (Neh. 8.9) is normally treated as a later insertion.[65] The use of the first person for Ezra in Ezra 7–10 and the use of the third person in Neh. 8 may lead one to separate Neh. 8 from Ezra 7–10. However, this change in person has been explained persuasively: Ezra is referred to using the third person in Neh. 8 to avoid confusion with Nehemiah, who occurs before and after the chapter.[66] This being so, scholarly debate is now chiefly concerned with the original location of Neh. 8 within Ezra 7–10.[67]

Neh. 9, on the other hand, is unlikely to have originated in the Ezra material, and thus was originally separate from Neh. 8.

Some scholars have argued that Neh. 9 was originally part of the Ezra material, treating both Neh. 8 and 9 together as one unit, and presuming that they were

---

61. Among those in support of this position are Norman H. Snaith, 'The Date of Ezra's Arrival in Jerusalem', *ZAW* 63 (1951), pp. 53–66, esp. pp. 64–65; Kellermann, *Nehemia*, pp. 90–92; McCarthy, 'Covenant and Law in Chronicles-Nehemiah', pp. 25–44; Clines, *Ezra, Nehemiah, Esther*, p. 181; Williamson, *Ezra and Nehemiah*, pp. 42–43; and Grabbe, *Ezra–Nehemiah*, pp. 53–54. The fact that these three chapters were combined into one unit may also be confirmed by the literary device called 'repetitive resumption' at the beginning of Neh. 11, showing that the narrative beginning with Neh. 7 continues in Neh. 11. See Williamson, *Ezra, Nehemiah*, pp. 268, 283, 344.

62. A few scholars do not find any heterogeneous nature among those chapters and believe that they reflect a genuine historical context. See, for example, Y. Kaufmann, *History of the Religion of Israel; IV: From the Babylonian Captivity to the End of Prophecy* (trans. C.W. Efroymson; New York: KTAV, 1977), pp. 638–49; J.S. Wright, *The Date of Ezra's Coming to Jerusalem*, p. 26.

63. Cf. Williamson, *Ezra, Nehemiah*, p. 283.

64. I.e., the dates for day and month are numbered (e.g., Ezra 8.31; Neh. 8.1). This contrasts with the way months are named in most of the book of Nehemiah (e.g., Neh. 1.1; 2.1; 6.15).

65. Cf. Rudolph, *Esra und Nehemia*, p. 148; Blenkinsopp, *Ezra–Nehemiah*, p. 288. More references and discussion related to this can be found in the next section.

66. Williamson, *Ezra and Nehemiah*, p. 24.

67. Although certain scholars locate Neh. 8 after Ezra 9, most scholars argue that its original place was after either Ezra 8 or Ezra 10. For a detailed discussion, see Williamson, *Ezra, Nehemiah*, pp. 283–86 and 308–309, where he offers a scholarly survey on this issue and supports Torrey, who initially claimed that Neh. 8 originally stood immediately after Ezra 8.

interrupted by Neh. 1–7.[68] This argument is untenable, however. Above all, as noted by Williamson, seeing Neh. 9 as the sequel to Neh. 8 implies that the events in Neh. 9 should precede those of Ezra 9, since it is widely accepted that Neh. 8 originally followed Ezra 8 (thus, Ezra 8 → Neh. 8 → Neh. 9 → Ezra 9).[69] This order obviously engenders an awkward situation, for the separation from foreigners takes place in Neh. 9, but has not yet happened in Ezra 9.[70]

It is true that there are linguistic affinities between Neh. 9 and the Ezra material, as seen in the references to 'separating themselves from foreigners' or 'the seed of Israel' in both (Neh. 9.2; cf. Ezra 9.1-2). These affinities, however, are confined only to Neh. 9.1-5,[71] and not to the remaining substantial part of the chapter (9.6-37). The prayer in Neh. 9.6-37, which is theologically consistent and coherently structured, is normally regarded as a source independent of verses 1-5.[72]

The argument that Neh. 9 is not part of the Ezra material is also supported by the contention that its compositional date preceded the time of Ezra, who was responsible for the Ezra material. According to scholarly analysis, there are numerous indications to show a close correlation in vocabulary, notions, and historical settings between the prayer in Neh. 9 and other literature composed *before*, rather than around or shortly after, the time of Ezra.[73] In the light of this, therefore, we conclude

68.   E.g., Johannes Geißler, *Die literarischen Beziehungen der Esramemoiren insbesondere zur Chronik und den hexateuchischen Quellschriften* (Chemnitz: Pickenhahn, 1899); E. Sellin, *Geschichte des israelitisch-jüdischen Volkes* (Leipzig: Quelle-Meyer, 1932), p. 140; Clines, *Ezra, Nehemiah, Esther*, pp. 10, 180–81.

69.   Williamson, *Ezra, Nehemiah*, pp. 308–309.

70.   Williamson adds that the absence of Ezra in Neh. 9 lends evidence to the notion that Neh. 8 and 9 are independent sources (*Ezra, Nehemiah*, p. 309). Grabbe also speculates, from the sudden disappearance of Ezra and Nehemiah in Neh. 9, that 'this episode is separate from the main Ezra and Nehemiah traditions' (*Ezra–Nehemiah*, p. 54). However, unlike others in the text above, these arguments are somewhat weak because the LXX has the word Εσδρας in 9.6 and in the light of Clines's argument that the ceremony described in Neh. 9 arose from a popular reaction to the law and was led by the Levites, implying that it was not necessary for Ezra to lead it. Cf. Clines, *Ezra, Nehemiah, Esther*, pp. 189–90.

71.   Thus, it has been suggested that Neh. 9.1-5 originally stood somewhere within Ezra 9–10. Observing the awkward connection between the joyful festival at the end of Neh. 8 and a sudden request for fasting and confession of sins in Neh. 9, Rudolph and Williamson both locate this fragment after Ezra 10, while Ahlemann argues that it was originally placed between Ezra 10.15 and 16. Cf. Rudolph, *Esra und Nehemia*, pp. 153–55; Frieder Ahlemann, 'Zur Esra Quelle', *ZAW* 59 (1942–43), pp. 77–98, esp. p. 89; Williamson, *Ezra, Nehemiah*, pp. 309–10.

72.   R. Rendtorff, 'Nehemiah 9: An Important Witness of Theological Reflection', in M. Cogan *et al.* (eds.), *Tehillah le-Moshe: Biblical and Judaic Studies in Honor of Moshe Greenberg* (Winona Lake: Eisenbrauns, 1997), pp. 111–17.

73.   Except for Martin Rehm, 'Nehemiah 9', *BZ* N.F. 1 (1957), pp. 59–69, who ascribes the compositional date of the prayer to the time of Nehemiah, most scholars agree with the book of an early date for the prayer in the chapter: e.g., the late seventh century BCE (Welch); the exilic period (Williamson); the early Persian period (Chrostowski, Rendsburg, Tollington, Boda). Cf. A.C. Welch, 'The Source of Nehemiah ix', *ZAW* 47 (1929), pp. 130–37; *idem*, 'The Share of North Israel in the Restoration of the Temple Worship', *ZAW* 48 (1930), pp. 175–87, esp. p. 177; H.G.M. Williamson, 'Structure and Historiography in Nehemiah 9', in Moshe Goshen-Gottstein (ed.), *Proceedings of the Ninth World Congress of Jewish Studies; Panel Session: Bible Studies and*

that the chapter must have been an independent source and did not stem from the Ezra material.[74]

As far as the origin and setting of Neh. 10 are concerned, no view has reigned unchallenged,[75] but it has widely been agreed that the chapter has close connections with Neh. 13 in terms of subject matter, though not of style.[76] This implies that Neh. 10 was not originally part of the Ezra material which includes Neh. 8, nor was it originally composed together with Neh. 9.

In summary, regardless of the exact origin of each chapter, none has a common origin. What is of significance is the fact that these diverse materials have been put together here. Some have argued that the present displacement took place accidentally through a scribal error.[77] However, more credible is the notion that the three chapters were deliberately assembled and carefully structured, as can be seen in their pattern of arrangement: proclamation of the law (Neh. 8) → confession (Neh. 9) → renewal of commitment to the covenant (Neh. 10).[78] It is highly likely that the author scrupulously arranged these chapters in their final form to present the climax of the reformational work on the basis of his ideology.[79] Thus, an examination of Neh. 8–10 may provide the best opportunity in E–N to detect the author's ideology.

Ancient Near East, Jerusalem 1988 (Jerusalem: Magnes, 1988), pp. 117–32; Waldemar Chrostowski, 'An Examination of Conscience by God's People as Exemplified in Neh. 9.6-37', *BZ* n.s. 34 (1990), pp. 253–61; Rendsburg, 'The Northern Origin of Nehemiah 9', *Biblica* 72, pp. 348–66; Janet E. Tollington, *Tradition and Innovation in Haggai and Zechariah 1–8* (JSOTSup, 150; Sheffield: JSOT Press, 1993); Mark J. Boda, *Praying the Tradition: The Origin and Use of Tradition in Nehemiah 9* (Berlin and New York: Walter de Gruyter, 1999).

74. For the same conclusion, see also Galling, *Die Bücher der Chronik, Esra und Nehemia*, p. 239; Coggins, *Ezra and Nehemiah*, p. 118; Rendtorff, 'Nehemiah 9', p. 112; Grabbe, *Ezra–Nehemiah*, pp. 55–56.

75. Among influential earlier views on the chapter are those of A. Bertholet, *Die Bücher Esra und Nehemia* (KHAT; Tübingen: Mohr, 1902) and Schaeder, *Esra der Schreiber*, pp. 5–26, who both ascribed Neh. 10 to the Nehemiah Memoir; A.C. Welch, 'The Share of North Israel', *ZAW* 48 (1930), pp. 175–87, who regarded it as a programme for restoring identity to a Jewish community in great confusion, a programme which was presented during the exilic period; and Alfred Jepsen, 'Nehemia 10', *ZAW* 66 (1954), pp. 87–106, who compared the list in the chapter with that contained in E–N and concluded that it must have been written before Nehemiah, thus denying any connection between the chapter and Neh. 13.

76. The similarities in subject matter between these two chapters have been observed by many scholars. For a useful summary, see Mowinckel, *Studien III*, pp. 142–55; Williamson, *Ezra, Nehemiah*, pp. 325–31. On the other hand, for a study of stylistic similarities between them, see Bertholet, *Die Bücher Esra und Nehemia*, p. 76. His view has been criticized by numerous scholars, however. E.g., Torrey, *Ezra Studies*, p. 246; Hölscher, 'Die Bücher Esra und Nehemia', pp. 545–46; Rudolph, *Esra und Nehemia*, p. 173.

77. Cf. Torrey, *Composition*, pp. 29–34; Rudolph, *Esra und Nehemia*, pp. xxii–xxiii; Paul P. Saydon, 'Literary Criticism of the Old Testament: Old Problems and New Ways of Solution', *Sacra Pagina* I (1951), pp. 316–24.

78. Kellermann, *Nehemia*, pp. 90–92, finds this pattern in Ezra 9–10; 2 Chron. 15.1-18; 29–31; 34.29–35.19. Cf. Williamson, *Ezra, Nehemiah*, pp. 275–76.

79. E.g., Williamson, *Ezra, Nehemiah*, p. xxxiv.

5.2.2.2 *Ideological Findings of Nehemiah 8–10*
(a) *Nehemiah 8*

Since Neh. 8 originally belonged with the Ezra material, it is difficult to distinguish between Ezra's and the author's contribution. Nonetheless, a close reading of the text as it stands reveals some distinctive ideological characteristics in the redactional material.

Firstly, the redactor tends to place emphasis on the *people*. In this chapter, they are depicted as those who took the initiative for the assembly: that is, they requested the reading of the law at the peak of the process of restoration (v. 1), not Ezra who was under obligation to read it (cf. Ezra 7.10, 25).

This emphasis on the initiative of the people may also be reinforced by the structure of the chapter. It consists of two sections (vv. 1-12 and vv. 13-18), and each section begins with the same verb, אסף ('to gather'). What is of note here is that the Niphal form, which frequently produces a reflexive meaning,[80] is used in both opening verses (ויאספו; vv. 1, 13). This allows us to translate it as 'they gathered *themselves* together', implying that the assembly was not prompted by the leaders but voluntarily performed by the people.[81] The verb is repeated again at the opening verse of the following section (Neh. 9.1), thus starting all three of the sections which speak of covenant renewal in Neh. 8–10.[82] On the basis of this observation, it may be said that it was a spontaneous gathering of the people that resulted in the reading of the law (8.1-12), the celebrating of the festival of tabernacles (8.13-18), and the repentance of sins and the making of a covenant (9.1–10.39).

Since this chapter was originally part of the Ezra material, where the focus is usually on Ezra's actions, this tendency to stress the role of the people is especially striking,[83] and it is probable that the description was a redactional change made by the author who adapted the original Ezra material. It displays one key aspect of his ideology: an emphasis on the common people.

Another feature of this chapter is its emphasis on the unity of the whole community, and their cooperative relationship. Since the chapter deals with the reading of the law, it is natural for both the reader, Ezra, and the audience, the people, to be present. However, the author appears to be trying to show that the reading was communal. For example, he painstakingly lists the names of thirteen people who stood up beside Ezra (v. 4).[84] As Williamson points out, these were probably leading

---

80. GKC, §51c. The following כאיש אחד in verse 1 makes a passive sense improbable.

81. Williamson, *Ezra, Nehemiah*, p. 287, also affirms that 'the initiative for the gathering is attributed to the people'.

82. For this division of Neh. 8–10, see Throntveit, *Ezra–Nehemiah*, pp. 94–111, where he divides these chapters into three sections: (1) 7.73b–8.12, Scene One: Joyous Renewal; (2) 8.13-18, Scene Two: Festive Renewal; and (3) 9.1–10.39, Scene Three: Covenant Renewal. See also Eskenazi, *Age of Prose*, p. 96; R.B. Dillard and Tremper Longman III, *An Introduction to the Old Testament* (Grand Rapids: Zondervan Publishing House, 1994), p. 179.

83. This feature is particularly distinctive when compared with 1 Esdras and Josephus where the efforts of the leaders (Zerubbabel, Ezra and Nehemiah) are glorified. Cf. Eskenazi, 'Current Perspectives on Ezra–Nehemiah', p. 74.

84. Due to a few textual uncertainties, there exist many theories on the exact number of the names in the list. Cf. Keil, *Ezra, Nehemiah, and Esther*, p. 229; Rudolph, *Esra und Nehemia*, p. 146;

members of the laity rather than clerics, who are normally designated as priests or Levites elsewhere.[85] Williamson argues that they are mentioned here to add weight to Ezra's authority. This may be true, but it is perhaps more likely that their inclusion was motivated by the author's aspiration to show that the whole group of people were taking part and cooperating in the restoration work.

The insertion of the phrase נחמיה הוא התרשׁתא ('Nehemiah who was the governor') in verse 9 is also in all likelihood caused by this desire to show unity. The phrase is widely believed to be a redactional addition,[86] but why was it inserted? There have been several different responses,[87] but it may be agreed that this insertion was less motivated by a desire for historical accuracy than by a wish to create, for this epochal event, a *cooperative* image of the two leaders, who respectively represent both the sacred (Ezra) and secular realms (Nehemiah).[88]

In addition to the leaders of the lay people (v. 4) and Nehemiah the governor (v. 9), the author of Neh. 8 embraces the Levites, mentioning them several times in the chapter (vv. 7, 9, 11, 13) and the people, as well. The references to the people are particularly notable. They are qualified by *all* (thus, כל־העם; 'all the people') in most of the references (vv. 1, 3, 5 [×3], 6, 9, 11, 12, 13, 17).[89] This is in significant

---

A.H.J. Gunneweg, *Nehemia* (KAT, 19.2; Gütersloh: Gerd Mohn, 1987), p. 109. For a defence of the Hebrew text as given without emendations, see Williamson, *Ezra, Nehemiah*, p. 278.

85.   Williamson, *Ezra, Nehemiah*, pp. 288–89. His view is shared with scholars such as Fensham, *Ezra and Nehemiah*, pp. 216–17, and Blenkinsopp, *Ezra–Nehemiah*, p. 286. On the other hand, without giving any evidence, others speculate they are priests. See Keil, *Ezra, Nehemiah, and Esther*, p. 229; Kidner, *Ezra & Nehemiah*, p. 105.

86.   That a singular verb precedes a plural subject is common in the Hebrew sentence: e.g., Neh. 2.19; 9.4. Cf. GKC, §145o; Carl Brokelmann, *Hebräische Syntax* (Neukirchen: Neukirchener Verlag, 1956), p. 51. This rule may not be applicable here, however. It is impossible for the Levites to be the subject of verse 9, since the following verse (v. 10) begins with a singular verb (ויאמר). This is also confirmed by the location of the Levites in verse 11, where the subject הלוים is placed in the beginning to *contrast* it with the subject of verse 10. If so, then two possibilities for the subject of verse 10 – Nehemiah or Ezra – are left, but in the light of the content of the chapter, Ezra must be its subject. Cf. Williamson, *Ezra, Nehemiah*, p. 279; Blenkinsopp, *Ezra–Nehemiah*, p. 284. Therefore, we may well conclude that the phrase 'Nehemiah who was the governor' in verse 9 is a later addition.

87.   For example, Blenkinsopp, *Ezra–Nehemiah*, p. 54, argues that the compiler intentionally made Ezra and Nehemiah contemporaries in the text to equate Ezra's partial success with Nehemiah's success. For a brief summary of the theological reason for that insertion, see Shaver, 'Ezra and Nehemiah: On the Theological Significance of Making them Contemporaries', pp. 76–86.

88.   Some have argued that Nehemiah was not only a lay person but also a eunuch, on the grounds that he could not enter the temple (cf. Neh. 6.10ff) and was present before the queen (Neh. 2.6). This is also supported by LXX[B.S]. Cf. Batten, *Ezra and Nehemiah*, p. 45; W. Bayer, *Die Memoiren des Statthalters Nehemia* (Speyer a. Rh: Pilger Druckerei, 1937), p. 76; A.T. Olmstead, *History of Palestine and Syria to the Macedonian Conquest* (New York: Charles Scribner's Sons, 1931), p. 588; Myers, *Ezra–Nehemiah*, pp. lxxvii and 96. For a useful summary of the discussion involved, see Edwin M. Yamauchi, 'Was Nehemiah the Cupbearer a Eunuch?', *ZAW* 92 (1980), pp. 130–42, who, after a thorough examination of the arguments, concludes they are untenable. Williamson, *Ezra, Nehemiah*, p. 174, also disagrees that Nehemiah was a eunuch, since Haman, who was not a eunuch (cf. Est. 7.8), also had access to the queen.

89.   Except only two references in verses 7, 16.

contrast to simple expressions ('the people') in the original sources attributed to Ezra or Nehemiah (cf. Ezra 8.15; 9.1; Neh. 4.6, 13; 5.1, 13, etc.), suggesting that the word כל was intentionally added to show the participation of the *whole* people in the event. This intention is also alluded to in other expressions: e.g., כאיש אחד ('as one man', v. 1) used to emphasize oneness (cf. Judg. 20.8; 1 Sam. 11.7), and מאיש ועד־אשה (both men and women', v. 2; cf. v. 3), a rare expression in the Old Testament, showing that *women* are also a necessary component of the new community.[90]

This ideology which embraces all groups of people in the community is not confined to the congregation who are gathering in the square before the Water Gate. They are requested to share their joy with 'any who have nothing ready' (v. 10) and to celebrate the Feast of Tabernacles not only in Jerusalem but everywhere in Judah (v. 15).

The emphasis on unity and cooperation between all tiers of people is clearly demonstrated in the accounts which show everyone working together and participating positively: Ezra brings and reads the law (vv. 2-3); the thirteen leaders of the laity participate and cooperate in the restoration work (v. 4); Levites help the people to understand and explicate the meaning of the text (vv. 7-8); Nehemiah encourages and admonishes the people (v. 9); and the people ask Ezra to bring the law, listen to it carefully, rejoice when the words are understood, and put it into practice as advised (vv. 1-18). Over and over again, the text portrays cooperation and a unified relationship between the social classes.

Finally, the chapter also reveals the author's opinion of the prevailing religious circumstances. On several grounds we can claim that he was dissatisfied with the religious status quo. For example, with regard to keeping the Feast of Booths, he claims that 'from the days of Jeshua the son of Nun to that day the people of Israel had not done so' (v. 17). This assertion seems strange and somewhat exaggerated, for mention is made of the regular celebration of the festival in several other texts (e.g., Judg. 21.19; 1 Sam. 1.3; 1 Kgs 8.2, 65; 2 Chron. 7.8-10; 8.13; Ezra 3.4).[91] The claim can only be understood if those earlier celebrations are being written off as inadequate in some respect, and so the comment becomes comprehensible as an expression of the author's discontent with the conventional observance of festivals, and might imply criticism of the clerical group who had led the previous festivals.

Another example of the author's discontent with current religious practices is found in his emphasis on the importance of making the people 'understand' (בין) the law.[92] The message of the chapter as a whole is clear and simple: when the people *understand* the meaning of the law, they experience great joy and determine to follow holy and sharing lives (v. 12). The implication is that they never had the opportunity to understand the profound meaning of the law prior to this occasion. We may conclude, therefore, that, in addition to having a strong interest in the

---

90. This verse (v. 2) may also include children or younger members, if we follow Ackroyd and Williamson on כל מבין לשמע. Cf. Ackroyd, *I & II Chronicles, Ezra, Nehemiah*, p. 293; Williamson, *Ezra, Nehemiah*, p. 288.

91. Cf. Grabbe, *Ezra–Nehemiah*, p. 54.

92. The word בין ('to understand') recurs several times in this chapter (vv. 2, 3, 9, 12).

common people and in unity and cooperation between the social classes, the author was also most likely a person who found the religious status quo unsatisfactory for some reason.

(b) *Nehemiah 9 and 10*
The ideologies evident in Neh. 8 are also to be found, though less obviously, in Neh. 9 and 10.

The author's emphasis on the public rather than their leaders is reflected in these chapters, too. For example, Neh. 10.35 reports that lots were cast in connection with the wood offering. This lot-casting practice was a common cultic affair and was normally performed in the Old Testament tradition, under priestly supervision (Lev. 16.8-10; 1 Chron. 24.5, 7, 31; 25.8, 9; 26.13, 14, etc.),[93] or by leaders (Josh. 14.2; 18.10; 1 Sam. 10.19-20, etc.). It is striking, then, that this verse refers to the *people* casting lots. This peculiarity, however, is understandable if we read the passage in the light of the author's broader attitude to the public, which has a somewhat 'demo-cratic' edge.

The author most likely inserted the prayer of Neh. 9.6-37 into the text because he wanted to emphasize the *unity* of the whole group of people. On the face of it, it seems incongruous that the author should have included this material, which differs from his own ideological perspective on Persia, in such a crucially important con-text.[94] The incongruity has, indeed, been noted by scholars, although no satisfactory explanation has been offered.[95] Before commenting on that question, however, let us first note that the prayer otherwise corresponds closely to the social perspectives which we have already identified as characteristic of E–N. First, it singles out the previous rulers (and, interestingly, the priests) as particularly responsible for the present plight of the people (vv. 34ff). Secondly, though, it regards that plight as the plight of the whole people. Indeed, the interest of the prayer overall is to por-tray the history of the people, and it makes no attempt to impose distinctions or to exculpate any group.

As regards the attitude to Persia, it is important to observe that blame for the current situation is in no way attributed to the foreign kings, who are explicitly set over the people as part of the divine punishment (v. 37). Equally, there is no sugges-tion that that power is being abused or is undeserved. The prayer is not anti-Persian, then, and is distinctive simply because it portrays Persian rule as a continuation of punishment, rather than a sign that the punishment has ended. There is nothing here

93. Cf. Williamson, *Ezra, Nehemiah*, p. 346.
94. While E–N is generally full of favourable attitude toward the Persian authorities, the prayer here seems to harbour resentment toward them, especially in verses 36-37 ('Behold, we are slaves this day; in the land that thou gavest to our fathers to enjoy its fruit and its good gifts, behold, we are slaves. And its rich yield goes to the kings whom thou hast set over us because of our sins; they have power also over our bodies and over our cattle at their pleasure, and we are in great distress').
95. Cf. Rudolph, *Esra und Nehemia*, pp. 156–57; Coggins, *Ezra and Nehemiah*, p. 118; Williamson, *Ezra and Nehemiah*, p. 26; P.R. Ackroyd, 'Rigorism and Openness in the Theology of the Persian (Achaemenian) Period', in *The Chronicler in His Age* (JSOTSup, 101; Sheffield: JSOT Press, 1991), pp. 360–78, esp. p. 369.

that would be objectionable to a supporter of Persian policy. Indeed, it is important to note that, immediately following the prayer, relief is sought through a public commitment, by the whole people, to the laws codified in the covenant – a procedure which, as we have seen, would certainly have met with Persian approval.

The prayer in Neh. 9, then, is completely in line with E–N's interest in the whole people, its suspicion of leaders and its emphasis on communal action. If it was originally a separate composition, as usually supposed, that fact may explain its distinctive understanding of the current situation as continuing divine punishment, but it expresses no criticism of the Persians or of imperial policy which might have proved unacceptable to the redactor.

The author's strong belief in unity can perhaps also be observed in the list which constitutes the first section of Neh. 10 (10.2-28). Most scholars again conclude that this list was interpolated into its present place: (1) because of the reverse ordering of signatories between 10.1b (laity – Levites – priests) and verses 2-28 (priests – Levites – laity); (2) because of the awkward repetition of some phrases in verses 1 and 2;[96] and (3) because of its interruption of a consecutive narrative which begins at 10.1 and continues until 10.29-30.[97] As regards the origin of this list, some argue that it is a genuine record of the signatories, whereas others consider it to be the author's own compilation.[98] Whatever the case, I believe that the author interpolated it here to emphasize the more general comment in verses 29-30, which declared that the whole community was unified in signing the pledge, by specifying the representatives of the community.[99]

Lastly, we can perhaps also find some evidence of the author's dissatisfaction with the religious status quo in Neh. 10, albeit only by implication. The last sentence of the chapter summarizes all the obligations of verses 32-39 by saying, 'we will not neglect the house of our God'. On the basis that one does not seek to remedy non-existent problems, this commitment might well be taken to suggest that the writer considered that there had been neglect in the past, a view consonant with the explicit criticism of the priesthood by the prayer in the preceding chapter.

---

96. Viz., the singular form על החתום (literarily, 'on the sealed'; i.e., 'on the seal') in verse 1 and the plural form על החתומים (literarily, 'on the sealed things'; i.e., 'on the seals') in verse 2.

97. Cf. Williamson, *Ezra, Nehemiah*, pp. 325–26; Blenkinsopp, *Ezra–Nehemiah*, p. 311.

98. Favouring the former view, Rudolph, *Esra und Nehemia*, pp. 173–74, presents five grounds as evidence, including (1) the reference to Nehemiah, who led the reformation recorded in Neh. 13 following the pledge, while no mention of Ezra is made, and (2) the reference to Zedekiah in verse 2, who is an *unknown* figure to us, thus suggesting that the list was not fabricated. Disagreeing with Rudolph, Williamson, *Ezra, Nehemiah*, pp. 327–30, argues that it is unnecessary for Ezra to be mentioned in the list since he was the instigator of the proceedings, and that the name of Zedekiah could be derived from the word 'Zadok the Scribe' (p. 327). He suggests that the author probably expanded the list on the basis of verse 29.

99. The fact that the whole community participated in this crucial event is confirmed by the subsequent accounts in vv. 31-40, which report that the covenant is being made by *us* (the Hebrew text repeatedly uses the first-person plural form: בנתינו, נקח, and עלינו), thus denoting the whole community referred to in verse 29.

5.2.2.3 *Summary*

So far, we have explored the ideology of E–N by using Neh. 8–10 as a case study. Originally, these three chapters were of independent origin: (1) Neh. 8 originated in the Ezra material; (2) Neh. 9 was composed during the early Persian period; and (3) Neh. 10 was connected to the Nehemiah Memoir. There is no doubt that these heterogeneous materials were intentionally placed together by the author in this sequence to describe the climax of the restoration work. Since he gathered and arranged them in this order, they provide a window on to the author's ideology. Through these chapters, we have identified three major ideological concerns: (1) decentralization of power; (2) an emphasis on unity and cooperation among the social classes; and (3) dissatisfaction with the religious status quo.

5.2.3 *Ideology in Ezra–Nehemiah*

After identifying three principal socio-political concerns in Neh. 8–10, we can finish by briefly indicating the extent to which each is characteristic of E–N as a whole.

We begin by focusing on the concern with decentralization of power, which leads E–N to emphasize the public as a whole, rather than its leadership.[100] Interestingly, in most instances where crucial events are described, such as the ceremonies of the temple dedication (Ezra 6.16-18) and the passover (Ezra 6.19-22), the leaders are not mentioned. Their status is played down, moreover, even when the context requires that they be mentioned. In the list of returning exiles, for instance, they are named without titles (Ezra 2.2).[101] In contrast, as pointed out by Japhet, the public play such a significant role that they are present in all important matters, even in the appointment of the Levites as overseers of the building work (Ezra 3.8).[102] This ideology certainly seems to characterize E–N as a whole.

Secondly, an ideology of unity or cooperation among social classes is also present throughout E–N. It is widely agreed that, in the post-exilic period, there were a number of class struggles: between returnees and remainees, between rich and poor, and between priests and Levites.[103] Curiously, little mention is made in E–N of these conflicts, and unity between the classes is emphasized instead. For example, while there is a sharp distinction between the people of Judah and their opponents called עם הארץ ('the people of the land'),[104] there is no dichotomy between any *true Israel* and *untrue Israel* within the people of Judah. Likewise, rather than endeavouring to recognize the existence of two groups of Israelites, i.e., the returned

---

100. Cf. Japhet, 'Sheshbazzar and Zerubbabel', p. 83, examines historical reasons for the process of decentralization of power to the people (pp. 87ff); Eskenazi, 'Current Perspectives on E–N', p. 74, also says 'E–N shuns the heroic model of history'.

101. Cf. Japhet, 'Sheshbazzar and Zerubbabel', p. 83.

102. Japhet, 'Sheshbazzar and Zerubbabel', p. 83. For more examples, see pp. 82–86.

103. Cf. Schultz, 'The Political Tensions Reflected in Ezra–Nehemiah', pp. 221–43; Berquist, *Judaism in Persia's Shadow*, pp. 133–40; McNutt, *Reconstructing the Society of Ancient Israel*, pp. 184, 200–202; and Grabbe, 'The Persian and Hellenistic Periods', p. 406. This position is widely accepted except by a few scholars, who argue that the land was the empire's and thus a class struggle between the returnees and the remainees over land rights could not have taken place. See Hoglund, 'The Achaemenid Context', pp. 59–60; Williamson, 'Exile and After', pp. 255–60.

104. For a discussion of the identity of עם הארץ, see section 6.1.2.2 below.

exiles and those who remained in the land, the author seeks to present both as *one* Israel by legitimating the people who were not exiled. This idea is shown in several places in E–N, but perhaps most clearly in the list of returnees in Ezra 2, which purposely amalgamates those who returned (vv. 3-20) with those who remained (vv. 21-35).[105]

Finally, dissatisfaction with the current religious status quo is also reflected throughout the book. Two points suffice for demonstration. First, there are a number of strong challenges to the religious leaders to take the lead in holy living (e.g., Ezra 9.1; Neh. 13.4-9, 28). Second, similar to Neh. 8–10, the law is highlighted throughout E–N with the same emphasis on reading and teaching it, because knowledge of it would prevent people from going astray: when the people hear the law, it leads them to separate themselves from the mixed multitude (Neh. 13.1-3). This can be regarded as an implicit criticism of existing religious practices, implying that the leaders had neglected their duties to teach the law and guide the people's spiritual lives.

In conclusion, we hold that the author infused E–N with these three ideologies: (1) decentralization of power; (2) unity and cooperation between social classes; and (3) dissatisfaction with the current religious situation.

5.3 *Conclusion*

We now have two clues for resolving the authorship issue. From an examination of the author's political perspective and the ideology in E–N, we have concluded that he is most likely to have been a person who held some stake in the success of imperial policy, and who may therefore have been sponsored by Persia. He also held particular views on (1) decentralization of power; (2) unity and cooperation among social classes; and (3) problems with the religious status quo.

We shall now turn to an examination of who – priests or Levites – were more likely to fit this description in the days of E–N's composition.

105. Japhet, 'People and Land in the Restoration Period', pp. 103–17.

Chapter 6

LEVITICAL AUTHORSHIP

In seeking to assess the likely correspondence between priestly or Levitical groups and the criteria uncovered in the last chapter, we have again to face the difficulty that our evidence is very limited. At this stage, the constraints are imposed principally by the biblical material, and by the impossibility of cross-checking most of the information which it offers.

6.1 *Persian Support*

6.1.1 *Preliminary Assumptions*
As we have seen, there is evidence to suggest that the author of E–N may have come from a group that had the support of the empire during the post-exilic period. Which of the two potential originators of E–N,[1] the priestly or the Levitical group, is known to have had Persian support?

Those familiar with a widely known theory, put forward particularly by Otto Plöger and Paul Hanson,[2] may answer immediately that it was the priests.[3] Though differing on certain points, Plöger and Hanson both agree that an analysis of post-exilic Jewish literature shows there to have been two major trends of thought within the post-exilic Jewish community.[4] According to them, parties representing each

---

1.   See section 2.3.
2.   Otto Plöger, *Theokratie und Eschatologie* (WMANT, 2; Neukirchen–Vluyn: Neukirchener Verlag, 1959), esp. pp. 129–42; Hanson, *The Dawn of Apocalyptic*, pp. 71–77 and 209–79; *idem*, 'Israelite Religion in the Early Postexilic Period', in P.D. Miller *et al.* (eds.), *Ancient Israelite Religion*, pp. 485–508. Their arguments (especially Plöger's) have been developed or modified by a number of scholars: e.g., Klaus Baltzer, 'Das Ende des Staates Juda und die Messias-Frage', in R. Rendtorff *et al.* (eds.), *Studien zur Theologie der alttestamentlichen Überlieferungen: Festschrift G. von Rad* (Neukirchen: Neukirchener Verlag, 1961), pp. 33–43; Kellermann, *Nehemia*, pp. 147ff and 174ff; Odil H. Steck, 'Das Problem theologischer Stromungen in nachexilischer Zeit', *EvTh* 28 (1968), pp. 445–58; Martin Hengel, *Judaism and Hellenism* (London: SCM Press, 1974); and Gunneweg, *Geschichte Israels*, pp. 140ff.
3.   See, for example, Gottwald, *The Hebrew Bible*, p. 509; Grabbe, *Judaism*, pp. 74–75.
4.   According to political and ideological perspectives preserved within each book, they distinguish between Isaiah 24–27, Zechariah 12–14, Joel and Daniel, and the Priestly Writing and the Chronicler's work (*Plöger's* division), or between Isaiah 56–66 and Zechariah 9–14, and Ezekiel, Haggai, Zechariah 1–8 and the Chronicler's work (*Hanson's* division), characterizing the former group of literature as eschatological and the latter as theocratic.

line of thought retained their own perspectives regarding restoration and developed opposing attitudes to each other with regard to the political reality of Persian rule.

To one party, the current status quo was an optimal environment, because the theocracy which it had long pursued was now believed to have been realized, as shown in Neh. 12.44–13.3.[5] Thus, Persian rule was regarded as desirable and worth supporting. Naturally, an eschatological dimension was completely absent in the ideology of this group.[6]

The other group, however, harboured discontent with their current situation; they believed themselves to have been subordinated and oppressed, and any change seemed a distant prospect. Thus, they eventually developed a strong eschatological belief which looked forward to the day when God would intervene in history to deliver and vindicate them and, as final judge, punish the unjust and reward the righteous.

The scholars who favour this dichotomy have designated the first group as *theocrats* or *hierocrats* and the second as *eschatologists* or *visionaries*. Who, then, belonged to the first group, the group that are believed to have obtained the imperial backing? Plöger identifies the *theocrats* as clerics, including both priests and Levites, while Hanson believes the Levites belonged only to the second group, *visionaries*. Hanson bases his conclusion on the age-old rivalry and conflict that is thought to have existed between the Zadokite priests, who resumed their controlling power over the rebuilt temple, and the Levites (plus the Abiathar priests), who had been disenfranchised of the share allotted to them in the cult.

We note that both scholars agree that *priests* were clearly among those who obtained Persian support. Furthermore, a few biblical passages impel us to believe that it is unlikely that Levites were the beneficiaries of imperial backing. For example, if they had truly been championed by the empire, it then becomes difficult to understand a passage which states that the Levites seriously hesitated to participate in the return to Jerusalem under Ezra's leadership (cf. Ezra 8.15-19).[7]

If we accept this widely held view, it may be concluded that it was the priests, rather than the Levites, who gained the support of the empire during the post-exilic period.[8] However, there are a few further points to consider.

---

5.   The notion that the realization of theocracy can be glimpsed in Neh. 12.44–13.3 was initially presented by Rudolph (*Chronikbücher*, p. xxiii) and was followed by several scholars: e.g., Myers, 'The Kerygma of the Chronicler', pp. 259–73. This view has been critically examined by Im, *Das Davidbild in den Chronikbüchern*, pp. 164–85, who pointed out that theocracy is not completely realized. He refers to the fact that 'trotz erfüllter Prophetie und angebrochener Gottesherrschaft hören wir die Gemeinde seufzen im Gebet Esras (Esr 9) und auch im Gebet Nehemias (Neh. 9)' (p. 168). For other criticisms on Rudolph's argument, see William F. Stinespring, 'Eschatology in Chronicles', *JBL* 80 (1961), pp. 209–19, esp. p. 219; R. North, 'Theology of the Chronicler', pp. 378–79.

6.   See Plöger, *Theokratie und Eschatologie*, p. 52, who argues that 'die konkrete jüdische Gemeinde, wie sie uns vor allem in Neh. 12.44–13.3 entgegentritt, für den Chronisten so sehr das Ideal der Theokratie verwirklicht, daß es keiner eschatologischen Erwartung mehr bedarf'.

7.   Cf. de Vaux, *Ancient Israel*, p. 388; Holmgren, *Ezra & Nehemiah*, p. 152.

8.   It is debatable whether using the theory represented by Plöger and Hanson is relevant to the present discussion or not. In fact, there have been some serious challenges to this theory: e.g.,

6.1.2 *Varied Agents of the Empire*

6.1.2.1 *The Problem*

Although we generally agree with the conclusion just stated, it does not necessarily mean that E–N originated in a priestly group. While it might be undeniable that priests were sponsored by the empire in the *early* post-exilic period, the pivotal point here is whether they were also supported *when E–N was composed* (i.e., in the late fifth century BCE according to our working date[9]). Proponents of the theory outlined above tend to believe that the dichotomy distinguishing the two opposing parties characterized the whole Persian as well as the early Hellenistic periods, since quite a few books whose dates are safely ascribed to these periods appear to support these dichotomous features.[10] Hence, most advocates of the theory continue to argue that the priests had been chosen, from the very outset, to play a role as the Persian agent and that the empire was loath to change its agent.[11]

This argument is far from persuasive, however, and it seems more plausible to contend that the empire used the priests as their agents at times, but not always. One text which particularly supports this contention is Ezra 1–6, which recounts a period of temple rebuilding during which Persia used an agent other than the priests. This point requires more elaboration. Cyrus's decree, which begins the account, focused on the permission given to the Jews to rebuild the temple (Ezra 1.2-4; cf. 6.3-5).[12] As noted earlier, the issuing of this decree was based entirely on perceived advantage to the empire, which not only could claim to be providing a benefit for the

---

Williamson, 'Eschatology in Chronicles', pp. 115–54 and *Israel*, pp. 132–40, argues that such a dichotomy should be applied *within* theocratic or hierocratic circles; R.P. Carroll, 'Twilight of Prophecy or Dawn of Apocalyptic?' *JSOT* 14 (1979), pp. 3–35, doubts the relevance of the models upon which Hanson's theory depends; P.R. Davies, 'The Social World of Apocalyptic Writings', in R.E. Clements (ed.), *The World of Ancient Israel: Sociological, Anthropological and Political Perspectives Essays by Members of the Society for Old Testament Study* (Cambridge: Cambridge University Press, 1989), pp. 251–71, criticizes as naive the assumptions that acceptance of the status quo is anti-visionary and that a fringe-like book (e.g., the book of Daniel) is necessarily the product of a fringe; Grabbe, *Judaism*, pp. 109–10, points out the danger of circular reasoning; Berquist, *Judaism in Persia's Shadow*, pp. 182–84, maintains that it is ridiculous to believe that the empire allowed a true theocracy to be established; and Brooks Schramm, *The Opponents of Third Isaiah: Reconstructing the Cultic History of the Restoration* (JSOTSup, 193; Sheffield: JSOT Press, 1995), claims that the targets of Third Isaiah were abhorrent and improper forms of cultic practices, not the hierocratic priests. While saying nothing of the merits of these challenges, it should be noted that no criticism has been made of the assertion that the priests gained Persian support.

9.   See section 2.1.

10.   See n. 4 above.

11.   For example, Hanson, *The Dawn of Apocalyptic*, p. 210, says: 'the Zadokite priests [which] controlled the high priesthood from the first year of the Solomon temple down to the second century B.C.' See also Schaper, *Priester und Leviten*, pp. 162–225.

12.   There are scholars who doubt mass return from the exile and argue that the main point of the decree was to permit the rebuilding of the temple. See, for example, Noth, *The History of Israel*, p. 308, where he says that a repatriation of the exiles was not necessary for the work of rebuilding, since many people had remained in the land. In contrast, no suspicion has been cast on the rebuilding of the temple.

province, but also stood to gain an institutional centre for more effective imperial control in the future.[13]

In this situation, the empire most likely sponsored the *priests*, who were in the majority among the exiles in Babylon, because they were concerned to restore the cult by rebuilding the temple and therefore had an interest in the implementation of Persian policy, and could be considered loyal to the empire. Indeed, there are several indications in E–N which demonstrate that certain previous events related to the rebuilding work were led chiefly by the priestly group. For example, Jeshua, the *high* priest,[14] was among the leaders to have brought the exiles to Judah (Ezra 2.2). He and his fellow priests took the initiative in the work of preparing for the rebuilding of the temple, setting up the altar, making sacrifices, and laying the foundations (Ezra 3). In addition, compared with other groups recorded in the list of the returnees in Ezra 2, the number of priests is extremely large (4.289; Ezra 2.36-39). This probably indicates that the priests did not hesitate to come back to Judah, and were confident of Persian support.[15]

Had the priests continued to receive strong imperial support, one would expect to see evidence of their role and effectiveness in the subsequent accounts of temple-rebuilding (Ezra 4.1–6.16). Interestingly, however, they are not even mentioned there, except in Ezra 6.9, which is only a reference to specific priestly business. Priests, moreover, are never shown acting as a channel for dialogue with the empire. The task of the rebuilding now seems to have been entrusted to others (cf. Ezra 6.7).[16] This unexpected change is puzzling and overturns our expectation that the priests were Persian agents receiving imperial support during the period of

13. Cf. Ahlström, *The History of Ancient Palestine*, pp. 841–42.

14. Jeshua is not designated with this title ('*high* priest') in E–N, probably because of its tendency to emphasize the public rather than the leader (cf. Japhet, 'Sheshbazzar and Zerubbabel', p. 83). It is clear, however, from other texts (e.g., Hag. 1.1, 12, 14; 2.2, 4) that his position was that of high priest.

15. Rooke may object to this contention by arguing that, unlike political leaders, the priests lacked independent authority and thus never exercised civil power, mainly because the high priest Joshua is frequently placed after Zerubbabel in E–N (Ezra 2.2; 3.8; 4.3; 5.2), implying that Joshua was in a secondary position to him. Cf. Rooke, *Zadok's Heirs*, pp. 155–56. This argument seems weak, however. The order of name-listing and having authority are two different things, one not always implying the other. The people named in the lists of cited passages, rather, indicate that they were all leaders of society. In addition, the passages cited are normally regarded as portions for which the author was responsible. The second position of Joshua, a priest, may show the author's tendency to discount the role of the priests or restrict them. For a useful argument, counter Rooke who maintains that Jewish high priests were not political leaders through Israelite history until the time of the Maccabees, see C.T. Robert Hayward, 'Book Review of *Zadok's Heirs: The Role and Development of the High Priesthood in Ancient Israel*', *Biblical Interpretation* 9 (2001), pp. 227–30.

16. Again, on the basis of this fact, Rooke, *Zadok's Heirs*, pp. 152–74, esp. pp. 156–57, jumps to conclusions that the priests were not involved in things unrelated to their proper tasks and so did not exercise any secular leadership. It is, however, questionable whether the *temple-rebuilding* work is really a matter with no bearings on their own tasks. Rooke has already defined the laying of the foundation for a new altar (Ezra 3.2) as 'an occasion on which the high priest would be expected to take priority' (p. 155). Therefore, it seems more plausible to believe that the priests were no longer allowed by Persia to play a leading role in the rebuilding work.

rebuilding. This perplexing situation calls for further examination of the facts. In what follows, therefore, we shall investigate this matter in more detail, focusing on Ezra 4–6, which deals with the whole process of temple-rebuilding from beginning to end.

Ezra 4–6 is composed of two parts: (1) Ezra 4, which focuses on hindrance to the rebuilding work by 'adversaries', and (2) Ezra 5–6, which reports the completion of the temple. The account is split into two by the change of imperial policy regarding the rebuilding: the work was suddenly *stopped* (Ezra 4) and then permitted to *resume* again (Ezra 5–6).[17] Why did the Persians change their minds on this matter twice in such a short period of time? As will be shown below, the answer to this question may shed light on imperial policy toward their agents in the subjugated area.

We will look more closely at this issue by posing two questions: (1) why was the work stopped (Ezra 4)?; and (2) why was it resumed (Ezra 5–6)?

6.1.2.2 *The Cessation of Temple Building*

Ezra 4 provides the rationale for the cessation of work. According to the text, the returned exiles planned to rebuild the temple, but the plan was thwarted by opponents called עם הארץ ('the people of the land'), who hired counsellors against the Jews to frustrate the work (vv. 4-5). Presumably, the accusation that the counsellors made against the Jews was accepted by the Persian leadership from the days of Cyrus to the second year of the reign of Darius (cf. vv. 5 and 24).

Two questions immediately arise here. First, who are the people of the land? Second, why did they hinder the work and, more importantly, what did the counsellors accuse the Jewish people of? The answers to these questions may account for the reason why the work was stopped.

There have been two main opinions on the identity of the people of the land. Regarding Ezra 4.1-3 and 4.4-5 as coming from two separate source materials,[18] one group of scholars argues that עם הארץ in 4.4 cannot be identical with the adversaries of Judah and Benjamin in verse 1, who are commonly conceived of as the Samaritans or their forebears.[19] According to these scholars, עם הארץ refers rather to a particular group of Jews and this can be verified from other Jewish literature, in which the term is seldom used for foreigners.[20] Furthermore, because they take

---

17. Bright, *A History of Israel*, p. 366, approaches this matter from an economic, rather than a political, viewpoint. He argues that the cessation of the temple work was due to a shortage in the supply of resources. His argument is likely, since the building work might have needed entailed considerable cost. Admittedly, however, it seems more reasonable to think that stopping and resuming the temple work was politically motivated; for it was not because Persia now came to be capable of supplying resources that permission for the work was again given (cf. Ezra 6).

18. This is mainly due to the opposing descriptions of the adversaries: for example, Ezra 4.1-3 describes the adversaries as those who were willing to help, whereas Ezra 4.4-5 describes the adversaries as those who bore hostility to the workers. See Coggins, *Ezra and Nehemiah*, p. 27.

19. R.J. Coggins, 'The Interpretation of Ezra IV.4', *JTS* n.s. 16 (1965), pp. 124–27; Fensham, *Ezra and Nehemiah*, p. 68; Gunneweg, *Geschichte Israels*, pp. 135–36; idem, *Esra*, p. 80; B.W. Anderson, *Understanding the Old Testament*, pp. 516–17.

20. Cf. Aharon Oppenheimer, *The 'Am ha-Aretz: A Study in the Social History of the Jewish*

the Chronicler to have been responsible for the composition of E–N, and believe that he considered the exiles alone to have represented *true* Israel, proponents of this view maintain that the people of the land must refer to the Jewish people *left behind in the land* during the exilic period. Admitting that the term had a positive connotation in some post-exilic writings,[21] they further ask why in Ezra 4.4 עם הארץ appears to describe opponents of the Jews, and have generally responded by pointing to a change of circumstances: the nationalistic עם הארץ, who resented imperial interference, came to be regarded by the Chronicler as anachronistic and an obstacle to the plan of Yahweh.[22]

This view is unpersuasive, however. First, there is no reason to presuppose that Ezra 4.1-5 is composed of two different units with two different origins. It is true that there are two episodes of opposition in Ezra 4.1-5, but the passage was most likely composed as one unit, as it is otherwise inexplicable that the people should be called 'adversaries' in 4.1, where they are still amicable and supportive of the building work.[23] This expression can be properly understood only in the light of verse 4, which mentions the subsequent hindrance of the work by the עם הארץ. This implies that the people of the land in verse 4 are treated as identical with or, at least, including those spoken of in verses 1-3.

Another major problem with this view is its assumption that the inhabitants left in the land, who had not been exiled, must be seen as opponents of the returned exiles, *ipso facto*. As we saw earlier, E–N does not distinguish between true and untrue Israel within the Jewish people, but it does dichotomize *true Israel* and *non-Jewish people*.[24] Other scholars, therefore, believe that the term עם הארץ in verse 4 must indicate *non-Jewish* people rather than a particular group within the Jewish community. Some argue that the people of the land are identified simply with the proto-Samaritans, alluded to in verses 1-3.[25] In all probability, however, the term indicates the non-Jewish inhabitants, including the Samaritans,[26] mainly because in

---

People in the Hellenistic-Roman Period (ALGHJ, 8; Leiden: Brill, 1977); A.H.J. Gunneweg, 'עם הארץ – A Semantic Revolution', *ZAW* 95 (1983), pp. 437–40.

21.   For example, they are described as those who took part in the rebuilding work and they were also closely associated with Zerubbabel, who was a central figure of the messianic movement (Hag. 2). Cf. Coggins, 'The Interpretation of Ezra IV.4', pp. 125–26.

22.   Cf. Coggins, 'The Interpretation of Ezra IV.4', pp. 125–26.

23.   Cf. Holmgren, *Ezra & Nehemiah*, p. 28.

24.   Japhet, 'People and Land in the Restoration Period', pp. 112–18. See also Williamson, *Ezra, Nehemiah*, p. 171. The force of the argument that there was a dichotomy between true Israel and untrue Israel, with the former identified with the returned exiles, seems to be weakened because of certain verses referring to the *unfaithfulness* of the exiles (e.g., Ezra 9.4; 10.6).

25.   For example, Ernst Würthwein, *Der 'amm ha' arez im Alten Testament* (Stuttgart: W. Kohlhammer, 1936), pp. 57–64, argues that the term had been used to imply the common Jewish people, but came to mean the Samaritans after they came into Judah and took over the titles and status of עם הארץ. M. Cogan, 'For We, like You, Worship your God: Three Biblical Portrayals of Samaritan Origins', *VT* 38 (1988), pp. 286–92, also regards the people of the land in Ezra 4.4 as the Samaritans in the belief that E–N reflects the struggle of the Gōlāh-community to establish the cult and thus identifies their adversaries with the Samaritans.

26.   Batten, *Ezra and Nehemiah*, pp. 125ff and 157ff; de Vaux, *Ancient Israel*, pp. 70–72; H.H. Rowley, 'The Samaritan Schism in Legend and History', in B.W. Anderson *et al.* (eds.), *Israel's*

E–N the עם הארץ is always contrasted with the whole of the people of Judah (Ezra 4.4) or the people of Israel (Ezra 9.1).[27] It thus refers to foreigners, including the non-Israelite peoples dwelling in Judah (Ezra 9.1, 2, 11; 10.2, 11; Neh. 10.31), and is simply a singular form of the term used to describe foreign nations in Neh. 9.30.[28]

We may conclude, therefore, that 'the people of the land' in Ezra 4.4, who hired counsellors to frustrate the work, are non-Jewish people dwelling in Judah, or foreigners in the neighbouring countries.[29] Of course, terms such as 'Jewish' or 'foreign' may themselves be problematic in this period, and we cannot be sure of the precise criteria which would have been used to identify either. By 'non-Jewish' in this context, then, we really mean 'perceived as non-Jewish by E–N'.

We have next to ask, of course, why this non-Jewish people chose to hinder the rebuilding work. According to the biblical accounts, they bribed the counsellors to stop the work and it seems that the accusation made against the Jews must have been accepted by Cyrus or his representatives, so that he presumably issued another official decree banning the Jews from rebuilding the temple. Knowing that such bribery was common in Persia,[30] it is easy to believe the report of this incident. Even accompanied by a bribe, however, the accusation must have been incriminating, dangerous and urgent to Persia, to the extent that Cyrus took it as a grave threat and withdrew his former decree, which had permitted and encouraged the building of the temple.

What, though, were the Jews accused of? This question is very important for an accurate understanding of the whole picture of the story presented in the text. Surprisingly, however, scholars have overlooked its importance or, at best, only scratched the surface of this matter.[31] Their conclusions have generally been merely along the lines that it is impossible 'to explain the failure to follow through on the construction of the temple until the time of Darius'.[32]

One would expect to find the answer in the subsequent narrative (Ezra 4.6ff). However, a rather bizarre story follows, one which is all the more confusing,

---

Prophetic Heritage: James Muilenburg Festschrift (New York: Harper & Brothers, 1962), pp. 208–22; Clines, *Ezra, Nehemiah, Esther*, p. 75; Japhet, 'People and Land in the Restoration Period', pp. 106–18; Williamson, *Ezra, Nehemiah*, pp. 49–50; Bruce C. Birch, *Let Justice Roll Down: The Old Testament, Ethics and Christian Life* (Louisville: Westminster/John Knox, 1991), p. 309; Grabbe, *Ezra–Nehemiah*, pp. 17–19 and 136–38.

27.   De Vaux, *Ancient Israel*, p. 72.

28.   Cf. Batten, *Ezra and Nehemiah*, p. 157; Grabbe, *Ezra–Nehemiah*, p. 18.

29.   A recent article by Stefan C. Matzal, 'The Structure of Ezra IV-VI', *VT* 50 (2000), pp. 566–68, also supports this conclusion. On the supposition that Ezra 4.4-5 should be treated as a proleptic summary for 4.6-23, he argues that the people of the land in verse 4 are sure to mean the non-Jewish adversaries who wrote a hostile letter in verse 6ff.

30.   Cf. R.N. Frye, *The Heritage of Persia* (Cleveland: World, 1963), p. 110; Josephus, *Ant.* XI.2.1.

31.   As far as I am aware, few commentators deal with this matter seriously. For example, see R.A. Bowman, 'Ezra and Nehemiah', p. 598, who says that 'the accusation is not explicit. Presumably the Chronicler (or the author of the Aramaic source) did not regard it as being as important or as relevant as those letters given in full.'

32.   Myers, *Ezra–Nehemiah*, p. 36.

because it appears out of context. The text of Ezra 4 names five Persian kings: Cyrus (v. 5), Darius (v. 5), Xerxes (v. 6), Artaxerxes (vv. 7-23), and Darius again (v. 24). Artaxerxes, in verses 7-23, is described as the king who stopped the building of the *walls* of Jerusalem, while Darius, in verse 24, reauthorized the building of the *temple*. Thus, these biblical accounts put the work of the temple-rebuilding chronologically *after* the rebuilding of the wall. If so, this means that the second temple was built in the reign of Darius II Ochus (424–405 BCE), rather than Darius I Hystaspes (522–486 BCE).[33] This interpretation, however, creates further confusion, since other sources clearly indicate that the temple was rebuilt in the time of Darius I Hystaspes.[34]

This awkward text has long been the subject of scholarly dispute. In an attempt to solve its problems, some scholars have investigated it from a historical point of view, and have reached the conclusion that it lacks any historical reliability.[35] Others have examined it from a literary point of view, and have argued that the author here used a technique, often called 'resumptive repetition', by which the preceding narrative in 4.1-5 is picked up again by repeating its wording in 4.24. On the basis of this argument, it is claimed that the narratives in 4.6-23 must have been interpolated between 4.1-5 and 4.24.[36]

If so, why did the author interpolate these out-of-context narratives in this position? One of the most persuasive explanations is that of Williamson, who argues that, because Ezra 7–Neh. 13 had already been presented in a complete form, the final editor had to find a place where the Aramaic material, currently placed in Ezra 4.6-23, could make a positive contribution to the whole context of E–N. He chose the present location hoping that the material 'would help explain and justify the apparently harsh rejection of the northerners' offer of assistance in 4.1-3 and show how that group's successors were indeed adversaries of Judah and Benjamin'.[37]

The resumptive repetition indicates redactional activity rather than simple error, and Williamson is surely correct in regarding the interpolation as something that happened intentionally, not as something that transpired haphazardly because of the author's confusion regarding the chronology of Persian kings.[38] However, his argument fails to provide a cogent reason for 4.24's separation from 4.1-5 and its location at the end, if the interpolation was intended simply to show a connection between the adversaries of 4.1-5 and 4.6-23. Instead, I believe that this structure is likely to suggest that the central narrative is sandwiched so that it would be read as

33. This proposition has been advanced by Luc Dequeker, 'Darius and Persian, and the Reconstruction of the Jewish Temple in Jerusalem (Ezra 4.24)', *Orientalia Lovaniensia Analecta* 55 (1993), pp. 67–92, esp. pp. 75–76.

34. See Japhet, 'Composition and Chronology', pp. 204–205, who discusses the difficulty in dating the reconstruction of the second temple during the time of Darius II Ochus.

35. See notes 3 and 4 in the introduction to Part III.

36. Talmon, 'Ezra and Nehemiah', pp. 317–28; Williamson, *Ezra, Nehemiah*, p. 57; Baruch Halpern, 'A Historiographic Commentary on Ezra 1–6', in W.H. Propp *et al.* (eds.), *The Hebrew Bible and Its Interpreters* (Winona Lake: Eisenbrauns), pp. 81–142, esp. p. 110.

37. Williamson, *Ezra and Nehemiah*, pp. 44–45.

38. This view has been argued by those who date E–N to a period so late that the author was confused about the chronology of the Persian kings. Cf. Bright, *A History of Israel*, pp. 396–97.

an *example* of the way in which the counsellors frustrated the work. In other words, the author probably wished to present a forceful ground for the accusation. Because he had no other material for that at hand, he most likely used the most accessible source – that of referring to a similar process of accusation – even though it dealt with different matters. If this assumption is sound, then we can find the structure of the chapter under discussion neatly organized as follows:

> vv. 1-5　　An accusation lodged
> vv. 6-23　The process of the accusation: an example
> v. 24　　　The outcome of the accusation.

In that case, we may surmise, from the parallel accounts in verses 6-23, a hint of what the Jews were accused of. According to those accounts, the Persian bureau-crats accused the Jews, who were in the middle of building the wall, of the *possibility* of rebellion. The latent logic behind this is simple: if allowed to complete the work, they would be in a position to rebel against the empire and refuse to pay taxes, or even to seek independence (vv. 12-16). The response of the royal court to this accusation is also made from the presumption of the *possibility* of rebellion (vv. 17-22).

Judging from this process of accusation recorded in the parallel accounts, the counsellors who took the bribe offered by the people of the land (v. 5) may have made a report to the king, similar to that in the parallel accounts (vv. 13-16), exag-gerating a *probable* aggravation of the situation: i.e., if the temple is rebuilt, the power will be centralized in the priests, inevitably leading to a rebellion.[39] This is nothing but a *potential* rebellion, however, and it might seem hard to believe that the Persian king *withdrew* his decree on the basis of such a wild accusation, but the accusation lodged in the following, interpolated accounts was also accepted on this same basis![40]

The decision made by Persia can be understood more easily if we consider that, at the same time, the Persian king might have received reports of a messianic movement whose final goal was to gain political independence and to resume a Davidic kingdom.[41] Our suspicion also dovetails well with the conclusion reached

---

39.　Myers, *Ezra–Nehemiah*, p. xxxi, has also argued that complaints made by the opponents of the Jews to Darius (Ezra 4.5), Ahasuerus (v. 6), and Artaxerxes (vv. 7-23), might be of the same character.

40.　It would be helpful to consider Persia's attitude from *their* perspective. It is well known that in its early period the empire was desperate to secure stability in its occupied areas, to the extent that the Persians decided to send, for example, the Jews *immediately* after they became the new masters of ANE (Ancient Near East), since Jews were expected to support imperial design. The empire probably knew that false incrimination was prevalent at that time but at the same time thought it the best policy to obviate a possible rebellion. For a useful summary of the main rebelli-ons during the early Persian period, see E. Stern, 'The Persian Empire and the Political and Social History of Palestine in the Persian Period', in W.D. Davies *et al.* (eds.), *The Cambridge History of Judaism* (Cambridge: Cambridge University Press, 1984), pp. 70–87, esp., pp. 71ff.

41.　Cf. Japhet, 'Sheshbazzar and Zerubbabel', pp. 76ff. We can also presume that the Persian king might possibly have come across the ambitious restoration programme mapped out by Ezekiel, who emphasized the initiative role of the priests when they returned to Jerusalem (Ezek. 40–48). Cf. Pfeiffer, *Introduction*, p. 554; Duguid, *Ezekiel and the Leaders of Israel*, pp. 78–79; W. Stewart

above, that the עם הארץ, who bribed the counsellors, were foreigners in Judah or in neighbouring countries. The completion of a religious centre for the Jews and the ramifications of national solidarity were presumably regarded as a grave threat to עם הארץ. It is under these circumstances that they strove to stop the work, even by means of bribery, once they perceived that they would be excluded from sharing in its benefits.

In short, the urgent and radical change of imperial policy from permitting the rebuilding of the temple in Jerusalem to prohibiting it should be understood as a situation where the bribed counsellors provoked a ban by exaggerating the danger of rebellion by the priests, who would possess more power if the temple was built. The king, who rated the maintenance of political stability in outlying territories as of the utmost importance, decided to withdraw his permission, perhaps regretting his previous trust in the priests. We have argued this conclusion on the basis of the way the text is arranged. Of course, it is possible to arrive at the same point through a simple reflection on the historical circumstances: what else other than a suspicion of disloyalty could have persuaded the Persians to withdraw support from a project that corresponded so closely to their policies, and promised both financial and political benefits for the empire?

6.1.2.3 *The Resumption of Temple-building*
We have asserted above that the rebuilding of the temple was probably stopped because the empire thought that holding the priests' increasing power in check was more important than the anticipated benefits of a new cult centre. It is reasonable to suppose that the Persian authorities, if they had lost confidence in the priests, would, under these circumstances, have looked for another agent to implement their policies. If this supposition is correct, it would mean that the empire did not limit its support only to the priests, and that there were other Persian agents. That is not, perhaps, improbable in any case: the Persians were too shrewd to have put all their eggs in one basket.

Let us explore this matter in more detail on the basis of the accounts of Ezra 5–6, which describe what transpired after the ban on the rebuilding of the temple. We can begin by investigating the process by which the Jews eventually gained permission to rebuild once more. If the ban was caused by the empire's own perception, however badly informed, that their priestly agents had not faithfully implemented their duty, resumption of the work correspondingly implies that Persia was no longer concerned by this problem. Our first task, then, is to establish the change of circumstances which reassured the Persians that no threat existed.

As in the story of the ban, the text itself here emphasizes the role of outsiders, and it is noteworthy that the Persian officials Tattenai, the governor of Beyond the River, and Shethar Boznai are described as neutral or sympathetic rather than as prejudiced against the Jews. Their attitude stands in sharp contrast to that of Rehum and Shimshai, who had accused the Jews of malicious intent in Ezra 4: i.e., Tattenai

McCullough, *The History and Literature of the Palestinian Jews from Cyrus to Herod 550 BC to 4 BC* (Toronto: University of Toronto Press, 1975), p. 56.

and Shethar Boznai first come to Jerusalem to find out what is happening (5.3) and then write a report to the Persian king on the basis of what they had heard from the Jewish leaders, not on the basis of what they had seen for themselves (vv. 9-16). They thus influence the royal decision, and lead the king to change his mind (6.1ff), purportedly on the basis of unsupported Jewish testimony.

The text also, moreover, asserts that permission was granted (5.13-17), simply because the Jews reminded the empire of the decree originally made by Cyrus. We are asked to believe, then, that the empire simply forgot its previous worries, and was happy to accept a Jewish assertion that they were simply obeying an earlier decree. All this is possible, but it implies an absent-mindedness on the part of the empire, and a lack of local knowledge in its officials, which is hard to credit.

It is interesting to note, however, that the Judeans who represent the community to Persian delegates in Ezra 5–6 are no longer Zerubbabel, Jeshua and the heads of the fathers' houses, as in 4.3, but the *elders* of the Jews. Before the ban on the work of temple-rebuilding, the priests were among the central members of the Judean camp propelling the project. After the ban, however, it is the elders who seem to be recognized as the community's channel of communication with the empire (5.9; 6.7, 8).[42] Putting aside the redactional material,[43] the Aramaic source in Ezra 5–6, which potentially provides earlier information on whom the Persian authorities regarded as their agent, does not make any mention of Jeshua. What is more, it is worth noting that this Aramaic source recognizes Sheshbazzar (5.14, 16), rather than Zerubbabel (cf. 3.8ff) as the person who laid the foundation of the temple. This is most likely to be because Zerubbabel was of Davidic descent and was apparently regarded as the bearer of their hopes of redemption by some Jews, which would have made him suspect in the eyes of the Persians. Furthermore, 6.9 seems to limit the function of the priests to the cultic realm alone – sacrificial affairs, rather than political matters.

From these observations, we may infer that, during the period when the priests represented the Judean community, Persia, rightly or wrongly, sensed a threat of rebellion and attempted to quash it by stopping the rebuilding. When the elders later took the lead role in representing the Jews, however, Persia relaxed its vigilance and the Jews began to rebuild again (cf. 5.8). The Persian officials asked the elders what was going on (5.9) and reported to the king in a way which was sympathetic toward the Jews. The elders based their case on reminding Persia of Cyrus's earlier decree, and tried to reassure the Persians that this work was anything but dangerous. They wisely replaced Zerubbabel with Sheshbazzar, who had been appointed by Cyrus for the mission (1.8) and was probably regarded as a suitable person by the empire, at least for the purpose of resuming the work (5.13-17).

---

42.   This is also observed by Gunneweg, 'Zur Interpretation der Bücher Esra-Nehemia', p. 150, who says, 'auch teilen die aramäischen Stücke die Chr Vorliebe für Priester und Leviten nicht, sondern lassen die 'Ältesten' als Vertreter des Volkes auftreten (Esra v 5, 9)'. Noth, *The History of Israel*, p. 313, also says that 'it is striking that in his report the satrap only passes on the information given by the elders in Jerusalem'.

43.   Viz., 5.1-5; 6.1-2 and 13-22. Cf. Williamson, *Ezra, Nehemiah*, pp. xxiv–xxxiii. Thus, the references to Jeshua in 5.2 and elders in 5.5 and 6.14 are ruled out from consideration.

6.1.2.4 *Conclusion*

Our examination suggests that Persia did indeed treat the priests as its agents in the province of Yehud – but only initially. Following a dispute with the 'the people of the land', the Persians withdrew their original order to rebuild the temple, and this episode probably marks a change in their attitude toward the priests. The details are unclear, but it seems probable that the Jews rejected the participation of foreigners who were resident in the land and worshipped the Jewish God, thereby asserting their exclusive right to control of the temple and, perhaps, local government. The foreigners responded by persuading the Persians to withdraw permission for the rebuilding. According to the biblical text, they accomplished this through bribery, which was not unknown in the Achaemenid bureaucracy. However, it does seem likely that the Persians were led to believe that the rebuilding had become associated with anti-Persian interests, and possibly with a potential rebellion. We might add that, in any case, the clash between the Jews and 'the people of the land' would hardly have inspired Persian confidence in the Jewish leadership: it was Persian policy to consolidate their provinces, not to sow discord and encourage civil unrest. It is also possible, of course, that a quasi-messianic enthusiasm among some Jews was indeed turning the temple-rebuilding into a dangerously nationalistic project.

Whatever the precise reasons, it does seem likely that the Persians lost confidence in their priestly protégés during this period. When the Jews later communicate with Persian officials, the priesthood is notably absent from the discussion, as in the nationalist figurehead Zerubbabel. Either Persian insistence or good sense on the part of the Jews led to a substitution of the elders. At least temporarily, after the fall from grace of the priests, the group acted as the de facto channel of communication between the Jewish community and the Persian empire, and it was this group that obtained permission for the rebuilding of the temple to be resumed. It might imply too formal an arrangement to claim that the elders were actually appointed to be imperial agents, but their role makes it clear that any previous arrangement with the priesthood was now effectively void.

6.1.3. *Levites as Imperial Agents in the Late-Fifth Century* BCE

6.1.3.1. *The Nehemiah Memoir as the Primary Source*

Our conclusion casts significant doubt on the adequacy of the common assumption that Persia supported the priests throughout its whole period of dominance, and thus that the priests would have been in the best position to compose E–N, a book which we believe to have originated in a pro-Persian group. It also implies that, in order to answer the principal question of this thesis – who was responsible for the composition of E–N? – we need to discover who enjoyed imperial backing *during the time when the book was composed*. The answer to this question must be closely connected to the implementation of imperial policy during the period of the late fifth century, since Persia's recognition of particular groups would have been primarily dependent on this. We might again attempt to establish Persia's policy in Yehud via an investigation into the general imperial polices implemented throughout the empire. This approach, however, does not seem appropriate for the present task, partly because it cannot adequately specify the particular situation in each country, and partly because the amount of available evidence for this period is too small for us to establish more than a vague outline of general imperial policy.

This situation directs our attention to the Nehemiah Memoir (=NM).[44] Not only was it written in the late fifth century BCE, but it is also widely regarded as a reliable historical source.[45] In addition, as Emerton has noted, our knowledge of Nehemiah's loyalty to the Persians gives us a basis on which to reconstruct Persian policy.[46]

6.1.3.2 *Why was Nehemiah Sent?*
6.1.3.2.1 *Current Approaches*

If we are to use NM as our primary source for the present study, the best way to investigate Persian policy in Yehud is simply to ask why the empire sent Nehemiah. Previous studies have taken a broad approach,[47] and most scholars have considered the issue within a wider political and historical context.[48] Thus, they look first into the history of the eastern Mediterranean countries during the fifth century BCE, where several revolts threatened the Achaemenid empire, threats which were engendered by Egyptian ferment (*circa* 464–450 BCE), by Megabyzos (449/8 BCE), or possibly

---

44.   The extent of NM we have adopted in this book is as follows: Neh. 1–2; 3.33–7.4; 12.27–29, 31-32, 37-40; 13.4-31. Cf. note 86 in Chapter 2. We here do not consider the Ezra Memoir (=EM) as a source relevant to this discussion for the following two reasons. First, we have favoured the traditional view of Ezra's return as dating to 458 BCE. On the other hand, since Nehemiah's date is agreed to be 445 BCE, NM is a source nearer to the compositional date of E–N. Second, EM is normally regarded as a less reliable source than NM, although a few scholars have argued that it is as reliable as NM. For the former view regarding EM as historically unreliable, see Herbert Donner, 'Das persische Zeitalter', *Geschichte des Volkes Israel und Seiner Nachbarn in Grundzügen, Teil 2: Von der Königszeit bis zu Alexander dem Großen, mit einem Ausblick auf die Geschichte des Judentums bis Bar Kochba* (Göttingen: Vandenhoeck & Ruprecht, 1986), p. 431; and works mentioned in note 3 in the introduction to Part III. For the latter view, see Eduard Meyer, *Die Entstehung des Judenthums* (Halle: Max Niemeyer, 1896), p. 65; Janzen, 'The "Mission" of Ezra', pp. 619–43.

45.   Cf. Harrison, *Introduction*, p. 1145; Williamson, 'Exile and After', pp. 240ff. By contrast, there have been scholars who claim that the narratives reporting Nehemiah's second visit to Judah are simply a later gloss because of the grave chronological confusion in Neh. 12.43, 44 and 13.1, 4, and thus are unreliable. Cf. S. Mowinckel, *Studien zu dem Buche Ezra-Nehemia II: Die Nehemia-Denkschrift* (SUNVAO. II. Hist.-Filos. Klasse. Ny Serie. No. 7; Oslo, 1964), pp. 35–37; Kellermann, *Nehemia*, pp. 48–51. Recently, Clines, 'The Perils of Autobiography', pp. 124–64, has continued to challenge the tendency to take the biblical statement at its face value and argues that we must entertain a hermeneutic of suspicion prior to using NM as source for historical reconstruction. Clines does not so much deny that the Memoir originated in the context to which it is usually attributed, as emphasize that it is far from being an objective account of events, and that we must treat it with appropriate caution as a historical source. With others (e.g., Williamson, *Ezra, Nehemiah*, pp. 382–84) I treat NM as a reliable source, though not an impartial one.

46.   J.A. Emerton, 'Review of *Nehemia: Quellen, Überlieferung und Geschichte* by U. Kellermann', *JTS* 23 (1972), pp. 171–85, esp. p. 182.

47.   Some conservative scholars understand that permission for Nehemiah to build the wall was granted simply as a result of his *devotional* approach to God and the Persian king's *tolerance* of him. E.g., Fensham, *Ezra and Nehemiah*, p. 161.

48.   Cf. Rowley, 'Nehemiah's Mission and Its Background', pp. 237–38; J.M. Myers, *The World of the Restoration* (Englewood Cliffs: Prentice-Hall, 1968), pp. 109–11; P.R. Ackroyd, *Israel Under Babylon and Persia* (Oxford: Oxford University Press, 1970), pp. 175–76; Widengren, 'The Persian Period', pp. 524–29.

by an Athenian challenge to the Levant.[49] They then conclude that the official sending of Nehemiah to Yehud should be understood in the context of the empire's interest in restoring stability to that area and its consequent openness to Nehemiah's request, agreement to which was expected to appease the people there.[50]

This view, which regards Nehemiah's mission as a combination of his nationalism and Persia's political need, serves to enhance the understanding of some enigmatic passages. For example, it has been asked why Artaxerxes so swiftly changed his mind about the policy to ban the building of a wall round Jerusalem, which had been formulated not so many years previously (cf. Ezra 4.7ff).[51] His strong prohibition against the Jews building the wall (Ezra 4.17-22) suddenly dissolved (Neh. 2.8-9), and this rapid change of heart is not difficult to understand if we take account of the historical situation confronting Persia. The perception of danger persuaded the empire to overturn its former policy without hesitation, and to refortify Jerusalem by sending a loyal official. Since the work had already proceeded to a considerable extent (Ezra 4.12), the Persian court may have believed that it would be better to give permission for this project than to invest in any other attempts to secure the province.

Such an interpretation of Nehemiah's mission also sheds light on certain passages which are otherwise difficult to understand. For example, in Neh. 2.8, Nehemiah asks the king to forward a letter to Asaph, the keeper of the king's forest, so that he can get materials to build not only the citadel and city wall, but also his own house. In reply to what seems a presumptuous request, the king surprisingly grants all that Nehemiah asks for, and furthermore sends officers and cavalry to escort him to Yehud (vv. 8-9).[52] These measures taken by the king are unexpected, and some

49. Cf. Ctesias, 'Epit 68', *La Perse, L'Inde: les sommaires de Photius*, P. Henry (ed.), *Collection le Begne 7*, ser. no. 84 (Bruxelles: Office de Publicité, 1947); Olmstead, *History of the Persian Empire*, pp. 312–13; Hoglund, *Achaemenid Imperial Administration*, pp. 97–205. For more detailed discussion about supposed historical events during the fifth century BCE, see Julian Morgenstern, 'Jerusalem – 485 B.C.', *HUCA* 27 (1956), pp. 101–79 and *HUCA* 28 (1957), pp. 15–47.

50. Noth, *The History of Israel*, p. 318; Schaper, *Priester und Leviten*, pp. 230–31.

51. The ban occurred less than thirteen years earlier, because the attempt to build the wall in Ezra 4 probably dates to after 458 BCE when Ezra came back to Judah (Ezra 4.12), while the dialogue between Artaxerxes and Nehemiah in Neh. 2 is suspected to have happened in 445 BCE. Cf. Rudolph, *Esra und Nehemia*, pp. 44–45; Williamson, *Ezra and Nehemiah*, p. 75. As to what event the calamity in Neh. 1.3 refers to, several proposals have been put forward. Fensham, *Ezra and Nehemiah*, p. 152, argues that the calamity does not refer to the event reported in Ezra 4.7ff since, unlike the Nehemiah text, the text there preserves no impression of the wall's collapse and thus it is better to associate the disaster expressed in Neh. 1.3 with the destruction of Jerusalem which transpired, almost 140 years earlier, in the time of Nebuchadnezzar. This argument has recently been supported by Grabbe, *Ezra–Nehemiah*, p. 40. If so, however, Nehemiah's bitter reaction to the news in Neh. 1.4 becomes ridiculous. Cf. Williamson, *Ezra, Nehemiah*, p. 172. In addition, the phrase 'by force', in Ezra 4.23 implies that there might have been damage to the wall. Therefore, the majority of scholars find its background in the sequence in Ezra 4.7-23. See Rudolph, *Esra und Nehemia*, p. 103; Brockington, *Ezra, Nehemiah and Esther*, p. 105; Kidner, *Ezra & Nehemiah*, p. 7; Clines, *Ezra, Nehemiah, Esther*, p. 136, *et al.*

52. That this request is unusual has been pointed out by several scholars. For example, see Hoglund, *Achaemenid Imperial Administration*, p. 211; Grabbe, *Ezra–Nehemiah*, p. 41.

scholars therefore doubt the reliability of the account.[53] Since the building work was impossible without those materials, however, and since it would not be too surprising for a governor to be supported and protected by the empire, they may well be true.[54] The otherwise inexplicable indulgence shown toward Nehemiah indicates that his mission and his loyalty were regarded as being of considerable importance to the empire.

This approach, which sets Nehemiah's original mission within a broader political and historical context, certainly sheds light on the political motive behind that mission, and the reasons for rebuilding the wall. It fails, however, to bring into focus his other missions during the remainder of his term as governor. In fact, Nehemiah stayed in Yehud for at least twelve years (cf. Neh. 5.14; 13.6),[55] and it is difficult to believe that he stayed there for such a long time without implementing any other Persian policy after the completion of the wall. Our discussion of his role must include his other activities, too, if we are to gain any broader insight into the character of that policy. In particular, there has been no thorough examination of the reason for his *second* mission, which is, in terms of the date, more crucial to the present study.

Going further in this direction than most scholars, Hoglund has sensibly sought to frame Nehemiah's mission in the light of his achievements during the whole of his tenure as governor.[56] In addition to the refortification of Jerusalem,[57] he discusses other tasks undertaken by Nehemiah – particularly, the economic reform in Neh. 5, and the settlement of social problems in Neh. 13.[58] More specifically, Hoglund believes that it was part of the mission given to Nehemiah to alleviate economic burdens caused by the heavy taxes required for Persia's military presence in Yehud. This activity by Nehemiah would abate the impact of imperial activity (5.1-13), and any consequent discontent.[59] With regard to Neh. 13, Hoglund notes particularly Nehemiah's response to the ill-treatment of the Levites (13.10-14), the profanation of the Sabbath (13.15-22), and the problem of intermarriage (13.23-29).[60]

53.   See especially, Torrey, *Composition*, p. 36; Batten, *Ezra and Nehemiah*, p. 194.

54.   Cf. R.A. Bowman, 'Ezra and Nehemiah', p. 675.

55.   On the grounds of Neh. 2.6, many argue that his first term of office in Yehud was only for a limited time. Cf. Emerton, 'Review of *Nehemia*', p. 180; Kidner, *Ezra & Nehemiah*, p. 81; Williamson, *Ezra, Nehemiah*, p. 386. However, it is doubtful whether the phrase in Neh. 2.6 ואתנה לו זמן (literally, 'and I set him a time') denotes a short period of time. In addition, the obvious reference to his stay in Neh. 5.14 has convinced scholars to accept his twelve-year governorship. Cf. Kellermann, *Nehemia*, pp. 12, 151–54; Clines, *Ezra, Nehemiah, Esther*, p. 238.

56.   Hoglund, *Achaemenid Imperial Administration*, pp. 207–26.

57.   Cf. note 62 in Chapter 5.

58.   Hoglund's original purpose adding these tasks in his book, *Achaemenid Imperial Administration*, pp. 212ff, was to defend his seminal argument that Nehemiah's mission was to refortify Jerusalem in response to an Athenian threat to the Levant, since similar fortifications were not erected in other cities in the Levant. According to him, Nehemiah was also sent because of these additional tasks.

59.   Hoglund, *Achaemenid Imperial Administration*, pp. 212–14.

60.   Hoglund, *Achaemenid Imperial Administration*, pp. 217ff.

Hoglund's thesis may increase our understanding of the scope of Nehemiah's mission, but it provides little specific reason for the empire's choice of Nehemiah for these tasks and does not really distinguish actual policy from day-to-day management. For example, Hoglund associates Nehemiah's intervention in economic hardship matters with his mission,[61] but it is difficult to believe that the empire sent its official to lessen taxes, and noteworthy that, in Neh. 5, the outcry of the people was primarily against their fellow Judeans, not against the Persians who levied the taxes (vv. 1, 7). Thus, the economic reforms recorded in Neh. 5 may have no bearing on the tasks for which Nehemiah was commissioned. Hoglund also includes concern for the Levites among Nehemiah's assigned missions, but gives no explanation as to what such activities might have to do with Persian national interest.

Previous studies, then, have not constructed a satisfactory overall picture of Nehemiah's mission: most scholars have failed to see it in terms of the work Nehemiah undertook during his whole stay in Yehud, and Hoglund, though attempting to do this, has failed to explain adequately the wider Persian motives. In addition, no previous studies have investigated seriously the reason for Nehemiah's second mission, which may possibly offer a clue to our present concern.

6.1.3.2.2 *Nehemiah's Second Mission*

In order to understand Nehemiah's mission more completely, let us first examine his second visit by posing the question: why was he sent *again*?

The text itself says that Nehemiah came back to the king, Artaxerxes, after twelve years away, but did not stay in Persia for long. After only a 'short' time[62] he sought and gained royal permission to return to Jerusalem (Neh. 13.6). The motivation to return is said, therefore, to have been Nehemiah's own. This is to be regarded, perhaps, as a desire not to present himself in the Memoir as a Persian lackey: Nehemiah was a royal cupbearer (1.11) and personal companion of the king (cf. 2.2); it seems incredible that such an individual would rush back from the court, after a long journey, without a good, and presumably official reason for doing so. If his mission was not actively devised by the Persian government, it was apparently approved by them, and regarded as sufficiently important to warrant his immediate return to Jerusalem. What, then, provoked such urgency?

Because of a shortage of data reporting his subsequent activities, we have no option but to deduce his mission from the information given in Neh. 13.4-31. This section recounts the expulsion of Tobiah from his room in the temple (vv. 4-9); the restoration of Levitical support (vv. 10-14); the prevention of profanation of the Sabbath (vv. 15-22); action against mixed marriages (vv. 23-27); the expulsion of Sanballat's son-in-law (vv. 28-29); and a summary (vv. 30-31). If some or all of

---

61. This position is also supported by Halligan, 'By Way of a Response to Hoglund and Smith', saying that 'I would argue that Nehemiah's testimony concerning the integrity of his term of office covers his conduct during the period of economic crisis rather than following it' (note 1 on p. 147).

62. Unlike the case of מִקֵּץ (e.g., Gen. 8.6; Esth. 2.12), לְקֵץ in Neh. 13.6 implies that it was an *indefinite* time (cf. BDB, p. 893). But, due to the following word יָמִים ('days'), it most likely denotes a very short period of time.

these tasks were undertaken by Nehemiah to fulfil his mission, we must ask what Persia might have intended to gain from each. As noted earlier, the issues regarding the Sabbath and intermarriage are understandable in the light of the policies of rituals and ethnic grouping,[63] but there is nothing urgent about them. The others seem, at first glance, to have nothing directly to do with imperial interests, and one might be forgiven for being sceptical of the idea that this passage can provide an understanding of the mission given to Nehemiah during his second stay in Judah.[64]

However, there is more to this text than meets the eye, and the chapter is characterized by a curious literary device, the so-called 'remember formula', which is typically found in the form זכרה־לי אלהי לטובה ('Remember me, O my God, for good'; vv. 14, 22, 29, 31). This style is so distinctive that no parallel is found in the Old Testament literature, with the possible exception of 2 Kings 20.3,[65] and it may be said that the remember formula is one of the most distinctive literary features of NM. Moreover, as Eskenazi has observed, repetition in literature is a device for emphasis,[66] and here in Neh. 13 the formula is repeated *four times* within only twenty-eight verses (vv. 4-31). What, then, did the author intend to emphasize with such a regular repetition of the formula?

When we read this section (13.4-31) closely, it is of the utmost significance to note that the Levites are referred to immediately before each remember formula (vv. 13, 22, 29, 30).[67] Thus, it seems possible to presume that what Nehemiah wanted God to remember is closely connected to the Levites and that the word לוי serves as a linking word for each unit. On further examination, moreover, we see that in each of the units separated by the remember formula, Nehemiah is described as paying special attention to the Levites. In the unit where the formula occurs for the first time, Nehemiah values the Levites by equating ill-treatment of them with

---

63. See section 5.1.2.

64. Cf. note 45 above.

65. '*Remember* now, *O Lord*, I beseech thee, *how* I have walked before thee … and *have done what is good* in thy sight'. As shown in italics, there is a literary similarity between this verse and the remember formula in NM. There are several significant differences, too, however. First, the verb for 'remember' in NM is always expressed emphatically (זכרה) while, in 2 Kings, a simple imperative form (זכר) is employed. Ackroyd, *I & II Chronicles, Ezra, Nehemiah*, p. 28, says that this form is attested in several Old Testament passages, but as far as I know, apart from NM, it occurs only in 2 Kings 20.3. Secondly, the addressees are different: אלהי (my God) in NM versus יהוה (Lord) in 2 Kings. Avoiding the use of יהוה for God is characteristic of NM. The word אלהים occurs 37 times (Neh. 1.4, 5[×2]; 2.4, 8, 12, 18, 20; 3.36[4.4]; 4.3[4.9], 9[4.15], 14[4.20]; 6.9, 10, 12, 14, 16; 7.2; 12.40; 13.4, 7, 9, 11, 14[×2], 18, 22, 25, 26[×2], 27, 29, 31) in NM, while יהוה occurs only twice (Neh. 1.5, 5.13). It appears that 1.5 came to have the word under the influence of the following technical term אלהי השמים ('God of heaven') in order to avoid the double use of אלהים, and 5.13 uses the term to reflect the liturgical context where ויהללו את־יהוה ('and praised the Lord'; e.g., Ezra 3.10, 11; cf. Neh. 8.6; 9.3, 5) is more frequently used than ויהללו את־האלהים. Therefore, it may be concluded from this literary distinction that the use of אלהים for God forms a distinctive feature of NM.

66. Eskenazi, 'The Structure of Ezra–Nehemiah', pp. 647–48.

67. The word לוים, which occurs nine times in the whole of NM, occurs here in Neh. 13.4-31 seven times.

neglect of the house of God and by ensuring payment of tithes to them (vv. 10-14).[68] In the next unit, the restoration of the Sabbath is completed by nominating the Levites as gate guards to sanctify it (vv. 15-22). It is noteworthy that this task was originally assigned to Nehemiah's own servants in verse 19, but is given to the Levites. No explicit reason is offered for this switch, but the measures are comprehensible in the light of Nehemiah's apparent confidence in the Levites.[69] Preceding the third occurrence of the formula (v. 29), there are two episodes: one dealing with the inability of Jewish children to speak the language of Judah and with mixed marriages (vv. 23-27); and the other with the expulsion of Sanballat's son-in-law (vv. 28-29).[70] We might expect a remember formula to separate these two episodes, since they each focus on a different matter, and the absence of the formula after the first is best explained by the supposition that it functions not simply as a device to separate episodes but as a way of marking these mentions of the Levites. After the second episode, the remember formula appears again in relation to the protection of the Levitical covenant (v. 29). Finally, in the last unit, Nehemiah establishes duties for the Levites (vv. 30-31). In short, most of the units in Neh. 13.4-31 show great concern for the Levites, treat them favourably, and end with the remember formula, which emphasizes their promoted status and seems especially to be linked to the mention of Levites.[71]

Such special attention to the Levites stands in sharp contrast to a very unflattering description of the priests. Eliashib, for example, is condemned twice in the chapter: once for his provision of a temple room to Tobiah (vv. 4-9), and a second time for the marriage of his grandson to Sanballat's family (v. 28). This strongly negative characterization of the priests is rarely found in the remainder of NM.

These findings stand out all the more if we look at Neh. 10, which is unanimously agreed to bear a close general resemblance to Neh. 13.[72] Despite dealing with similar matters, that chapter shows no hint of favouritism toward the Levites, but rather emphasizes a harmonious relationship between the clerical orders.[73] This goes to show that Neh. 13 intentionally and extraordinarily focuses on the elevation of the Levites and a denigration of the priests. Just in case he has not made the point clearly enough, moreover, the writer apparently emphasizes it through repeated use

---

68. Note that ריב is used in verse 11, thus making it possible to deduce that we have here a *court trial* between Nehemiah and the officials (cf. Fensham, *Ezra and Nehemiah*, p. 262) and Nehemiah took this matter that much seriously.

69. Some have responded to the switch by arguing that the duty entrusted to Nehemiah's servants was temporary and the Levites were chosen to permanently undertake the sacred tasks (cf. Ryle, *Ezra and Nehemiah*, p. 306; Williamson, *Ezra, Nehemiah*, p. 396). In addition, commercial activities at the gate of Jerusalem on the Sabbath probably began immediately after the wall-building was completed during Nehemiah's *first* term as governor. If this presumption is right, why, then, does Nehemiah criticize this conventional practice now? Therefore, it may be possible to argue that this unit was devised to highlight Nehemiah's care for the Levites, rather than aimed at preventing profanation of the Sabbath.

70. For this division, see Brockington, *Ezra, Nehemiah and Esther*, p. 164.

71. Cf. Holmgren, *Ezra & Nehemiah*, p. 152.

72. See notes 82 in Chapter 5.

73. See section 4.1.2.

of the remember formula. Consequently, if anything in Neh. 13 indicates the reason for Nehemiah's rapid return to Jerusalem, it must surely be this strongly emphasized treatment of the priests and the Levites.[74]

6.1.3.2.3 *The Purpose of Nehemiah 13*
It is clear, then, that the account of Nehemiah's second visit stresses the favour shown to the Levites and the imposition of restraints upon the priests. What led Nehemiah to describe the situation in this way? In order to answer this question, we must explore more closely the general character of the Nehemiah Memoir. Many attempts have been made to explain the genre or nature of NM, usually by comparing it with biblical or extra-biblical materials.[75] These attempts, however, have been unsatisfactory and, in fact, have faced harsh criticism.[76] Most theories believe that it is addressed to God, but fail to explain why, if it is supposed to present Nehemiah's action on God's behalf, as the remember formula suggests, there is no mention of the building work, which was obviously Nehemiah's most brilliant achievement before God.

One possible way to address this problem may be to postulate that the work was not originally addressed to God, but to the Persian king. Not surprisingly, some

---

74. Since I originally formulated this argument, a similar position has been adopted on other grounds by Schaper, *Priester und Leviten*, pp. 226–68. He argues that the Levites were promoted by Nehemiah's positive support during the late fifth century BCE. According to Schaper, Nehemiah, who was commissioned to build the wall, needed people's help for the building work. But, when Nehemiah came to Jerusalem, there was irreconcilable conflict between the aristocracy and the people and between the priests and the Levites. In this situation, he decided to form a coalition, and to undertake his work with the people and the Levites. During his stay in Judah as Persian governor, Nehemiah openly sponsored the Levites in many ways, as seen in several texts of Nehemiah (7.1; 13.10, 11, 13, etc.).

75. Many scholars think that no passage in the biblical literature is comparable to NM, while Kellermann, *Nehemia*, pp. 84–88, compares NM with 'prayers of the accused in the Psalms' on the basis of earlier studies of Hans Schmidt, *Das Gebet der Angeklagten im Alten Testament* (Giessen: Ricker, 1928), and Hans J. Boecker, *Redeformen des Rechtslebens im Alten Testament* (Neukirchen–Vluyn: Neukirchener Verlag, 1964). Among those who compare NM with extra-biblical documents are Mowinckel, *Studien II*, pp. 50–92, who compares NM with 'royal inscriptions of ANE'; G. von Rad, 'Die Nehemia-Denkschrift', *ZAW* 76 (1964), pp. 176–87, with 'late Egyptian votive inscriptions'; Pfeiffer, *Introduction*, p. 838, with the 'apology of Hattushil III'; Blenkinsopp, 'The Nehemiah Autobiographical Memoir', in S.E. Balentine *et al.* (eds.), *Language, Theology, and the Bible: Essays in Honour of James Barr* (Oxford: Clarendon Press, 1994), pp. 199–212, esp. pp. 207–12, with 'the Udjahorresnet inscription'. On the other hand, Bowman, 'Ezra and Nehemiah', pp. 556–57, sees NM as an appeal made to God to remember Nehemiah's good works since he was a eunuch (Neh. 2.6). Ackroyd, *Israel under Babylon and Persia*, p. 248, argues that Neh. 13.4-31 was not part of NM but an addition by a later editor who wanted to glorify Nehemiah as a hero of the faith.

76. See Kellermann, *Nehemia*, pp. 76–84; Emerton, 'Review of *Nehemia*', pp. 173–77; Williamson, *Ezra, Nehemiah*, pp. xxiv–xxviii; Blenkinsopp, 'The Nehemiah Autobiographical Memoir', pp. 199–212. For a discussion related to Bowman's thesis about whether or not Nehemiah was a eunuch (cf. n. 75 above), see Yamauchi, 'Was Nehemiah the Cupbearer a Eunuch?', pp. 132–42, where he examines the existing theories and concludes that 'any dogmatic statement that he was a eunuch is based upon a web of arguments which are in many cases untenable and in other cases less than convincing' (p. 142).

scholars have already proposed that NM should be understood in terms of Nehemiah defending himself to the Persian authorities after being accused by his opponents.[77] But they have failed to note the crucially important fact that Neh. 13 has a strong interest in the promotion of the Levites, which is hard to explain in such terms.

It is easiest to comprehend the present form and content of Neh. 13 if we view it as having developed in the following sequence: (1) Nehemiah's special attention to the Levites, emphasized by the remember formula, must have been associated with the concerns which impelled his sudden return to Jerusalem in about 433 BCE. (2) After taking measures to deal with those concerns, Nehemiah wrote the king a report which demonstrated his faithful resolution of the situation and reminded the king of his loyalty. (3) A copy of this report, which had been written immediately after the events, underwent a slight change in the addressee from king to God, because the redactor, responsible for the whole of E–N, wanted to depict Nehemiah as a devotional reformer.[78]

We, therefore, submit that the best way to interpret Neh. 13.4-31 is to regard it as a report devised to the Persian king to show how faithfully Nehemiah performed an imperial mission which involved supporting the Levites and restraining the priests.

6.1.3.3 *A Proposed Reconstruction*

On the basis of our research so far, we may propose a partial and tentative reconstruction of Jewish history in the early Second Temple period, in terms of the imperial support for particular groups in Yehud:

(1) Although the priests had been held in check during the rebuilding of the temple, its completion inevitably enhanced their status, and as time went on, their functions and roles in the temple, a key administrative centre, were increasingly enlarged.[79] Persia had no other choice than to accept the status

---

77. E.g., W. Erbt, 'Esra und Nehemia', *OLZ* 12 (1909), cols. 154–61; Max Haller, *Das Judentum* (SAT; Göttingen: Vandenhoeck & Ruprecht, 1914), p. 149.

78. Williamson, *Ezra, Nehemiah*, pp. xxiv–xxviii, has suggested another plausible understanding of NM. With the observation that the remember formula never refers to the building of the wall as what Nehemiah wishes God to remember, Williamson claims that NM was composed in two stages: the first NM dealt with the task of the wall building, while the second was added later, by using the remember formula. As regards the later addition, he argues that 'Nehemiah may have felt that justice was not being done to him within his own community... We suggest that he was thus moved to rework his old report, points for which he felt he was not being given due credit' (p. xviii). In other words, according to him, Nehemiah came to compose the section in Neh. 13 in order to defend himself by showing that he was not a person who had performed differently from the community's stance. If so, since it is a major message of the section that the Levites should be favoured more than ever before, it directly shows that they were living after the time when the Levites had been ignored. Therefore, though following Williamson's thesis, it is not denied that the second NM reveals the situation of those who lived in the late fifth century BCE, where the Levites were favoured over the priests.

79. Cf. Albright, *Biblical Period*, p. 88; Noth, *The History of Israel*, pp. 335–36; Gunneweg, *Geschichte Israels*, p. 139; Gottwald, *The Hebrew Bible*, p. 189.

quo, and watch the increasing power of the priests within Yehud. This situation probably led the empire to resume their prior relationship where the priests served as agents of the empire and representatives of the Jews.

(2)   During a period of revolts elsewhere in the empire, Persia felt a strong need to take a more 'hands-on' approach to its provinces, and to enforce greater compliance with imperial policy. Under these circumstances, Ezra was sent to Yehud in 458 BCE. He brought a law, which contained not only traditional laws and customs of Judah, but also aspects of imperial control.[80] In the first year, he devoted himself to teaching and establishing the law in an attempt to make it a basic national principle. This effort of his was unsuccessful, most likely due to the radical character of his reformation and suspicion of his motives as a Persian agent.[81]

(3)   Another important mission assigned to Ezra was to inquire about Jerusalem and Yehud (Ezra 7.14). Specifically, he had to assess whether there existed a possibility of rebellion by the priests to whom power had been centralized in the community.[82] Ezra was probably, however, involved in the attempt to build the wall (Ezra 4.7ff), which came to be viewed with suspicion by the Persians, and was prohibited.[83]

(4)   Nehemiah, who had been in support of the previous attempt to build the wall, learned that the effort had been frustrated, and decided to ask the Persian king for permission to continue the building work. This request was accepted, since the empire thought that it was wiser to give permission: the completion of the wall with Persia's authorization, and under the supervision of a Persian loyalist, would ultimately provide a fort defending an imperial fringe. The empire was aware that the accumulation of power by particular groups in occupied countries was undesirable, as it created an alternative source of authority, and could lead to rebellion. Thus, providing Nehemiah with full support for rebuilding the wall, on the one hand, the empire also required that he should attempt to check the accumulation of power by the priesthood in Yehud, who had previously aroused suspicions of disloyalty, and antagonized other groups locally.

---

80.   Cf. Balentine, *The Torah's Vision of Worship*, p. 51.

81.   It is notable that Ezra's reform received little favour by the priests in Yehud, though he was also a priest. The priests are often described as the object, rather than the subject, of the reformation in the Ezra Memoir (Ezra 9.1; 10.18-22), while his reformation was supported by the chiefs (שׂרים; 9.1), the people (10.1) and Shechaniah, whose descent is disputed, though he is clearly not of a priestly family. The failure of Ezra's reform has been pointed out by several scholars: e.g., Morton Smith, *Palestinian Parties and Politics that Shaped the Old Testament* (New York: Columbia University Press, 1971), p. 179; Douglas, 'Responding to Ezra', pp. 4–5.

82.   As noted by commentators (e.g., Williamson, *Ezra, Nehemiah*, p. 101), it is hard to elucidate the meaning of לבקרא על־יהוד ולירושלם (literally, 'to inquire concerning Judah and Jerusalem'). If we favour our earlier thesis that the nomination of the imperial agent to Yehud was totally dependent upon its policy to get rid of any potential rebellions, our proposal should be regarded as the best of several plausible interpretations.

83.   Rudolph, *Esra und Nehemia*, pp. 44–45.

(5)   During his first term in office, Nehemiah was careful not to neglect this second mission of checking the priests and decentralizing their power. From the outset, he let all the people share in the building work, rather than limiting it to a specific group of people (cf. Neh. 3). He was also interested in promoting the status of the common people (cf. Neh. 5). Following a brief recall to the court, during which the priesthood took advantage of his absence, Nehemiah took a new and more forceful approach to the problem, by supporting the Levites, who were the only credible alternative to the priests.[84] Upon returning to Jerusalem, he concentrated his efforts on supporting the Levites in various ways, and reported these efforts to the king.

From this plausible reconstruction of post-exilic Jewish history, and certainly from Neh. 13, we may deduce that the Levites received support from Persia after about 433 BCE.

6.1.3.4 *Conclusion*
Based on our research so far, we can characterize Achaemenid imperial policy toward particular groups in Yehud as follows:

538–520 BCE	Priests supported
520–515 BCE	Elders supported
515–458 BCE	Priests supported (reluctantly?)
458–433 BCE	Support for various groups, to reduce priestly power
433 BCE and following	Levites supported.

We may conclude, therefore, that E–N, which was composed in the late fifth century BCE and was probably penned by someone with Persian backing, originated in all likelihood from a Levitical group.

6.2 *Ideological Examination of Ezra–Nehemiah*

6.2.1 *Introduction*
In the previous section, we began our discussion by observing that E–N portrays a favourable attitude toward the Persian empire, even when Persian policy did not coincide with Jewish interests. This led us to suppose that the book would only have such a perspective if the author was a person on good terms with, or backed by, Persia. On the basis of this, we further asked which group – priestly or Levitical – was in that position during the late fifth century BCE, the date which has been suggested for the composition of the book.

In particular, our historical study of Nehemiah's *second* visit to Jerusalem demonstrated that the Levites probably enjoyed the best relationship with Persia during that period, while the priests, by contrast, were held in check. This led us to contend

---

84.   Since Nehemiah was presumably the principal Persian expert on Yehud, this policy may have been his own idea, and it is certainly in line with his previous actions, as Schaper has shown (*Priester und Leviten*, pp. 226–68). The urgency of his return, and his strong line thereafter, may be connected with a perceived failure to constrain the priests sufficiently.

that the Levites were most likely to have been under the patronage of the empire during that time and that E–N most likely originated in a Levitical group.

There remains the possibility that some within the priestly group still retained a good relationship with the Persians, regardless of the current Persian support for the Levites and, therefore, could have penned E–N. There is no particular evidence to support such a contention, but it might permit further precision if we explore the matter of ideologies, raised earlier in section 5.2, which offers our 'second clue'. It will be recalled that the author of E–N is likely to have been a person who valued the ideologies of (1) decentralization of power; (2) unity and cooperation among social classes; and (3) dissatisfaction with the religious status quo. We will approach this issue by asking which group – priestly or Levitical – is more likely to have held such views.

6.2.2 *Priests* vis-à-vis *the Ideological Emphasis of Ezra–Nehemiah*
It seems unlikely that the priesthood, with their long-standing status as the spiritual elite of Jewish society, and a corresponding investment in leadership and hierarchical relationships, would have attributed importance to any of the social and religious values which we have identified in E–N.[85] In order to convince us even of the plausibility of priestly authorship, it would have to be demonstrated that some turning-point or epochal event had brought about a change in priestly perspectives at, or before, the time of E–N's composition.

Japhet's thesis, which explains the decentralizing tendency in the context of a more prevalent democratization in the period, might, at first glance, undermine this objection.[86] It suggests that the ideology of decentralization in E–N should be understood in terms of a contemporary social phenomenon, rather than just as the author's personal viewpoint. However, because the author of E–N himself would have been deeply influenced by this ideology, it is obvious that the Levitical group was in a position more easily to accept the new trend which centred on *the public*.

In searching for a historical watershed which might have led the priestly group to endorse the second (unity and cooperation among social classes) and third ideologies (dissatisfaction with the religious status quo), we may note Williamson's hypothesis, which connects the composition of E–N to an unknown event that occurred *circa* 300 BCE, and gave rise to the secession of a number of priests from Jerusalem to Shechem in order to found another religious community.[87] This theory might provide the basis for understanding a change in priestly attitude, by which the priests became so determined to prevent another split and so anxious to retain the Levites, that they began strongly to encourage unity and cooperation between all groups of people.

---

85.   Cf. Chapter 3.

86.   See Japhet, 'Sheshbazzar and Zerubbabel', pp. 87–88, where she argues that the abolition of the monarchy brought a change in the social structure which eventually provided an opportunity for popular representative bodies to be established, as attested in the Great Assembly and the Gerusia.

87.   Williamson, 'The Composition of Ezra i–vi', pp. 26–29.

There are, however, several difficulties with this proposal. The first is that E–N was most likely written in about 400 BCE, and not 300 BCE.[88] Secondly, this theory lacks internal cohesion. If Williamson is correct in assuming that the event in 300 BCE prompted a reorganization, or a change in ideology, within the priesthood, then one would expect the remaining priests in Jerusalem to focus on their *own* internal solidarity, promising betterment in the future rather than focusing on the laity or every man. In this context, therefore, if we read the text assuming priestly authorship, then no explanation is offered for the narratives which show the ideologies of decentralization and unity, such as the reading of the law initiated by the people (Neh. 8), or lot-casting, in which the people were also invited to participate (Neh. 10.35).

A third difficulty concerns dissatisfaction with the religious status quo. While one might claim that a criticism of existing religious practices was presented within the priestly groups as an orientation for future restoration, it is seriously doubtful whether the priests, who were in the middle of suffering from the effects of a secession, were mature enough to criticize themselves in such a harsh tone. The overall tone of the text is dismissive of many previous religious practices,[89] thus making it highly unlikely that these accounts originated in a priestly group who had previously been in charge of religious matters.

Based on the ideologies preserved in E–N, therefore, we would have to reject the notion that E–N was the product of a priestly group.

6.2.3 *Levites* vis-à-vis *the Ideological Emphasis of Ezra–Nehemiah*
As examined above, it is hard to understand the ideological emphasis of E–N if we accept priestly authorship. Therefore, we will now examine the possibility of Levitical authorship in relation to the ideological emphasis of E–N.

We begin our exploration by focusing on a general understanding of the Levites in Jewish society. It appears that their status was relatively low *vis-à-vis* that of the priests.[90] They were also a group who needed to be taken care of financially (cf. Deut. 12.12, 19; 14.27, 29, *et passim*), and were regularly treated as *clerus minor*. Because they were so marginalized, it is very likely that *decentralization of power* was exactly what the Levites would have hoped for. In addition, if some process of democratization had indeed happened in Jewish society, the Levites would surely have been less hesitant to accept it than the priests. As a corollary, one would expect the Levites also to endorse the ideology of the *unity of the whole people*, and to have emphasized the *cooperative relationship* between the clerical orders. Congruent with this understanding is the presumption that the Levites, throughout most of the post-exilic period, requested a harmonious relationship between the priests and themselves rather than stressing their difference in function and status. Finally, the last ideology, *dissatisfaction with the religious status quo*, also dovetails with Levitical authorship. Since it was the priests who had been in charge of religious matters, a strong request for the reformation of the existing religious practices was

---

88. Cf. section 2.1; Williamson, *Ezra and Nehemiah*, p. 46.
89. See section 5.2.
90. Cf. Chapter 3.

mostly likely to have come from another source: the Levites. In sum, the ideologies emphasized in E–N are congruent with the probable desires of the Levites, as far as we can ascertain historically.

Lastly, we turn our attention to the conclusion, reached in section 6.1, that there was a time when the Levites had the support of society with the help of patronage from the empire. Once again, the ideologies emphasized in E–N are congruent with this conclusion. It is highly likely that the Levites composed E–N as an idealistic programme for future restoration on the basis of the bitter experiences they had undergone, hoping that a society would be created where power was no longer centralized in a specially ranked group of people; where the marginalized would be invited to participate in national affairs if they wanted to; where a harmonious and cooperative, not feuding and hierarchical, relationship reigned in the clerical orders; and where religious practices corrected by the law were prevalent in their cultic lives.

From an examination of the possibility of Levitical authorship in terms of the ideologies emphasized in E–N, then, we may conclude that it was the Levites who were in the best position to harbour and value those ideologies, and that Levitical authorship for E–N is most compatible with the historical context.

Summary of Part III

In this part of the book, we aimed to examine the authorship issue of E–N within a historical context. While it might be desirable to do so by first reconstructing history on the basis of other sources and then exploring which group – priestly or Levitical – was in the best position to produce the book, we have not had the luxury to take such an approach, since it is virtually impossible to reconstruct an accurate history in that way. Instead, we have had to pursue a more circumstantial examination, trying to establish the broad political context, and the probable reaction to it by different groups.

Two clues to authorship were presented in Chapter 5. The first came from a study of Achaemenid policy: after becoming the new master of ANE, Persia mapped out an imperial policy which, while liberal when compared to those of previous empires, was definitely intended primarily to benefit Persia and which inflicted certain burdens on the Jewish people. Since E–N was composed during the time of Persian rule, it might be expected that the author would have harboured animosity toward the Persians. A close reading of the book, however, confounds this expectation. Instead, the Persian kings are described as channels for God's benevolence and there is no negative or critical mention of imperial policy. This situation is inexplicable unless we think that the author was on good terms with, or sponsored by, the empire.

The other clue concerned the ideology preserved in the book. An author's ideology will necessarily be reflected in a text. We chose Neh. 8–10 as a case study, since these chapters were from different sources which were then comprehensively edited by the author, and thus they might be considered to reflect the author's ideology through both selection and redaction. From our study of these chapters, we reached the conclusion that the author was someone who valued the ideologies of (1) decentralization of power; (2) unity and cooperation among social classes; and (3) dissatisfaction with the religious status quo. This conclusion was vindicated by noting the presence and emphasis of these ideologies throughout the remainder of the book.

The purpose of Chapter 6, therefore, was to investigate the two possible candidates for authorship of E–N; i.e., a priestly or the Levitical group, in the light of these two clues.

The first question posed was: who gained Persian backing during the compositional period of E–N? Most scholars commonly assume that the empire supported the priests from the beginning of the Persian period to the end. It is true that the priests were supported at first, but our study of Ezra 4–6 clearly shows that it is not the case that they were always supported. This led us more closely to explore who received Persian support during the late fifth century BCE, the supposed date for the composition. We focused our attention on Neh. 13.4-31 since it is believed to have been penned nearest in time to the composition of E–N. Our study of this passage, particularly emphasizing the remember formula in Neh. 13, suggested that one of Nehemiah's important missions was to support the Levites and to hold the priests in check. Therefore, we concluded that it is highly probable that the author, with a pro-Persian tendency, came from a Levitical group.

The second clue was examined by asking which authorship theory – priestly or Levitical – provides us with a better understanding of the three ideologies. The assumption that E–N originated in a priestly group troubled us in many ways; in order for this to be true, we would have to believe that the priests were those (1) who had an interest in decentralizing power and sharing it with the common people, (2) who disliked the hierarchical relationship between clerical orders, and (3) who were dissatisfied with the conventional religious practices for which they themselves had been primarily in charge. We found this to be highly unlikely, finding no evidence, historical or otherwise, to support such a conclusion. In contrast, Levitical authorship was found to fit well with these ideologies. The Levites' status as *clerus minor* may have put them in a position to identify with the marginalized over a long period of time. Thus, it seems highly plausible that the Levites would have supported such ideologies.

Therefore, from our examination of the authorship issue through the available clues, we now conclude that E–N most likely came from a Levitical group who received Persian backing during the late fifth century BCE and who valued the ideologies of decentralization of power, unity and cooperation among social groups, and dissatisfaction with the religious status quo.

The primary purpose of this book has been to determine the authorship of Ezra–Nehemiah, especially in the light of modern assumptions that it originated as an independent, unified work. Pre-critical assumptions, which took Ezra to have been the author of E–N, were challenged 170 years ago by Leopold Zunz, who found that only a few portions of the book could be ascribed to Ezra. However, in view of what he took to be shared linguistical and ideological traits, Zunz argued that E–N was composed by the Chronicler, and this theory of common authorship enjoyed a position of consensus for almost 150 years, especially excluding any separate consideration of authorship in E–N. Sara Japhet's seminal article, published in 1968, substantially weakened this consensus. Her thesis was taken up and elaborated by Hugh Williamson, and now a growing number of scholars are convinced by their arguments that E–N should be treated as a discrete composition. With this change has come a need to address questions of authorship and context for the work.

The thesis of common authorship still remains influential, and so we began by examining the four main arguments involved in the relationship between Chronicles and E–N, in order to affirm the unity and independence of E–N. We concluded both that the arguments for common authorship are weak, and that there are substantial reasons to support separate authorship. We also reviewed and rejected the position of those scholars who suggest that E–N has to be regarded as two distinct works.

If E–N can be treated as a single unified work, composed independently of the Chronicler, who, then, wrote it? Some scholars have discussed this issue and made useful contributions. For example, the studies of Tamara Eskenazi and Japhet have led us to take seriously the possibility that E–N might have been composed all at once by one author, rather than over a long period of time by different editors. Likewise, Williamson's study has shown that the author of E–N had knowledge of cultic matters and most likely was a person who could have had access to temple archives. However, none of these studies has taken proper account of E–N's most peculiar feature, its strong interest in the Levites, and none has linked this feature to a discussion of authorship. Perhaps because of widespread belief in the Levitical authorship of Chronicles, scholars who assert E–N's independence have been reluctant to consider the possibility of separate Levitical authorship for E–N also. In any case, priestly authorship seems to have been adopted *faute de mieux*, with little specific consideration of the issue.

It is difficult, however, to overlook the fact that E–N has the most frequent occurrence of the word לוי in the Old Testament, at a rate of more than once every five verses.[1] Of course, this frequent occurrence of לוי *per se* does not necessarily imply any partiality to the Levites or show Levitical authorship. But it can be said to show, at least, E–N's strong interest in the Levites, and to offer a significant clue for resolving the question of authorship.

The common occurrence of לוי does not rule out the possibility of priestly authorship for E–N, and the word כהן also occurs frequently, though not as much. We can say, with some certainty, however, that the book must have originated in a clerical group: it apparently uses numerous sources from temple archives, and its frequent references to לוי and כהן reflect a broader interest in clerical matters, particularly in the authorial portions. With these considerations in mind, our preliminary study in Part I left us with two possible candidates for authorship: the priests and the Levites.

In Part II, we attempted to narrow the choice, exploring the issue of authorship by looking first at the internal, literary evidence. We compared the descriptions of the Levites in other texts from the exilic or post-exilic period, with that presented in E–N, as a way of determining how the Levites are customarily described in contemporary priestly or Levitical texts. Our study of those texts identified some specific and clear-cut features: *priestly texts* (Ezekiel, P, and Chron.-P) tend to downgrade the Levites, depicting them as *clerus minor*; *Levitical texts* (Chron.-L), on the other hand, describe them favourably and promote their status to one of equality with the priests. Our subsequent study demonstrated that, among the 65 references in E–N, the Levites are *nowhere* described as *clerus minor*. Instead, it seems that, in all references to לוי, they are consistently favoured and presented as co-workers with the priests. In short, E–N is congruent, in its description of the Levites, with the Levitical Old Testament texts, and quite different from the priestly texts. In the light of this observation, therefore, we may conclude that E–N most likely originated in a Levitical group.

This evidence is compelling, and is sufficient in itself to make a good case for Levitical authorship. In the third part of the book, however, we sought to supplement it by examining the historical context for the composition. We first investigated the author's political perspectives, and examined the ideologies predominant in E–N, concluding that the author of E–N was most likely to have been a person who (1) gained support from the Persian empire and (2) valued the ideologies of (i) decentralization of power; (ii) unity and cooperation among social classes; and (iii) dissatisfaction with the religious status quo. We then sought to identify which of the clerical groups was most likely to have held these views during the period in which E–N was composed.

An analysis of the biblical accounts, particularly Ezra 4–6 and the Nehemiah Memoir, revealed that different groups in Judah enjoyed Persian support at different times, and that the Levites were probably sponsored by the time of E–N. These findings challenge a common assumption that Persia supported the priests throughout the whole Achaemenid period. We also argued that Levitical authorship for E–N offered the best explanation for the other ideological features of the work.

---

1.   Indeed, if we employ Rudolph's or Williamson's sources for the authorial portions, it occurs more frequently, i.e., once per less than three verses.

Historical research in the Persian period is always necessarily a somewhat speculative matter, and our historical arguments had to rely on sources of unknown veracity, such as the Nehemiah Memoir, or to deal briefly with such notorious problems as the identity of the עם הארץ. For that reason, this third part of the book offers a less secure basis for identifying the origin of E–N than did the internal evidence in the second part. All the same, I believe that it offers a plausible reconstruction of the historical context, and it indicates some of the historical implications of the thesis as a whole.

There are, of course, many other implications arising from our conclusions, and we may usefully finish by indicating some of the most important, and by highlighting questions which remain to be answered in this field.

(1) *The Relationship with Chronicles*

At first glance, an attribution of E–N to Levitical circles seems to imply that Chronicles and E–N share the same origin, since it is widely accepted that Chronicles also came from a Levitical group.[2] However, one of our key reasons for rejecting the common authorship of the two works was the apparent conflict between their views on a wide range of topics, many of them religious (cf. section 1.1.2.4). If the ascription of Chronicles to a Levitical source is correct, this leaves us in a strange situation, where two documents, which are supposed to have come from the same source, hold widely different views.

The only way to explain this is to insist on separate authorship: i.e., two different *Levitical* authors for Chronicles and E–N, but not separate authorship between a Levitical author for Chronicles and a priestly author for E–N. Had the authors of Chronicles and E–N belonged to the same period, they might well have subscribed to common ideologies, and the fact that they possessed divergent opinions, therefore, might suggest that they were composed at different times. If so, our study would lay a foundation for further discussion about the date of Chronicles, which was presumably *not* then composed around the late fifth century BCE, at the same time as E–N.

On the other hand, it is equally possible to argue that the differences resulted not from any gap in time, but from diversity within the Levitical group, so that Chronicles and E–N reflect voices of the different groups within the Levites. Such diversity might be expected, given the fact that the Levitical group in the post-exilic time consisted of Levites who had different backgrounds: some had remained in the land, and some had returned from Babylon. If that is the case, then, our conclusions may shed light on the internal situation or structure of the Levitical group in the post-exilic period. More generally, of course, this situation highlights the extent to which, whatever their affiliations, the writers must be considered as independent voices, not merely party spokesmen.

---

2.   Cf. note 11 in the Introduction.

(2) *The Theme of Restoration*

Restoration is a key theme in E–N, and has usually been interpreted there in terms of the restoration of theocracy, cult, or temple. E–N certainly contains these aspects of restoration. However, this is only one side of the coin, and the other side may arguably be more important. It is widely recognized that a feuding relationship existed between the clerical orders until post-exilic times, and this must constantly have undermined unity within the Jewish community. If E–N was produced as a programme for restoration of the post-exilic Jewish community, and if it was composed by a *Levite*, who was in a position to deplore this situation, it is easy to believe that the author's broader concept of restoration must have embraced the restoration of a harmonious relationship between priests and Levites. As pointed out in our main discussion, E–N clearly shows an interest in a harmonious and cooperative relationship between the clerical groups: they appear side by side during the most important events; the Levites are also mentioned in almost every place the priests appear; and there is no mention of any tension or conflict between the religious groups.

At the time of E–N, if our historical reconstruction is correct, Levites had just come into power for the first time, with the support of the Persian empire. The author of E–N, rather than denigrating the priesthood in this situation, may have decided to formulate a programme for restoration in which not only the cult but also human relationships are wholly to be restored. The priests and the Levites are therefore portrayed as cooperating in a common endeavour to restore Jewish society.

Read against the historical background, then, the author's treatment of the relationship between priests and Levites appears to be conciliatory, and, perhaps, idealistic. He is not seeking to assert Levitical parity from a position of weakness, but from a position of strength, and he apparently sees restoration not in terms just of reinstating the old, but as the creation of a better society. This is crucially important for understanding both the nature of E–N, and the ideological climate within which it was composed.

(3) *Levites and the Second Temple*

It has widely been observed that in the Second Temple period there was a tendency to promote the status of Levi and his descendants.[3] This trend stands out particularly in *Jubilees* 30–32, the *Testament of Levi* section of the *Testaments of the Twelve Patriarchs*, the *Aramaic Levi Document*, and *4Q541* and *540*. In these works, Jacob's son Levi appears already consecrated as a priest during his lifetime, and the priestly position is given to him and his descendants in perpetuity.

This runs against the older view that the Levites were not supposed to have been nominated for priestly office until the time of the golden calf incident (Exod. 32.25-29) or the death of Aaron (cf. Deut. 10.6-8), and some scholars suggest, therefore, that the Levites must have been in an elevated position during the Second Temple

---

3. For recent articles and books on this matter, see note 14 in the Introduction.

period.[4] This suggestion may be supported by the evidence that the Levites took the lead in the interpretation of the scriptures and religious teaching during the Hellenistic era.[5] In contrast, however, others argue that the mention of Levi's elevation to the priesthood reflects the disappearance of the Levites in the late post-exilic and Hellenistic periods.[6] In the Second Temple writings which contain the Levi traditions, there is no reference to the existence of non-priestly descendants of Levi: for example, Ben-Sira does not mention the Levites at all, and the tithe was apparently given not to the Levites but to the priests.[7] On this basis, these scholars conclude that 'there were no Levites in the Second Temple period. The story of Levi's elevation to the priesthood is one explanation for this reality.'[8]

In short then, these later writings have been taken either to show that the Levites were genuinely promoted to priestly status by Second Temple times, or that they had simply disappeared, being absorbed into the existing priesthood or some other group. A full examination of that question lies outside the scope of this book, but our conclusions may inform future discussion: as we have seen, the Levites probably enjoyed a much higher status by the late fifth century than they had done earlier, and there was some pressure for reconciliation with the priesthood. It is unlikely, therefore, that they simply disappeared, and the emphasis on Levi in Second Temple writings must be read as part of a somewhat older attempt to elevate the caste.[9]

To sum up, we conclude that E–N originated most likely in a Levitical group. This conclusion may contribute to a deeper understanding of E–N in many ways. In particular, it provides a foundation for further study of (1) the date of Chronicles and internal situation of the Levitical group in the post-exilic period; (2) the author's concept of restoration; and (3) the position of the Levites in the post-Achaemenid period onward.

---

4.   See especially Kugel, 'Levi's Elevation', pp. 1–2.

5.   For example, M. Hengel, ''Schriftauslegung' und 'Schriftwerdung' in der Zeit des Zweiten Tempels', in *Schriftauslegung im antiken Judentum und im Urchristentum*, M. Hengel *et al.* (eds.) (WUNT, 73; Tübingen: Mohr, 1994), pp. 1–71, says 'daß in den Wirren nach der Alexanderzeit durch den neuen hellenistischen Einfluß die politisch führende Priesterschaft teilweise 'verweltlichte' und nicht mehr in ausreichender Weise in der Lage war, der Aufgabe der schriftgelehrten Interpretation der heiligen Texte nachzukommen, und daß mehr und mehr die Leviten in diese Funktion eintraten' (p. 31). Cf. Schaper, *Priester und Leviten*, p. 306. According to him, this tendency lasted, at least, until the time of Johanan ben Zakkai (pp. 305–306).

6.   E.g., Werman, 'Levi and Levites', pp. 211–16.

7.   According to Werman, 'Levi and Levites', pp. 214–15, the Levites were absorbed into the singers' and the gatekeepers' families, and this had already happened since Ezra's time.

8.   Werman, 'Levi and Levites', p. 215.

9.   In addition to these implications presented so far, our conclusion can also furnish grounds for further scholarly discussions about other unsettled critical issues. For example, our study of *who* composed E–N allows us to proceed on a firmer ground to an examination of *how* it was composed. Furthermore, our conclusion may contribute to reinvigorating discussions about more puzzling issues, including the theological purpose of the present location of Neh. 8–10, the mission of Ezra, the mission of Nehemiah, and the nature of the Nehemiah Memoir.

BIBLIOGRAPHY

Abba, Raymond
    1962   'Priests and Levites', *IDB*, III, pp. 876–89.
    1977   'Priests and Levites in Deuteronomy', *VT* 27, pp. 257–67.
    1978   'Priests and Levites in Ezekiel', *VT* 28, pp. 1–9.
Achtemeier, Elizabeth
    1978   *Deuteronomy, Jeremiah* (Proclamation Commentaries: The Old Testament for Preaching; Philadelphia: Fortress Press).
    1982   *The Community and Message of Isaiah 56–66* (Minneapolis: Augsburg Publishing House).
Ackroyd, Peter R.
    1951   'Studies in the Book of Haggai', *JJS* 2 (1951), pp. 163–76.
    1968   *Exile and Restoration* (London: SCM Press).
    1970   *Israel under Babylon and Persia* (Oxford: Oxford University Press).
    1973   *I & II Chronicles, Ezra, Nehemiah: Introduction and Commentary* (London: SCM Press).
    1988   'Chronicles–Ezra–Nehemiah: The Concept of Unity', in O. Kaiser (ed.), *Lebendige Forschung im Alten Testament*, pp. 189–201.
    1991   'Rigorism and Openness in the Theology of the Persian (Achaemenian) Period', in *The Chronicler in His Age* (JSOTSup, 101; Sheffield: JSOT Press), pp. 360–78.
Ahlemann, Frieder
    1942–43 'Zur Esra Quelle', *ZAW* 59, pp. 77–98.
Ahlström, Gösta W.
    1993   *The History of Ancient Palestine from the Palaeolithic Period to Alexander's Conquest* (JSOTSup, 146; Sheffield: JSOT Press)
Albright, William F.
    1921   'The Date and Personality of the Chronicler', *JBL* 40, pp. 104–24.
    1965   *The Biblical Period from Abraham to Ezra: An Historical Survey* (New York: Harper & Row).
Allan, Nigel
    1982   'The Identity of the Jerusalem Priesthood during the Exile', *HeyJ* 23, pp. 259–69.
Alt, Albrecht
    1953   'Die Rolle Samarias bei der Entstehung des Judentums', in *Kleine Schriften zur Geschichte des Volkes Israel, Band II* (München: Beck), pp. 316–37.
Andersen, Francis I., and A. DeanForbes
    1989   *The Vocabulary of the Old Testament* (Roma: Editrice Pontificio Istituto Biblico).
Andreasen Niels-Erik A.
    1972   *The Old Testament Sabbath: A Tradition-Historical Investigation* (SBL, 7; Missoula, MT: SBL).

Anderson, Bernard W.
    1986   *Understanding the Old Testament* (Englewood Cliffs: Prentice-Hall, 4th edn).
Anderson B.W., and W. Harrelson (eds.)
    1962   *Israel's Prophetic Heritage: James Muilenburg Festschrift* (New York: Harper & Brothers).
Anderson, Francis I.
    1958   'Who Built the Temple?', *ABR* 6, pp. 1–35.
Anderson, George W.
    1994   *A Critical Introduction to the Old Testament* (London: Duckworth, 2nd edn).
Archer, Gleason L.
    1964   *A Survey of Old Testament Introduction* (Chicago: Moody Press).
Baker, David W., and Bill T. Arnold (eds.)
    1999   *The Face of Old Testament Studies: A Survey of Contemporary Approaches* (Grand Rapids: Baker Books).
Balentine, Samuel E.
    1999   *The Torah's Vision of Worship* (Minneapolis: Fortress Press).
Balentine S.E., and J. Barton (eds.),
    1994   *Language, Theology, and the Bible: Essays in Honour of James Barr* (Oxford: Clarendon Press).
Baltzer, Klaus
    1961   'Das Ende des Staates Juda und die Messias-Frage', in R. Rendtorff *et al.* (eds.), *Studien zur Theologie der alttestamentlichen Überlieferungen*, pp. 33–43.
Barag, D.P.
    1985   'Some Notes on a Silver Coin of Johanan the High Priest', *BA* 48, pp. 166–68.
    1986–87   'A Silver Coin of Yohanan the High Priest and the Coinage of Judah in the Fourth Century B.C.', *Israel Numismatic Journal* 9, pp. 4–21.
Bartlett, John R.
    1968   'Zadok and His Successors at Jerusalem', *JTS* n.s. 19, pp. 1–18.
Barton, John, and D.J. Reimer (eds.)
    1996   *After the Exile: Essays in Honour of Rex Mason* (Macon, GA: Mercer University Press).
Batten, Loring W.
    1913   *A Critical and Exegetical Commentary on the Books of Ezra and Nehemiah* (ICC; Edinburgh: T&T Clark).
Baudissin, Wolf W.G.
    1902   'Priests and Levites', *Hasting's Dictionary of the Bible*, IV (New York: Charles Scribners' Sons), pp. 67–97.
Bayer, W.
    1937   *Die Memioren des Statthalters Nehemia* (Speyer a. Rh: Pilger Druckerei).
Becker, Joachim
    1990   *Esra, Nehemia* (NEB, 25; Würzburg: Echter Verlag).
Becking, Bob
    1998   'Ezra on the Move… Trends and Perspectives on the Character and His Book', in F.G. Martínez *et al.* (eds.), *Perspectives in the Study of the Old Testament and Early Judaism*, pp. 154–79.
    1999   'Continuity and Community: The Belief System of the Book of Ezra', in B. Becking *et al.* (eds.), *The Crisis of Israelite Religion*, pp. 256–75.

Becking, Bob, and Marjo C.A. Korpel (eds.)
1999   *The Crisis of Israelite Religion: Transformation of Religious Tradition in Exilic and Post-Exilic Times* (OTS, XLII; Leiden: Brill).

Bedford, Peter R.
2001   *Temple Restoration in Early Achaemenid Judah* (JSJSup, 65; Leiden: Brill).

Berquist, Jon L.
1995   *Judaism in Persia's Shadow: A Social and Historical Approach* (Minneapolis: Fortress Press).

Berry, George R.
1923   'Priests and Levites', *JBL* 42, pp. 227–38.

Bertholet, Alfred
1902   *Die Bücher Esra und Nehemia* (KHAT; Tübingen: Mohr).

Bickerman, Elias J.
1966   *From Ezra to the Last of the Maccabees: Foundations of Post-Biblical Judaism* (New York: Schocken Books).
1976   'The Edict of Cyrus in Ezra 1', in *Studies in Jewish and Christian History: Part One* (Leiden: Brill), pp. 72–108.

Blenkinsopp, Joseph
1988   *Ezra–Nehemiah: A Commentary* (OTL; London: SCM Press).
1991   'Temple and Society in Achaemenid Judah', in P.R. Davies (ed.), *Second Temple Studies: 1*, pp. 22–53.
1994   'The Nehemiah Autobiographical Memoir', in S.E. Balentine *et al.* (eds.), *Language, Theology, and the Bible* (Oxford: Clarendon Press), pp. 199–212.
1996   'An Assessment of the Alleged Pre-Exilic Date of the Priestly Material in the Pentateuch', *ZAW* 108, pp. 495–518.

Birch, Bruce C.
1991   *Let Justice Roll Down: The Old Testament, Ethics and Christian Life* (Louisville, KY: Westminster/John Knox).

Boda, Mark J.
1999   *Praying the Tradition: The Origin and Use of Tradition in Nehemiah 9* (Berlin and New York: Walter de Gruyter).

Boecker, Hans J.
1964   *Redeformen des Rechtslebens im Alten Testament* (Neukirchen–Vluyn: Neukirchener Verlag).

Bowman, John W.
1955–56   'Ezekiel and the Zadokite Priesthood', *TGUOS* 16, pp. 1–14.

Bowman, Raymond A.
1954   'Introduction and Exegesis to the Book of Ezra and the Book of Nehemiah', *The Interpreter's Bible*, 3 (Nashville: Abingdon Press), pp. 551–819.

Braun, Roddy L.
1977   'A Reconsideration of the Chronicler's Attitude toward the North', *JBL* 96, pp. 59–62.
1979   'Chronicles, Ezra and Nehemiah: Theology and Literary History', in J.A. Emerton (ed.), *Studies in the Historical Books of the Old Testament*, pp. 52–64.

Briant, Pierre
1975   'Villages et communautés villageoises d'Asie achéménide et hellénistique', *JESHO* 18, pp. 165–88.

Bright, John
    1965   *Jeremiah* (AB, 21; Garden City, NY: Doubleday).
    1981   *A History of Israel* (Philadelphia: Westminster Press, 3rd edn).
Brockington, L.H.
    1969   *Ezra, Nehemiah and Esther* (NCB; Oliphants: Marshall, Morgan & Scott).
Brosius, M., and Amélie Kuhrt (eds.)
    1998   *Studies in Persian History: Essays in Memory of David M. Lewis* (Leiden: Nederlands Instituut voor het Nabije Oosten).
Brunet, Adrien M.
    1959   'La théologie du Chroniste: Théocratie et messianisme', *Sacra Pagina* 1, pp. 384–97.
Carroll, R.P.
    1979   'Twilight of Prophecy or Dawn of Apocalyptic', *JSOT* 14, pp. 3–35.
    1981   *From Chaos to Covenant - Prophecy in the Book of Jeremiah* (New York: Crossroad).
Carter, Charles E.
    1999   *The Emergence of Yehud in the Persian Period: A Social and Demographic Study* (JSOTSup, 294; Sheffield: JSOT Press).
Cazelles, Henry
    1954   'La Mission d'Esdras', *VT* 4, pp. 113–40.
    1979   'Review of H.G.M. Williamson's *Israel in the Book of Chronicles*', *VT* 29, pp. 375–80.
Childs, Brevard S.
    1979   *Introduction to the Old Testament as Scripture* (London: SCM Press).
Chrostowski, Waldemar
    1990   'An Examination of Conscience by God's People as Exemplified in Neh. 9:6-37', *BZ* n.s. 34, pp. 253–61.
Clements Ronald E. (ed.)
    1989   *The World of Ancient Israel: Sociological, Anthropological and Political Perspectives Essays by Members of the Society for Old Testament Study* (Cambridge: Cambridge University Press).
Clines, David J.A.
    1984   *Ezra, Nehemiah, Esther* (NCB; London: Marshall, Morgan & Scott).
    1990   'The Nehemiah Memoir: The Perils of Autobiography', in *What does Eve do to Help?* (JSOTSup, 94; Sheffield: JSOT Press), pp. 124–64.
    1995   'The Ten Commandments, Reading from Left to Right', in *Interested Parties: The Ideology of Writers and Readers of the Hebrew Bible* (JSOTSup, 205; Sheffield: JSOT Press), pp. 26–45.
Cody, Aelred
    1969   *A History of Old Testament Priesthood* (Rome: Pontifical Biblical Institute)
Cogan, Mordechai
    1988   'For We, like You, Worship your God: Three Biblical Portrayals of Samaritan Origins', *VT* 38, pp. 286–92.
Cogan, Mordechai, B.L. Eichler, and J.H. Tigay (eds.)
    1997   *Tehillah le-Moshe: Biblical and Judaic Studies in Honor of Moshe Greenberg* (Winona Lake: Eisenbrauns).
Coggins, Richard J.
    1965   'The Interpretation of Ezra IV.4', *JTS* n.s. 16, pp. 124–27.

1976   *Ezra and Nehemiah* (Cambridge: Cambridge University Press).
Cohen, Shaye J.D.
1983   'From the Bible to the Talmud: The Prohibition of Intermarriage, *HAR* 7, pp. 15–39.
Cook, Stephen L.
1995   'Innerbiblical Interpretation in Ezekiel 44 and the History of Israel's Priesthood', *JBL* 114, pp. 193–208.
Cox, Claude E. (ed.)
1991   *Seventh Congress of the International Organisation for Septuagint and Cognate Studies, Leuven 1989* (Atlanta: Scholars Press, 1991).
Croft, Steven J.L.
1979   'Review of Williamson's *Israel in the Books of Chronicles*', *JSOT* 14, pp. 68–72.
Cross, Frank M.
1973   'The Priestly Work', in *Canaanite Myth and Hebrew Epic* (Cambridge: Harvard University Press), pp. 293–325.
1975   'A Reconstruction of the Judean Restoration', *JBL* 94, pp. 4–18.
Cross, Frank M., Werner E. Lemke, and Patrick D. Miller (eds.)
1976   *Magnalia Dei: The Mighty Acts of God: Essays on the Bible and Archaeology in Memory of G. Ernest Wright* (Garden City, NY: Doubleday).
Crüsemann, Frank
1996   *Die Tora: Theologie und Sozialgeschichte des alttestamentlichen Gesetzes* (München: Chr Kaiser, 1992), ET *The Torah: Theology and Social History of Old Testament Law* (trans. Allan W. Mahnke; Minneapolis: Fortress Press).
Ctesias
1947   'Epit 68', *La Perse, L'Inde: les sommaires de Photius*, P. Henry (ed.), *Collection le Begne 7*, ser. no. 84 (Bruxelles: Office de Publicité).
Curtis, Edward L., and Albert A. Madsen
1910   *A Critical and Exegetical Commentary on the Books of Chronicles* (ICC; Edinburgh: T&T Clark).
Curtiss, Samuel I.
1877   *The Levitical Priests: A Contribution to the Criticism of the Pentateuch* (Edinburgh: T&T Clark).
Dahmen, Ulrich
1996   *Leviten und Priester im Deuteronomium: Literarkritik und redaktionsgeschichtliche Studien* (BBB, 110; Bodenheim: Philo Verlag).
Dandamaev, Mohammad A.
1989   *La Politique religieuse des Achéménides*; ET *A Political History of the Achaemenid Empire* (trans. W.J. Vogelsang; Leiden: E.J. Brill).
Dandamaev, Mohammad A., and V.G. Lukonin
1989   *The Culture and Social Institution of Ancient Iran* (trans. P.L. Kohl; Cambridge: Cambridge University Press).
Davies, Gordon F.
1999   *Ezra and Nehemiah* (Berit Olam; Collegeville, Minnesota: The Liturgical Press).
Davies, Philip R.
1989   'The Social World of Apocalyptic Writings', in R.E. Clements (ed.), *The World of Ancient Israel*, pp. 251–71.

1998   *Scribes and Schools: The Canonisation of the Hebrew Scriptures* (Louisville, KY: Westminster John Knox Press).

Davies, Philip R. (ed.)
1991   *Second Temple Studies: 1. Persian Period* (JSOTSup, 117; Sheffield: JSOT Press).

Davies, William D., and Louis Finkelstein (eds.)
1984   *The Cambridge History of Judaism* (Cambridge: Cambridge University Press).

Dequeker, Luc
1993   'Darius and Persian, and the Reconstruction of the Jewish Temple in Jerusalem (Ezra 4:24)', *Orientalia Lovaniensia Analecta* 55, pp. 67–92.

Dillard, Raymond B.
1984   'Reward and Punishment in Chronicles: The Theology of Immediate Retribution', *WTJ* 46, pp. 164–72.
1986   *2 Chronicles* (WBC, 15; Waco, TX: Word Books).

Dillard, Raymond B., and Tremper Longman III
1994   *An Introduction to the Old Testament* (Grand Rapids: Zondervan Publishing House).

Dirksen, Piet B.
1999   'The Future in the Book of Chronicles', in P.J. Harland *et al.* (eds.), *New Heaven and New Earth Prophecy and the Millennium*, pp. 37–51.

Donner, Herbert
1986   'Das persische Zeitalter', in *Geschichte des Volkes Israel und Seiner Nachbarn in Grundzugen, Teil 2: Von der Königszeit bis zu Alexander dem Großen, mit einem Ausblick auf die Geschichte des Judentums bis Bar Kochba* (Göttingen: Vandenhoeck & Ruprecht).

Dörrfuss, Ernst M.
1994   *Moses in den Chronikbüchern: Garant theokratischer Zukunftserwartung* (BZAW, 219; Berlin: Walter de Gruyter).

Douglas, Mary
2002   'Responding to Ezra: The Priests and the Foreign Wives', *Biblical Interpretation* 10, pp. 1–23.

Driver, Samuel R.
1906   *An Introduction to the Literature of the Old Testament* (New York: Charles Scribner's Sons).

Duggan, Michael W.
1996   'An Exegetical, Literary, Theological, and Intertextual Study of the Covenant Renewal in Ezra–Nehemiah (Neh 7:72b–10:40)' (unpublished PhD Dissertation, Catholic University of America).

Duguid, Iain M.
1994   *Ezekiel and the Leaders of Israel* (Leiden: E.J. Brill).

Duhm, Bernhard
1901   *Das Buch Jeremia* (Tübingen and Leipzig: Mohr).

Duke, Rodney K.
1988   'Punishment or Restoration: Another Look at the Levites of Ezekiel 44.6-16', *JSOT* 40, pp. 61–81.
1990   *The Persuasive Appeal of the Chronicler: A Rhetorical Analysis* (JSOTSup, 88; Sheffield: Almond Press).

Dumbrell, William J.
  1985   'Purpose of the Books of Chronicles', *JETS* 27, pp. 257–66.
  1986   'The Theological Intention of Ezra–Nehemiah', *The Reformed Theological Review* 45, pp. 65–72.
Dyck, Jonathan E.
  1998   *The Theocratic Ideology of the Chronicler* (Leiden: Brill).
Eichrodt, Walter
  1970   *Ezekiel* (OTL; Philadelphia: Westminster).
Eichhorn, J.G
  1830   *Einleitung in das Alte Testament*, Vol. 2 (Leipzig: Weidmann, 3rd edn).
Eisenstadt, Shmuel N.
  1963   *The Political Systems of Empires* (New York: Free Press of Glencoe).
Eissfeldt, Otto
  1965   *Einleitung in das Alte Testament* (Tübingen: Mohr, 3rd edn, 1964), ET *The Old Testament: An Introduction, including the Apocrypha and Pseudepigrapha and also the Works of Similar Type from Qumran* (trans. P.R. Ackroyd; New York: Harper & Row).
Emerton, J.A.
  1962   'Priests and Levites in Deuteronomy', *VT* 12, pp. 129–38.
  1966   'Did Ezra go to Jerusalem in 428 BC?', *JTS* n.s. 17, pp. 1–19.
  1972   'Review of *Nehemia: Quellen, Überlieferung und Geschichte* by U. Kellermann', *JTS* 23, pp. 171–85.
Emerton, John A. (ed.)
  1979   *Studies in the Historical Books of the Old Testament* (VTSup, 30; Leiden: Brill).
  1981   *Congress Volume, Vienna 1980: International Organisation for the Study of the Old Testament* (VTSup, 32; Leiden: Brill).
  1991   *Congress Volume, Leuven 1989: International Organisation for the Study of the Old Testament* (VTSup, 43; Leiden: Brill).
Eph'al, J.
  1988   'Syria-Palestine under Achaemenid Rule', *Cambridge Ancient History*, IV (Cambridge: Cambridge University Press, 2nd edn), pp. 139–64.
Erbt, W.
  1909   'Esra und Nehemia', *OLZ* 12, cols. 154–61.
Eskenazi, Tamara C.
  1986   'The Chronicler and the Composition of I Esdras', *CBQ* 48, pp. 39–61.
  1988   *In an Age of Prose: A Literary Approach to Ezra–Nehemiah* (Atlanta: Scholars Press).
  1988   'The Structure of Ezra–Nehemiah and the Integrity of the Book', *JBL* 107, pp. 641–56.
  1989   'Ezra–Nehemiah: From Text to Actuality', in J.C. Exum (ed.), *Signs and Wonders*, pp. 165–97.
  1993   'Current Perspectives on Ezra–Nehemiah and the Persian Period', *CR: BS* 1, pp. 59–86.
Eskenazi, T.C., and Kent H. Richards (eds.)
  1994   *Second Temple Studies. II. Temple and Community in the Persian Period* (JSOTSup, 175; Sheffield: JSOT Press).
Evans, C.D., W.W. Hallo, and J.B. White (eds.)
  1980   *Scripture in Context* (Pittsburgh: Pickwick).

Exum, J. Cheryl (ed.)
1989   *Signs and Wonders: Biblical Texts in Literary Focus* (Atlanta: Scholars Press).
Fensham, F. Charles
1982   *The Books of Ezra and Nehemiah* (NICOT; Grand Rapids: Eerdmans).
Fishbane, Michael
1985   *Biblical Interpretation in Ancient Israel* (Oxford: Clarendon Press).
Fishbane, M., Immanuel Tov, and Weston W. Fields (eds.)
1992   *Sha'arei Talmon: Studies in the Bible, Qumran, and the Ancient Near East. Presented to S. Talmon* (Winona Lake: Eisenbrauns).
Fohrer, Georg
1970   *Einleitung in das Alten Testament* (Quelle & Meyer: Heidelberg, 1965), ET *Introduction to the Old Testament* (trans. David Green; London: SPCK Press).
Freedman, David N.
1961   'The Chronicler's Purpose', *CBQ* 23, pp. 436–42.
Frei, P., and Klaus Koch
1996   *Reichsidee und Reichsorganisation im Perserreich; Zweite bearbeitete und stark erweiterte Auflage* (OBO, 55; Freiburg and Göttingen: Vandenhoeck & Ruprecht, 2nd edn).
Friedman, Richard Elliott *et al.* (eds.)
1987   *The Future of Biblical Studies: The Hebrew Scriptures* (Atlanta: Scholars Press).
Frye, Richard N.
1963   *The Heritage of Persia* (Cleveland: World).
1984   *The History of Ancient Iran* (Munich: C.H. Beckische).
Gabriel, Ingeborg
1990   *Friede über Israel: Eine Untersuchung zur Friedenstheologie in Chronik I 10–II 36* (Klosterneuburg, Austria: Osterreichisches Katholisches Bibelwerk).
Galling, Kurt
1951   'The "Gōlā List" According to Ezra 2/Nehemiah 7', *JBL* 70, pp. 149–58.
1954   *Die Bücher der Chronik, Esra, Nehemia* (ATD, 12; Göttingen: Vandenhoeck & Ruprecht).
1964   'Die Liste der aus dem Exil Heimgekehrten', in *Studien zur Geschichte Israels im persischen Zeitalter* (Tübingen: Mohr), pp. 89–108.
1964   'Bagoas und Esra', in *Studien zur Geschichte Israels im persischen Zeitalter*, pp. 149–84.
Garbini, Giovanni
1988   *History and Ideology in Ancient Israel* (trans. J. Bowden; London: SCM Press).
Gardner, Anne E.
1986   'The Purpose and Date of I Esdras', *JJS* 37 (1986), pp. 18–27.
Geißler, Johannes
1899   *Die literarischen Beziehungen der Esramemoiren insbesondere zur Chronik und den hexateuchischen Quellschriften* (Chemnitz: Pickenhahn).
Gelb, Ignace J., John A. Brinkman, and Miguel Civil (eds.)
1965   *The Assyrian Dictionary of the Oriental Institute of the University of Chicago*, 2 (Gluckstadt: J.J. Augustin).

Gelston, Anthony
1996   'The End of Chronicles', *SJOT* 10 (1996), pp. 53–60.
Gese, Hartmut
1957   *Der Verfassungsentwurf des Ezekiel (Kap. 40-48): Traditionsgeschichtlich Untersucht* (BHT, 25; Tübingen: Mohr–Siebeck).
1974   'Zur Geschichte der Kultsänger am zweiten Tempel', in *Vom Sinai zum Zion: Alttestamentliche Beiträge zur biblischen Theologie* (BEvT, 64; Munich: Kaiser Verlag), pp. 147–58.
Goshen-Gottstein Moshe (ed.)
1988   *Proceedings of the Ninth World Congress of Jewish Studies. Panel Session: Bible Studies and Ancient Near East, Jerusalem 1988* (Jerusalem: Magnes Press).
Gottwald, Norman K.
1985   *The Hebrew Bible: A Socio-Literary Introduction* (Philadelphia: Fortress Press).
Grabbe, Lester L.
1991   'Reconstructing History from the Book of Ezra', in P.R. Davies (ed.) *Second Temple Studies*, I, pp. 98–106.
1994   *Judaism from Cyrus to Hadrian* (London: SCM Press).
1994   'What was Ezra's Mission?', in T.C. Eskenazi *et al.* (eds.), *Second Temple Studies*, II, pp. 286–99.
1995   *Priests, Prophets, Diviners, Sages: A Socio-Historical Study of Religious Specialists in Ancient Israel* (Valley Forge: Trinity Press International).
1998   *Ezra–Nehemiah* (London and New York: Routledge).
2000   'The History of Israel: The Persian and Hellenistic Periods', in A.D.H. Mayes (ed.), *Text in Context*, pp. 403–27.
Graham, M. Patrick
1998   'The "Chronicler's History": Ezra–Nehemiah, 1–2 Chronicles', in S.L. McKenzie and M.P. Graham (eds.), *The Hebrew Bible Today,* pp. 201–15.
Greenberg, Moshe
1950   'A New Approach to the History of the Israelite Priesthood', *JAOS* 70, pp. 41–47.
Grol, Harm W.M. van
1990   'Ezra 7,1–10: Een Literair-stilistische Analyse', *Bijdragen* 51, pp. 21–37.
1997   'Schuld und Scham: Die Verwurzelung von Ezra 9,6–7 in der Tradition', *Estudios Bíblicos* 55, pp. 29–52.
Gunneweg, Antonius H.J.
1965   *Leviten und Priester: Hauptlinien der Traditionsbildung und Geschichte des israelitisch-jüdischen Kultpersonals* (FRLANT, 89; Göttingen: Vanden-hoeck & Ruprecht).
1972   *Geschichte Israels bis Bar Kochba* (Stuttgart: W. Kohlhammer).
1981   'Zur Interpretation der Bucher Esra–Nehemia', in J.A. Emerton (ed.), *Congress Volume, Vienna 1980*, pp. 146–61.
1983   'עם הארץ – A Semantic Revolution', *ZAW* 95, pp. 437–40.
1985   *Esra* (KAT, 19.1; Gütersloh: Gerd Mohn).
1987   *Nehemia* (KAT, 19.2; Gutersloh: Gerd Mohn).
Haller, Max
1914   *Das Judentum* (SAT; Göttingen: Vandenhoeck & Ruprecht).

Halligan, John M.
1991   'By Way of a Response to Hoglund and Smith', in P.R. Davies (ed.), *Second Temple Studies*, I, pp. 146–53.
Hallock, R.T.
1969   *Persepolis Fortification Tablets* (Oriental Institute Publications, 92; Chicago: University of Chicago Press).
Halpern, Baruch
1990   'A Historiographic Commentary on Ezra 1–6', in W.H. Propp *et al.* (eds.), *The Hebrew Bible and Its Interpreters*, pp. 81–142.
Hanhart, Robert
1977   'Zu Text und Textgeschichte des ersten Esrabuches', in I.A. Shinan (ed.), *Proceedings of the Sixth World Congress of Jewish Studies*, pp. 201–12.
Hanson, Paul D.
1979   *The Dawn of Apocalyptic: The Historical and Sociological Roots of Jewish Apocalyptic Eschatology* (Philadelphia: Fortress Press).
1986   *The People Called: The Growth of Community in the Bible* (San Francisco: Harper & Row), pp. 224–33.
1987   'Israelite Religion in the Early Postexilic Period', in P.D. Miller *et al.* (eds.), *Ancient Israelite Religion* (Philadelphia: Fortress Press), pp. 485–508.
1992   '1 Chronicles 15–16 and the Chronicler's Views on the Levites', in M. Fishbane *et al.* (eds.), *Sha'arei Talmon*, pp. 69–77.
Haran, Menahem
1978   *Temple and Temple-Service in Ancient Israel: An Inquiry into the Character of Cult Phenomena and the Historical Setting of the Priestly School* (Oxford: Clarendon Press).
1981   'Behind the Scenes of History: Determining the Date of the Priestly Source', *JBL* 100, pp. 321–33.
1985   'Catch-Lines in Ancient Palaeography and in the Biblical Canon', *Eretz-Israel* 18, pp. 124–29 (Hebrew).
1985   'Book-Size and the Device of Catch-Lines in the Biblical Canon', *JJS* 36, pp. 1–11.
1986   'Explaining the Identical Lines at the End of Chronicles and the Beginning of Ezra', *Bible Review* 2, pp. 18–20.
Harland, P.J., and C.T.R. Hayward (eds.)
1999   *New Heaven and New Earth Prophecy and the Millennium: Essays in Honour of Anthony Gelston* (Leiden: Brill).
Harrison, Roland K.
1970   *Introduction to the Old Testament* (London: The Tyndale Press).
Hayes, John H.
1986   *An Introduction to Old Testament Study* (Nashville: Abingdon Press).
Hayes, John H. (ed.)
1999   *Dictionary of Biblical Interpretation* (Nashville: Abingdon Press).
Hayes, J.H., and J. Maxwell Miller (eds.)
1977   *Israelite and Judean History* (London: SCM Press).
Hayward, C.T. Robert
2001   'Book Review of *Zadok's Heirs: The Role and Development of the High Priesthood in Ancient Israel*', *Biblical Interpretation* 9, pp. 227–30.
Hengel, Martin
1974   *Judaism and Hellenism* (London: SCM Press).

1994 ' "Schriftauslegung" und "Schriftwerdung" in der Zeit des Zweiten Tempels', in M. Hengel *et al.* (eds.), *Schriftauslegung im antiken Judentum und im Urchristentum* (WUNT, 73; Tübingen: Mohr), pp. 1–71.

Hengstenberg, Ernst W.

1867/8 *Die Weissagung des Propheten Ezechiel, für solche die in der Schrift forschen erläutert* (Berlin: Ludwig Oehmigke).

Hoglund, Kenneth

1991 'The Achaemenid Context', in P.R. Davies (ed.), *Second Temple Studies*, I, pp. 54–72.

1992 *Achaemenid Imperial Administration in Syria-Palestine and the Missions of Ezra and Nehemiah* (SBLDS, 125; Atlanta: Scholars Press).

Holmgren, Fredrick C.

1987 *Ezra & Nehemiah: Israel Alive Again* (ITC; Edinburgh: The Handsel Press).

Hölscher, G.

1922 *Geschichte der israelitisch-jüdischen Religion* (Giessen: Alfred Töpelmann).

1923 'Die Bücher Esra und Nehemia', in E. Kautzsch *et al.* (eds.), *Die heilige Schrift des Alten Testaments*, pp. 491–562.

1924 *Hesekiel, der Dichter und das Buch* (BZAW, 39; Giessen: Alfred Töpelmann).

Hoonacker, Albin van

1890 'Néhémie et Esdras: Nouvelle hypothese sur la chronolgie de l'époque de la restauration', *Muséon* 9, pp. 151–84, 317–51, 389–401.

1923 'La succession chronologique Néhémie-Esdras', *RB* 32, pp. 481–94.

Houtman, Cornelis

1981 'Ezra and the Law', *OTS* 21 (1981), pp. 91–115.

Howorth, H.H.

1893 'The Real Character and the Importance of the Book of I Esdras', *The Academy*, p. 43.

1901 'Some Unconventional Views on the Text of the Bible', *Proceedings of the Society of Biblical Archaeology*, vols. 23–29.

Hurvitz, Avi

1974 'The Evidence of Language in Dating the Priestly Code: A Linguistic Study in Technical Idioms and Terminology', *Revue Biblique* 91, pp. 24–56.

Im, Tae-Soo

1985 *Das Davidbild in den Chronikbüchern: David als Idealbild des theokratischen Messianismus für den Chronisten* (Frankfurt am Main: Peter Lang).

In der Smitten, Wilhelm Th.

1972 'Zur Pagenerzahlung im 3. Esra [3 Esr. III 1—V6]', *VT* 22, pp. 492–95.

1973 *Esra: Quellen, Überlieferung und Geschichte* (Studia Semitica Neerlandica 15; Assen: Van Gorcum).

Janssen, E.

1956 *Juda in der Exilszeit* (FRLANT, 69; Göttingen: Vandenhoeck und Ruprecht).

Janzen, David

2000 'The "Mission" of Ezra and the Persian-Period Temple Community', *JBL* 11, pp. 619–43.

Japhet, Sara

1968 'The Supposed Common Authorship of Chronicles and Ezra–Nehemiah Investigated Anew', *VT* 18, pp. 330–71.

1982   'Sheshbazzar and Zerubbabel: Against the Background of the Historical and
            Religious Tendencies of Ezra–Nehemiah', *ZAW* 94, pp. 66–98.
1983   'People and Land in the Restoration Period', in G. Strecker (ed.), *Das Land
            Israel in biblischer Zeit*, pp. 103–25.
1989   *The Ideology of the Book of Chronicles and its Place in Biblical Thought*
            (trans. A. Barber; Frankfurt am Main: Peter Lang [originally published in
            Hebrew; Jerusalem: Bialik, 1977]).
1991   'The Relationship between Chronicles and Ezra–Nehemiah', in J.A. Emerton
            (ed.), *International Organisation for the Study of the Old Testament Congress
            13th 1989 Louvain*, pp. 298–313.
1993   *I & II Chronicles* (OTL; Louisville, KY: Westminster/John Knox Press).
1994   'Composition and Chronology', in Eskenazi and Richards, *Second Temple
            Studies*, II, pp. 189–216.
Jenson, Philip
1997   'לוי' in *NIDOTTE*, II, p. 772–78.
Jepsen, Alfred
1954   'Nehemia 10', *ZAW* 66, pp. 87–106.
Johnson, M.D.
1969   *The Purpose of Biblical Genealogies with Special Reference to the Setting of
            the Genealogies of Jesus* (Cambridge: Cambridge University Press).
Johnstone, William
1986   'Guilt and Atonement: The Theme of 1 and 2 Chronicles', in J.D. Martin
            et al. (eds.), *A Word in Season: Essays in Honour of William McKane*, pp.
            113–38.
1990   'Which is the Best Commentary?: 11. The Chronicler's Work', *ExpTim* 102,
            pp. 6–11.
Jones, Gwilym H.
1993   *1&2 Chronicles* (OTG; Sheffield: JSOT Press).
Judge, H.G.
1956   'Aaron, Zadok and Abiathar', *JTS* n.s. 7, pp. 70–74.
Kaiser, Otto
1984   *Einleitung in das Alte Testament* (Gütersloh: Gerd Mohn).
Kaiser, Otto (ed.)
1988   *Lebendige Forschung im Alten Testament* (BZAW, 100; Berlin: de Gruyter).
Kapelrud, Arvid S.
1944   *The Question of Authorship in the Ezra-Narrative: A Lexical Investigation*
            (Oslo: I Kommisjon Hos Jacob Dybwad).
1964   'The Date of the Priestly Code (P)', *ASTI* III, pp. 58–64.
Kaufmann, Yehezkel
1961   תולדות האמונה הישראלית: מימי קדם עד סוף בית שני (8 vols.; Tel-Aviv: Bialik
            Institute-Dvir, 1937–56), ET *The Religion of Israel: From its Beginnings to
            the Babylonian Exile*, Moshe Greenberg (abridged and edited) (London:
            George Allen & Unwin Ltd, 1961).
1977   *History of the Religion of Israel. IV. From the Babylonian Captivity to the
            End of Prophecy* (trans. C.W. Efroymson; New York: KTAV).
Kautzsch, E., and A. Bertholet (eds.)
1923   *Die heilige Schrift des Alten Testaments* (Tübingen: Mohr, 4th edn).
Keil, Carl F.
1873   *Biblischer Commentar über die nachexilischen Geschichtsbücher: Chronik,*

Esra, Nehemia und Esther (Leipzig: Doerffling und Franke, 1870), ET *The Books of Ezra, Nehemiah, and Esther* (trans. S. Taylor; Edinburgh: T&T Clark).

Kellermann, D.
1984 'לוי', in *ThWAT*, Band IV, pp. 499–521.

Kellermann, Ulrich
1967 *Nehemia: Quellen Überlieferung und Geschichte* (BZAW, 102; Berlin: Töpelmann).
1968 'Erwägungen zum Problem der Esradatierung', *ZAW* 80, pp. 55–87.
1968 'Erwägungen zum Esragesetz', *ZAW* 80, pp. 373–85.

Kelly, Brian E.
1996 *Retribution and Eschatology in Chronicles* (JSOTSup, 211; Sheffield: JSOT Press).

Kennett, Robert H.
1905 'The Origin of the Aaronite Priesthood', *JTS* 6, pp. 161–86.

Kertzer, David
1988 *Ritual, Politics, and Power* (New Haven/London: Yale University Press).

Kidner, Derek
1979 *Ezra & Nehemiah: An Introduction & Commentary* (TOTC; Leicester: Inter-Varsity Press).

Kitchen, Kenneth A.
1965 'The Aramaic of Daniel', in D.J. Wiseman *et al.* (eds.), *Notes on some Problems in the Book of Daniel*, pp. 31–79.

Kittel, Rudolf,
1929 *Geschichte des Volkes Israel*, vol. 3 (Stuttgart: Kohlhammer).

Klein, Ralph W.
1976 'Ezra and Nehemiah in Recent Studies', in F.M. Cross *et al.* (eds.), *Magnalia Dei*, pp. 361–76.

Kleinig, John W.
1994 'Recent Research in Chronicles', *CR: BS* 2, pp. 43–76.

Knibb, Michael A.
1998 'Perspectives on the Apocrypha and Pseudepigrapha: The Levi Traditions', in Martinez *et al.* (eds.), *Perspectives in the Study of the Old Testament and Early Judaism*, pp. 197–213.

Knight, Douglas A. and Gene M. Tucker (eds.)
1985 *The Hebrew Bible and Its Modern Interpreters* (Philadelphia, Fortress Press).

Knoppers, Gary N.
1999 'Hierodules, Priests, or Janitors?: The Levites in Chronicles and the History of the Israelite Priesthood', *JBL* 118, pp. 49–72.

Koch, Klaus
1996 'Weltordung und Reichsidee im alten Iran und ihre Auswirkungen auf die Provinz Juhud', in P. Frei and K. Koch, *Reichsidee und Reichsorganisation im Perserreich*, pp. 220–39.

Kochavi, M. (ed.)
1972 *Judaea, Samaria, and the Golan: Archaeological Survey 1967–1968* (Jerusalem: The Survey of Israel [Hebrew]).

König, Eduard
1901 'The Priests and Levites in Ez 44:7-15', *ExpTim* 12, pp. 300–303.

Kooij, Arie van der
    1991   'Zur Frage des Anfangs des 1. Esrabuches', *ZAW* 103, pp. 239–52.
    1991   'On the Ending of the Book of I Esdras', in C.E. Cox (ed.), *Seventh Con-gress of the International Organisation*, pp. 37–49.
Kornfeld, Walter
    1983   *Levitikus* (NEB; Würzburg: Echter Verlag).
Kraemer, David
    1993   'On the Relationship of the Books of Ezra and Nehemiah', *JSOT* 59, pp. 73–92.
Krone, D.
    1983   *Proceedings of the Eight World Congress of Jewish Studies. Panel Sessions: Bible Studies and Hebrew Language* (Jerusalem: World Union of Jewish Studies).
Kropat, Arno
    1909   *Die Syntax des Autors der Chronik* (BZAW, 16, Berlin: Töpelmann).
Kugel, James
    1993   'Levi's Elevation to the Priesthood in Second Temple Writings', *HTR* 86, pp. 1–64.
Kugler, Robert A.
    1996   *From Patriarch to Priest: The Levi-Priestly Tradition from Aramaic Levi to Testament of Levi* (SBL Early Judaism and Its Literature, 9; Atlanta: Scholars Press).
Kuhrt, Amélie
    1983   'The Cyrus Cylinder and Achaemenid Imperial Policy', *JSOT* 25, pp. 83–97.
Laato, Antti
    1994   'The Levitical Genealogies in 1 Chronicles 5–6 and the Formation of Levitical Ideology in Post-exilic Judah', *JSOT* 62, pp. 77–99.
Levenson, Jon D.
    1976   *Theology of the Program of Restoration of Ezekiel 40–48* (HSM, 10; Missoula: Scholars Press).
Limburg, James
    1976   'Psalms, Book of', *IDB*, V, pp. 522–36.
Martin, James D., and Philip R. Davies (eds.)
    1986   *A Word in Season: Essays in Honour of William McKane* (JSOTSup, 42; Sheffield: JSOT Press).
Martinez, Florentino Garcia, and Noort Edward (eds.)
    1998   *Perspectives in the Study of the Old Testament and Early Judaism: A Symposium in Honour of Adams S. van der Woude on the Occasion of his 70th Birthday* (VTSup, 73; Leiden: Brill).
Mason, Rex
    1989   'Some Chronistic Themes in the "Speeches" in Ezra and Nehemiah', *ExpTim* 101, pp. 72–76.
    1990   *Preaching the Tradition: Homily and Hermeneutics after the Exile* (Cambridge: University Press).
Matzal, Stefan C.
    2000   'The Structure of Ezra IV–VI', *VT* 50, pp. 566–68.
Mayes, Andrew D.H. (ed.)
    2000   *Text in Context: Essays by Members of the Society for Old Testament Study* (Oxford: Oxford University Press).

Mays, James L., David L. Petersen, and K.H. Richards (eds.)
1995   *Old Testament Interpretation: Past, Present, and Future. Essays in Honor of Gene M. Tucker* (Nashville: Abingdon Press).

McCarthy, Dennis J.
1982   'Covenant and Law in Chronicles–Nehemiah', *CBQ* 44, pp. 25–44.

McConville, J. Gordon
1983   'Priests and Levites in Ezekiel: A Crux in the Conclusion of Israel's History', *TynBul* 34, pp. 3–32.
1985   *Ezra, Nehemiah and Esther* (DSB; Edinburgh: The Saint Andrew Press).

McCullough, W. Stewart
1975   *The History and Literature of the Palestinian Jews from Cyrus to Herod 550 BC to 4 BC* (Toronto: University of Toronto Press).

McEntire, Mark H.
1993   *The Function of Sacrifice in Chronicles, Ezra, and Nehemiah* (Lampeter, Wales: Edwin Mellen).

McFall, Leslie
1991   'Was Nehemiah Contemporary with Ezra in 458 B.C.?', *WTJ* 53, pp. 263–93.

McKenzie, Steven L.
1985   *The Chronicler's Use of the Deuteronomistic History* (HSM, 33; Atlanta: Scholars Press).

McKenzie, S.L., and M.P. Graham (eds.)
1998   *The Hebrew Bible Today: An Introduction to Critical Issues* (Louisville, KY: Westminster John Knox Press).

McNutt, Paula M.
1999   *Reconstructing the Society of Ancient Israel* (London: SPCK Press).

Meek, Theophile J.
1928–29 'Aaronites and Zadokites', *AJSL* 45, pp. 149–66.

Meshorer, Yaakov
1982   *Ancient Jewish Coinage, Vol. I: Persian Period through Hasmonaeans. II. Herod the Great through Bar Kochba* (New York: Amphora).

Meyer, E.
1896   *Die Entstehung des Judenthums* (Halle: Max Niemeyer).

Meyers, Eric M.
1987   'The Persian Period and the Judean Restoration: From Zerubbabel to Nehemiah', in P.D. Miller *et al* (eds.), *Ancient Israelite Religion*, pp. 509–21.
1994   'Second Temple Studies in the Light of Recent Archaeology: Part 1: The Persian and Hellenistic Periods', *CR:BS* 2, pp. 25–42.

Michaeli, Frank
1967   *Les livres des Chroniques, d'Esdras et de Nehemie* (Commentaire de l'AT 16; Neuchâtel: Delachaux & Niestle).

Milgrom, Jacob
1970   *Studies in Levitical Terminology. I. The Encroacher and the Levite; The Term 'Aboda* (Berkeley: University of California Press).
1999   'The Antiquity of the Priestly Source: A Reply to Joseph Blenkinsopp', *ZAW* 111, pp. 10–22.

Miller, J. Maxwell
1985   'Israelite History', in D.A. Knight *et al.* (eds.), *The Hebrew Bible and Its Modern Interpreters*, pp. 1–30.

Miller, J. Maxwell, and John H. Hayes
    1986   *A History of Ancient Israel and Judah* (Philadelphia: The Westminster Press).
Miller, Patrik D., Paul D. Hanson, and S.D. McBride (eds.)
    1987   *Essays in Honor of Frank Moore Cross: Ancient Israelite Religion* (Philadelphia: Fortress Press).
Morgenstern, Julian
    1956   'Jerusalem – 485 B.C.', *HUCA* 27, pp. 101–79.
    1957   'Jerusalem – 485 B.C.', *HUCA* 28, pp. 15–47.
Mosis, Rudolf
    1973   *Untersuchungen zur Theologie des chronistischen Geschichtswerkes* (Freiburg: Herder).
Movers, F.C.
    1834   *Kritische Untersuchungen über die biblische Chronik* (Bonn: T. Habicht).
Mowinckel, Sigmund
    1914   *Zur Komposition des Buches Jeremia* (Oslo: Jacob Dybwad).
    1964   *Studien zu dem Buche Ezra–Nehemia I: Die nachchronistische Redaktion des Buches. Die Listen* (SUNVAO. II. Hist. Filos. Klasse. Ny Serie. No. 3; Oslo: Universitetsforlaget).
    1964   *Studien zu dem Buche Ezra–Nehemia II: Die Nehemia-Denkschrift* (SUNVAO. II. Hist.-Filos. Klasse. Ny Serie. No. 5; Oslo: Universitetsforlaget).
    1965   *Studien zu dem Buche Ezra–Nehemia III: Die Ezrageschichte und das Gesetz Moses* (SUNVAO. II. Hist.-Filos. Klasse. Ny Serie. No. 7; Oslo: Universitetsforlaget).
Murray, Donald F.
    1993   'Dynasty, People, and the Future: The Message of Chronicles', *JSOT* 58, pp. 71–92.
Myers, Jacob M.
    1965   *Ezra–Nehemiah* (AB, 14; Garden City, NY: Doubleday).
    1966   'The Kerygma of the Chronicler: History and Theology in the Service of Religion', *Interpretation* 20, pp. 259–73.
    1968   *The World of the Restoration* (Englewood Cliffs: Prentice-Hall).
    1974   *I and II Esdras* (AB, 42; Garden City: Doubleday).
Nelson, Richard D.
    1993   *Raising up a Faithful Priest: Community and Priesthood in Biblical Theology* (Louisville, KY: Westminster/John Knox Press).
Newsome, James D. (Jr.)
    1975   'Toward a New Understanding of the Chronicler and His Purpose', *JBL* 94, pp. 201–17.
North, Francis Sparling
    1954   'Aaron's Rise in Prestige', *ZAW* 66, pp. 191–99.
North, Robert
    1963   'Theology of the Chronicler', *JBL* 82, pp. 369–81.
Noth, Martin
    1943   *Überlieferungsgeschichtliche Studien: Die sammelnden und bearbeitenden Geschichtswerke im Alten Testament* (Halle: Max Niemeyer).
    1960   *The History of Israel* (London: Adam & Charles Black, 2nd edn).
    1962   *Das dritte Buch Mose. Levitikus* (ATD, 5; Göttingen: Vandenhoeck & Ruprecht).

Nurmela, Risto
1998   *The Levites: Their Emergence as a Second-Class Priesthood* (Atlanta: Scholars Press).
O'Brien, Julia M.
1988   'Priest and Levite in Malachi' (unpublished PhD dissertation, Duke University).
Oded, Bustenay
1979   *Mass Deportations and Deportees in the Neo-Assyrian Empire* (Wiesbaden: L. Reichert).
Oeming, Manfred
1990   *Das wahre Israel: Die genealogische 'Vorhalle' 1 Chronik 1–9* (BWANT, 128; Stuttgart: Kohlhammer).
Olmstead, Albert T.
1931   *History of Palestine and Syria to the Macedonian Conquest* (New York: Charles Scribner's Sons).
1948   *History of the Persian Empire* (Chicago: University of Chicago Press).
Oppenheimer, Aharon
1977   *The 'Am ha-Aretz: A Study in the Social History of the Jewish People in the Hellenistic-Roman Period* (ALGHJ, 8; Leiden: Brill).
Pelaia, Bruno M.
1960   *Esdra e Neemia* (La Sacra Bibbia; Turin, Roma: Marieti).
Pfeiffer, Robert H.
1941   *Introduction to the Old Testament* (New York: Harper & Brothers Publishers).
Pietersma, Albert and C. Cox (eds.)
1984   *De Septuaginta: Studies in Honour of John William Wevers on his Sixty-fifth Birthday* (Mississauga: Benben Publications).
Plöger, Otto
1959   *Theokratie und Eschatologie* (WMANT, 2; Neukirchen–Vluyn: Neukirchener Verlag).
Pohlmann, Karl-Friedrich
1970   *Studien zum dritten Esra. Ein Beitrag zur Frage nach dem ursprünglichen Schluß des chronistischen Geschichtswerkes* (FRLANT, 104; Göttingen: Vandenhoeck & Ruprecht).
1991   'Zur Frage von Korrespondenzen und Divergenzen zwischen den Chronik-büchern und dem Esra/Nehemia Buch', in J.A. Emerton (ed.), *Congress Volume: Leuven 1989*, pp. 314–30.
Polzin, Robert
1976   *Late Biblical Hebrew: Toward a Historical Typology of Biblical Hebrew Prose* (HSM, 12; Missoula, MT: Scholars Press).
Propp, William Henry, Baruch Halpern, and David Noel Freedman (eds.)
1990   *The Hebrew Bible and Its Interpreters* (Winona Lake: Eisenbrauns).
Rad, Gerhard von
1930   *Das Geschichtsbild des chronistischen Werkes* (BWANT, IV/3; Stuttgart: Kohlhammer).
1953   *Studies in Deuteronomy* (London: SCM Press).
1962   *Theologie des alten Testaments, Band I: Die Theologie der geschichtlichen Überlieferungen Israels* (München: Chr Kaiser Verlag, 1958), ET *Old Testament Theology: 1: The Theology of Israel's Historical Traditions* (trans. D.M.G. Stalker; Edinburgh: Oliver and Boyd).

1964   'Die Nehemia-Denkschrift', *ZAW* 76, pp. 176–87.
1966   'The Levitical Sermons in I and II Chronicles', in *The Problem of the Hexateuch and Other Essays* (Edinburgh and London: Oliver and Boyd), pp. 267–80.

Rehm, Martin
1957   'Nehemiah 9', *BZ* N.F. 1 (1957), pp. 59–69.
Renan, E.
1891   *Histoire du peuple d'Israël, IV* (Paris).
Rendsburg, Gary
1980   'Late Biblical Hebrew and the Date of "P" ', *JANES* 12, pp. 65–80.
1991   'The Northern Origin of Nehemiah 9', *Biblica* 72, pp. 348–66.
Rendtorff, Rolf
1984   'Esra und das "Gesets"', *ZAW* 96, pp. 165–84.
1997   'Nehemiah 9: An Important Witness of Theological Reflection', in M. Cogan *et al.* (eds.), *Tehillah le-Moshe*, pp. 111–17.
Rendtorff R., and K. Koch (eds.)
1961   *Studien zur Theologie der alttestamentlichen Überlieferungen: Festschrift G. von Rad* (Neukirchen–Vluyn: Neukirchener Verlag).
Revell, E. John
1988   'First Person Imperfect Forms with *WAW* Consecutive', *VT* 38, pp. 419–26.
Richards, Kent H.
1995   'Reshaping Chronicles and Ezra–Nehemiah Interpretation', in J.L. Mays *et al.* (eds.), *Old Testament Interpretation*, pp. 211–24.
Riley, William
1993   *King and Cultus in Chronicles: Worship and the Reinterpretation of History* (JSOTSup, 160; Sheffield: JSOT Press).
Rooke, Deborah W.
2000   *Zadok's Heirs: The Role and Development of the High Priesthood in Ancient Israel* (OTM; Oxford: Oxford University Press).
Rooker, Mark F.
1990   *Biblical Hebrew in Transition: The Language of the Book of Ezekiel* (JSOTSup, 90; Sheffield: JSOT Press).
Rothstein, Johann W., and Johannes Hänel
1927   *Kommentar zum ersten Buch der Chronik* (KAT, 18/2; Leipzig: A. Deichert).
Rowley, Harold H.
1962   'The Samaritan Schism in Legend and History', in B.W. Anderson *et al.* (eds.), *Israel's Prophetic Heritage*, pp. 208–22.
1963   'Nehemiah's Mission and Its Background', in *Men of God: Studies in Old Testament History and Prophecy* (London: Thomas Nelson and Sons Ltd), pp. 211–45.
1965   'The Chronological Order of Ezra and Nehemiah', in *The Servant of the Lord and Other Essays* (Oxford: Blackwell, 2nd edn), pp. 137–68.
Rudolph, Wilhelm
1949   *Esra und Nehemia* (HAT, 20; Tübingen: Mohr).
1954   'The Problems of the Books of Chronicles', *VT* 4, pp. 401–409.
1955   *Chronikbücher* (HAT, 21; Tübingen: Mohr).
Ryle, Herbert E.
1897   *The Books of Ezra and Nehemiah* (Cambridge: Cambridge University Press).

Saldarini, Anthony J.
1992   'Scribes', *ABD*, V, pp. 1012–16.
Saydon, Paul P.
1951   'Literary Criticism of the Old Testament: Old Problems and New Ways of
           Solution', *Sacra Pagina I*, pp. 316–24.
Schaeder, Hans H.
1930   *Esra der Schreiber* (Tübingen: Mohr).
Schaper, Joachim
1995   'The Jerusalem Temple as an Instrument of the Achaemenid Fiscal Admini-
           stration', *VT* 45, pp. 528–39.
1997   'The Temple Treasury Committee in the Times of Nehemiah and Ezra', *VT*
           47, pp. 200–206.
2000   *Priester und Leviten im achämenidischen Juda: Studien zur Kult- und
           Sozialgeschichte Israels in persischer Zeit* (Forschungen zum Alten Testa-
           ment, 31; Tübingen: Mohr–Siebeck).
Schmidt, Hans
1928   *Das Gebet der Angeklagten im Alten Testament* (Giessen: Ricker).
Schmidt, Werner H.
1984   *Old Testament Introduction* (trans. M.J. O'Connell; New York: Crossroad).
Schramm, Brooks
1995   *The Opponents of Third Isaiah: Reconstructing the Cultic History of the
           Restoration* (JSOTSup, 193; Sheffield: JSOT Press).
Schultz, Carl
1980   'The Political Tensions Reflected in Ezra–Nehemiah', in C.D. Evans *et al.*
           (eds.), *Scripture in Context*, pp. 221–43.
Segal, Moses H.
1943   'The Books of Ezra and Nehemiah' (Hebrew), *Tarbiz* 14, pp. 81–103.
Sellin, Ernst
1932   *Geschichte des israelitisch-jüdischen Volkes* (Leipzig: Quelle-Meyer).
Sellin, Ernst, and Georg Fohrer
1968   *Introduction to the Old Testament* (Nashville: Abingdon Press).
Selman, Martin J.
1994   *First Chronicles: An Introduction and Commentary* (TOTC; Downers Grove:
           InterVarsity Press).
Shaver, Judson R.
1989   *Torah and the Chronicler's History Work* (BJS, 196; Atlanta: Scholars Press).
1992   'Ezra and Nehemiah: On the Theological Significance of Making Them
           Contemporaries', in E. Ulrich *et al.* (eds.), *Priests, Prophets and Scribes*, pp.
           76–86.
Shinan, I. Avigdor (ed.)
1977   *Proceedings of the Sixth World Congress of Jewish Studies* (Jerusalem:
           World Union of Jewish Studies).
Smith, David A.
1990   'Ezra, Book of', in W.E. Mills (ed.), *The Lutterworth Dictionary of the
           Bible* (Cambridge: The Lutterworth Press), pp. 258–59.
Smith, Morton
1971   *Palestinian Parties and Politics that Shaped the Old Testament* (New York:
           Columbia University Press).

Smith W. Robertson, and Alfred Bertholet
    1902   'Priest', in *Encyclopaedia Biblica*, III (New York: MacMillan and Co.),
               cols. 3837–47.
Smith-Christopher, Daniel L.
    1997   'Book Review of J.L. Berquist, *Judaism in Persia's Shadow: A Social and
               Historical Approach*', *The Journal of Religion* 77, pp. 656–58.
Snaith, Norman H.
    1951   'The Date of Ezra's Arrival in Jerusalem', *ZAW* 63, pp. 53–66.
Soggin, J. Alberto
    1993   *An Introduction to the History of Israel and Judah* (Valley Forge: Trinity
               Press International).
Spencer, John R.
    1992   'Aaron', in *ABD*, I, pp. 1–6.
Steck, Odil H.
    1968   'Das Problem theologischer Stromungen in nachexilischer Zeit', *EvTh* 28,
               pp. 445–58.
Steins, Georg
    1995   *Die Chronik als kanonisches Abschlußphänomen: Studien zur Entstehung
               und Theologie von 1/2 Chronik* (BBB, 93; Weinheim: Beltz).
Stern, Ephraim
    1982   *Material Culture of the Land of the Bible in the Persian Period 538–332
               B.C.* (Jerusalem: Israel Exploration Society; Westminster: Aris & Phillips).
    1984   'The Persian Empire and the Political and Social History of Palestine in the
               Persian Period', in W.D. Davies *et al.* (eds.), *The Cambridge History of
               Judaism*, pp. 70–87.
Stinespring, William F.
    1961   'Eschatology in Chronicles', *JBL* 80, pp. 209–19.
Strecker, Georg (ed.)
    1983   *Das Land Israel in biblischer Zeit* (Göttingen: Vandenhoeck & Ruprecht).
Strünbind, Kim
    1991   *Tradition als Interpretation in der Chronik: König Josaphat als Paradigma
               chronistischer Hermeneutik und Theologie* (BZAW, 201; Berlin: de Gruyter).
Talmon, Shemaryahu
    1976   'Ezra and Nehemiah', *IDBSup*, pp. 322–28.
Talshir, David
    1988   'A Reinvestigation of the Linguistic Relationship between Chronicles and
               Ezra–Nehemiah', *VT* 38, pp. 165–93.
    1988   'The References to Ezra and the Books of Chronicles in *B. Baba Bathra*
               15a', *VT* 38, pp. 358–60.
Talshir, Zipora
    1984   'The Milieu of I Esdras in the Light of its Vocabulary', in A. Pietersma *et al.*
               (eds.), *De Septuaginta*, pp. 129–47.
Theis, Johannes
    1910   *Geschichtliche und literarkritische Fragen in Esra 1–6* (Munich).
Throntveit, Mark A.
    1982   'Linguistic Analysis and the Question of Authorship in Chronicles, Ezra and
               Nehemiah', *VT* 32, pp. 201–16.
    1989   *Ezra–Nehemiah* (IBC; Louisville, KY: John Knox Press).

| 2000 | 'Nehemiah, Book of', in David Noel Freedman *et al.* (eds.), *Eerdmans Dictionary of the Bible* (Grand Rapids: Eerdmans). |

Tollington, Janet E.
1993   *Tradition and Innovation in Haggai and Zechariah 1–8* (JSOTSup, 150; Sheffield: JSOT Press).

Torrey, Charles C.
1896   *The Composition and Historical Value of Ezra–Nehemiah* (BZAW, 2; Giessen: Ricker).
1910   *Ezra Studies* (Chicago: University of Chicago).
1936   'The Foundry of the Second Temple at Jerusalem', *JBL* 55, pp. 247–60.
1945   'A Revised View of First Esdras', *Louis Ginzberg Jubilee Volume* (New York: The American Academy for Jewish Research).

Tuplin, Christopher
1996   *Achaemenid Studies* (Stuttgart: Franz Steiner Verlag Stuttgart).

Ulrich, E., John W. Wright, Robert P. Carrol and Philip R. Davies (eds.)
1992   *Priests, Prophets and Scribes: Essays on the Formation and Heritage of Second Temple Judaism in Honour of Joseph Blenkinsopp* (JSOTSup, 149; Sheffield: JSOT Press).

VanderKam, James C.,
1992   'Ezra–Nehemiah or Ezra and Nehemiah?', in E. Ulrich *et al.* (eds.), *Priests, Prophets and Scribes*, pp. 55–75.

Vaux, Roland de
1965   *Ancient Israel: Its Life and Institutions* (London: Darton, Longman & Todd Ltd, 2nd edn).
1967   *Bible et Orient* (Paris: Cerf).

Vink, J.G.
1969   'The Date and Origin of the Priestly Code in the Old Testament', in *The Priestly Code and Seven Other Studies* (*OTS*, XV; Leiden: E.J. Brill).

Vries, Simon J. de
1989   *1 and 2 Chronicles* (FOTL, 11; Grand Rapids: Eerdmans).

Weinberg, Joel P.
1992   *The Citizen-Temple Community* (trans. D. Smith-Christopher; JSOTSup, 151; Sheffield: JSOT Press).

Weinfeld, Moshe
1983   'Social and Cultic Institutions in the Priestly Source against their Ancient Near Eastern Background', in D. Krone, *Proceedings of the Eight World Congress of Jewish Studies*, pp. 95–129.
1991   *Deuteronomy 1–11: A New Translation with Introduction and Commentary* (AB, 5; Garden City, NY: Doubleday).

Weippert, Helga
1988   *Palästina in vorhellenistischer Zeit* (HdA, Vorderasien 2, Band I; München: Beck).

Welch, Adam C.
1929   'The Source of Nehemiah ix', *ZAW* 47, 130–37.
1930   'The Share of North Israel in the Restoration of the Temple Worship', *ZAW* 48, pp. 175–87.
1935   *Post-Exilic Judaism* (Edinburgh and London: William Blackwood & Sons Ltd).

1939   *The Work of the Chronicler: Its Purpose and its Date* (London: Oxford
            University Press).
Wellhausen, Julius,
1878/1994   *Geschichte Israels* (Berlin: G. Reimer, 1878), titled with *Prolegomena zur
            Geschichte Israels* since the second edition in 1883, translated in English
            Prolegomena to the History of Israel (Edinburgh: Adam and Charles Black,
            1885), and reprinted in 1994 (Atlanta: Scholars Press).
Welten, Peter
1973   *Geschichte und Geschichtsdarstellung in den Chronikbüchern* (WMANT,
            42; Neukirchen–Vluyn: Neukirchener Verlag).
Wenham, Gordon
1999   'The Priority of P', *VT* 49, pp. 240–58.
Werman, Cana
1997   'Levi and Levites in the Second Temple Period', *DSD* 4, pp. 211–25.
Wette, Wilhelm M.LD. de
1806–1807   *Beiträge zur Einleitung in das Alte Testament* (2 vols.; Halle: Schimmel-
            pfennig).
1843   *A Critical and Historical Introduction to the Canonical Scripture of the Old
            Testament* (trans. T. Parker; Boston: Little and Brown).
Wevers, John W.
1982   *Ezekiel* (NCB; Grand Rapids: Eerdmans).
Widengren, Geo
1977   'The Persian Period', in J.H. Hayes (eds.), *Israelite and Judaean History,*
            pp. 489–538.
Willi, Thomas
1972   *Die Chronik als Auslegung* (FRLANT, 106; Göttingen: Vandenhoeck &
            Ruprecht).
Williamson, Hugh G.M.
1977   'Eschatology in Chronicles', *TnyBul* 28, pp. 115–54.
1977   *Israel in the Books of Chronicles* (Cambridge: Cambridge University Press).
1979   'The Origins of the Twenty-four Priestly Courses', in J.A. Emerton (ed.),
            Studies in the Historical Books of the Old Testament, pp. 251–68.
1982   *1 and 2 Chronicles* (NCB; London: Marshall, Morgan & Scott).
1983   'The Composition of Ezra i–vi', *JTS* 34, pp. 1–30.
1985   *Ezra, Nehemiah* (WBC, 16; Waco, TX: Word Books).
1987   'Post-exilic Historiography', in R.E. Friedman (eds.), *The Future of Biblical
            Studies: The Hebrew Scriptures* (Atlanta: Scholars Press), pp. 189–207.
1987   'Did the Author of Chronicles Also Write the Books of Ezra and Nehemiah?',
            Bible Review 3, pp. 56–59.
1988   'Structure and Historiography in Nehemiah 9', in M. Goshen-Gottstein (ed.),
            Proceedings of the Ninth World Congress of Jewish Studies, pp. 117–32.
1988   *Ezra and Nehemiah* (OTG; Sheffield: JSOT Press).
1994   *The Book Called Isaiah: Deutero-Isaiah's Role in Composition and Redaction*
            (Oxford: Oxford University Press).
1996   'The Problem with First Esdras', in J. Barton (eds.), *After the Exile: Essays
            in Honour of Rex Mason*, pp. 201–16.
1998   'Judah and the Jews', in M. Brosius *et al.* (eds.), *Studies in Persian History*,
            pp. 145–63.

1999	'The Belief System of the Book of Nehemiah', in B. Becking *et al.* (eds.), *The Crisis of Israelite Religion*, pp. 276–87.
1999	'Ezra and Nehemiah, Books of', J.H. Hayes (ed.), *Dictionary of Biblical Interpretation*, pp. 375–82.
1999	'Exile and After: Historical Study', in D.W. Baker *et al.* (eds.), *The Face of Old Testament Studies*, pp. 236–65.

Wilson, Robert
1980   Prophecy and Society in Ancient Israel (Philadelphia: Fortress Press).
Wiseman, Donald J., *et al.* (eds.)
1965   *Notes on some Problems in the Books of Daniel* (London: Tyndale).
Wright, G. Ernest
1954   'The Levites in Deuteronomy', *VT* 4, pp. 325–30.
1954   'Deuteronomy', in *The Interpreter's Bible*, 2 (Nashville: Abingdon Press).
Wright, John S.
1958   *The Date of Ezra's Coming to Jerusalem* (London: Tyndale Press).
Würthwein, Ernst
1936   *Der 'amm ha'arez im Alten Testament* (Stuttgart: W. Kohlhammer Verlag).
Yamauchi, Edwin M.
1980   'Was Nehemiah the Cupbearer a Eunuch?', *ZAW* 92, pp. 130–42.
Zevit, Ziony
1982   'Converging Lines of Evidence Bearing on the Date of P', *ZAW* 94, pp. 321–33.
Zunz, Leopold
1832   'Dibre-Hajamim oder die Bucher der Chronik', in *Die gottesdienstlichen Vorträge der Juden, historisch entwickelt* (Berlin: Asher), pp. 13–36.

APOCRYPHA AND PSEUDEPIGRAPHA

OTHER ANCIENT REFERENCES

INDEX OF AUTHORS